A TRAILS BOOKS GUIDE

TASTES OF MINNESOTA

A FOOD LOVER'S TOUR

DONNA TABBERT LONG

TRAILS BOOKS
Black Earth, Wisconsin

Library of Congress Catalog Card Number: 2001088612
ISBN: 0-915024-95-0

Editor: Stan Stoga
Photos: Donna Tabbert Long
Design and Production: Impressions Book and Journal Services, Inc.
Map: Mapping Specialists
Cover Designer: John Huston
Cover Photo: Richard Hamilton Smith

Printed in the United States of America.
06 05 04 03 02 01   6 5 4 3 2 1

Trails Books, a division of Trails Media Group, Inc.
P.O. Box 317   •   Black Earth, WI 53515
(800) 236-8088   •   e-mail: info@wistrails.com
www.trailsbooks.com

To my husband, Rod, who made it all possible.

To my son Keith, whose always smiling face will appear in my next book.

To my dad, whose wanderlust spirit lives on.

And to all the restaurateurs, chefs, bakers, ice cream makers, apple growers, winemakers, and others who shared their time, their stories, their goodwill, their hopes, and their dreams with me. I hope they know this book is not only about them, it is for them.

Contents

Contents

Introduction

Within a state famous for its hot dish, Lutheran church suppers, and the homogenous Lake Wobegon, many folks are surprised to discover the "land of lakes" is not all Swedish pancakes and smorgasbords (the fact is, they're actually rather difficult to find!).

In truth, Minnesota has long offered an incredible range of edibles. Whether you're crazy for a kolacky, have a passion for pie, or crave some good eating apples or fresh spring rolls, Minnesota today is abundant with tasty bounty—and a world of flavors and aromas just waiting to be discovered.

Tastes of Minnesota: A Food Lover's Tour is designed to help lead you to some of these unforgettable—and often unheard-of and unsung—places where such bounty can be sampled: restaurants, small out-of-the-way orchards, hometown cafes, old-fashioned candy shops, and ethnic bakeries. Along with descriptions of food festivals that celebrate the diversity of the state, it also offers helpful tips for the best places to load up on local jams and jellies, find fresh grape juice, or purchase smoked fish. Favorite recipes from some of the top chefs in the region are included as well.

Although I hope that armchair gourmets may find pleasure merely reading about some of the state's bounty (and cooks may discover a great recipe or two), my main goal has been to write a book that will serve as a useful tool for travelers looking to experience the real flavor that is Minnesota.

I started this guidebook with the mission of finding and directing people to some of the best food sources in the state. It is meant to be selective, but it is in no way meant to be a comprehensive state food guide. Obviously, owing to time and word constraints, I could not include or even visit every place I would have liked. But I really do love the places that are within these pages—and I hope you love them as well. Some are well known and popular; many are "secrets." None, by the way, has paid to be included in the book. But all are spots I find myself returning to or directing my friends to visit—places that won my heart, but not simply because they served delicious food. For me, the joy of eating my way across the state has also been about the spirit of the place visited and something more than the sustenance served up. It's about people's hopes and dreams, too—where a hand-dipped chocolate cream, an apple from the family orchard, or a piece of homemade banana cream pie made from grandma's recipe reflects pride and craftsmanship as much as flavor.

Over the past year, I've journeyed several thousand miles, criss-crossing the state, stopping in bakeries early in the morning, watching candy makers hand-twist peppermint candy canes, eating raspberry pancakes while over-looking Lake Superior, savoring walleye in small lakeside eateries at sunset, slurping spicy noodles on Nicollet Avenue in Minneapolis, and sipping Mexican hot chocolate in St. Paul. Along the way I've made friends—and shared food, conversation, and laughter at many tables. And I gained 20 pounds.

All in all, I have to say it was a wonderful trip. Even so, I know there is lots more out there to explore, discover, and savor. A journey like this is never really finished.

But for now, it's your turn. May you have safe, fun-filled, and flavor-packed travels.

ACKNOWLEDGMENTS

No book is the work of one person, and this one would never have happened without the advice, recommendations, help, and belief of many. Besides family and friends, I am indebted to countless people all over the state who took the time to share their knowledge and provide me with insights and nuggets of information that in many cases were unavailable in print.

Specifically, I want to thank three of my dearest friends in life as well as in food and travel adventures: Angie Suchy Brown, Carole Peterson, and Rosemary Holman. The first two also tested recipes for this book, while Rosemary spent hours helping me select and organize my entire slide selection—and all three occasionally roamed the state with me (flat tires and all). They continually supported me and kept me going. All I can say is that I am truly blessed. This project would never have been completed without them.

Another sincere thank-you to my dear friend Judy Westergard, who was the first person to read the first chapter of this book; she immediately gave me her enthusiastic encouragement to pursue the dream of writing it. Her editing skills and her homemade chocolate treats helped me immensely. Thanks also go to my wonderful (and patient!) editor, Stan Stoga, who loved the idea from the start, shared my vision of what the book could be, kept me on task, made me smile, and put up with my sometimes strange sense of humor.

A huge and heartfelt thank-you to my family: My sons Kevin, Keith, and David traveled alongside me when necessary, eating and/or waiting while I asked questions and got into long conversations with strangers. Most of all, I am grateful to my husband, Rod. While I was traveling, he paid the bills and kept the home fires burning and the porch light on. The book could not have been written without his love and support.

Last, but certainly not least, a loving thank-you goes to my parents, Henry and Edna Tabbert, the original road-trip travelers and the ones who first taught me the joys of the journey and the pleasure of places along the way.

1. The Great River Road

Come September, roadside markets all along Minnesota's Great River Road are lush with color and fragrant produce. Bushel baskets spill out rosy apples, and bright orange pumpkins are heaped on hay wagons. Honey, fresh-pressed apple cider, homemade caramel apples, jelly and jams, squash and gourds, and branches of bright bittersweet fill wooden shelves and benches. Drive through some sleepy river town and you're likely to see a hand-lettered sign swinging from a porch proclaiming "Pie of the Day" or a sidewalk poster advertising "Apple Pancake Breakfast This Sunday."

With crimson leaves and gold, trees fill the majestic bluffs rising over Mark Twain's mighty Mississippi, and the highway curves to its shore in between. Although I've always felt each season brings a meandering strip of rural roadway its own enchantment, I admit that autumn remains my favorite time to wander this famous road.

Leaving the Twin Cities on Highway 61 takes you through the "front porch" river city of Hastings. From here it's just a matter of following the green-and-white signs bearing pilot's wheels (designating the Great River Road) into the first—and biggest—river town: historic Red Wing. Cradled between the river and towering Barn Bluff, the town is one of those postcard-perfect spots. Step into the lobby of the beautiful 1875 St. James Hotel, stroll by the river, admire the restored T.B. Sheldon Auditorium Theatre, or browse in the Red Wing Pottery Salesroom. Here you can watch as a potter makes salt-glazed pottery and then purchase kitchen crockery replicas of the traditional grayish blue–banded pottery with its trademark red wing logo stamped on.

There are plenty of inspiring views along the river road, but if you head up to Barn Bluff, be sure to pack a picnic or stuff some apples and a thermos of apple cider in a back pack. Early-morning types would be wise to stop in for fortifications at Braschler's Bakery: hot coffee and a bag of almond biscotti work for me. Then park at the end of East Fifth Street and plan at least an hour for the steep jaunt up to the bluff's broad, grassy top. The vista of the river and town is one that even Henry David Thoreau thought was worth the trek.

Travel downstream a few miles (turn off on County 2) and Frontenac State Park offers another choice spot (without quite the exertion) for an alfresco meal with a view. The park completely encircles the tranquil hamlet of Old Frontenac. Something of a well-kept secret these days, Old Frontenac was once known as the "Newport of the Northwest"—a summer resort for America's elite in the late nineteenth century. It's worth a detour for those who want to

Sunset on the Mississippi at Wabasha

see flower gardens and elegant 1860s-vintage homes; along Garrard Avenue, they face the river.

Back on the main road, more expansive overlooks of Lake Pepin lead you into Lake City, an area long known for its apple production. Orchards here produce about one-fourth of the 700,000 bushels of apples grown in Minnesota each year. They are also the nation's largest producer of Haralson apples—the crisp tart fruit prized for pies by many Minnesota cooks. At dinner time, find a table at Waterman's Restaurant overlooking Lake Pepin and the river. (Order the walleye, prepared in a homemade beer batter.)

You have to turn off Highway 61 to get into the river town of Wabasha, but it's worth it. Brick and sandstone facades dating to the 1850s line the town's quiet, sleepy Main Street, including the oldest operating hotel in the state, the Anderson House. In Grandma Anderson's dining room, Friday nights used to be all-you-can-eat fish fries; now they have a seafood buffet. No matter what they call it, it's still a good deal.

Continuing on past soaring bluffs, you'll recognize bustling Winona by the same landmark that early riverboat captains saw: Sugar Loaf Mountain. A town rich in architecture, don't miss the 1911 Watkins Administration Building, with its incredible Italian marble, mahogany woodwork, and a curved roof that encloses Tiffany stained-glass skylights. Around the corner is Watkins Heritage Museum, where you can see historical memorabilia and then stock up on their famous double-strength vanilla extract, sweet cinnamon, and black pepper.

Applefests abound throughout Minnesota, but by far the biggest celebration of the glossy red fruit takes place in La Crescent, the self-proclaimed apple capital of the state and the last town on Minnesota's Great River Road. It's been said the whole town is filled with the aroma of apple pies baking the week before the festival. Still, don't skip the smaller apple affairs should you serendipitously wander into one. I well remember the Sunday afternoon I happened on the Polish Cultural Institute's (aka the Polish Museum) event in Winona: accordion music drifting over the street, the heady scent of home-brewed apple cider in the making, and rosy-cheeked old guys in overalls on the sidewalk outside cutting apples. Inside, homemade pies filled every available space on the long tables, and later the pies that weren't cut were auctioned off for an incredible $5.00 each.

HASTINGS

Alexis Bailly Vineyard

18200 Kirby Avenue • Phone: (651) 437-1413
Web site: www.abvwines.com

The first time I stopped in at the Alexis Bailly Vineyard was a June day of sunshine and heat. It also happened to be the opening of the season—which the family-run vineyard celebrates by releasing a new vintage and staging an open house. Families picnicked outside the main building, babies slept on blankets, and folks strolled the grounds while others mingled, glass in hand, on the vine-covered deck overlooking the acres of perfectly symmetrical rows of grapes.

Inside the main building, in front of barrels of aging wine, someone was playing the grand piano, and platters of cheese under glass covers were set about on the tops of several upright, unused wooden wine barrels. At the tasting bar, at least five wine pourers were explaining the differences between various vintages.

In the Napa Valley, this kind of thing would not be unusual, I recall thinking. But this is Minnesota, where—as proprietor Nan Bailly's sign at the end of her gravel driveway states—"the grapes can suffer."

Indeed, grapes at this picturesque vineyard south of Hastings, have been suffering—but also producing some pretty great wine—for over 20 years. Founded in 1973, when the family planted a 10-acre site, the first commercial vintage was produced in 1977. Since then, Bailly's Maréchal Foch and Léon Millot wines have consistently won gold, silver, or bronze medals in New York's prestigious International Eastern Wine Competition every year. If you have room for only one bottle in your suitcase, pick up the Maréchal Foch: medium-bodied and dry with an intense purple color, it's Alexis Bailly Vineyard's signature wine. With a little more room, I'd stash a bottle of their Hastings Reserve, a rich dessert wine, alongside it.

Although the vineyard is named for a pioneer descendant, it was Nan Bailly's father, David, who first had the dream of a quality wine produced entirely in Minnesota. Although he died in the spring of 1990, he lived to see his vision realized. Today, says Nan, "I still feel a great deal of satisfaction in being part of bringing that dream about."

Visitors are free to stop in and taste-test the wines, wander the grounds, and observe the fermenting process from the first two weekends in June (when the annual open house takes place) until the first weekend in November—when the vineyard commemorates the end of the season with a harvest wine tasting.

Emily's Bakery and Deli
Midtown Shopping Center • 1212 Vermillion Street • Phone: (651) 437-2491

This is a friendly, sunny bakery and deli café located in a small shopping center in Hastings. It bakes a lovely round of golden sourdough bread, a popular sunflower loaf, and a hearty seven-grain bread. Another favorite—a hefty Normandy rye bread—is made with rye starter fermented in apple cider (no sugar or shortening in this loaf). Wander in the busy shop during strawberry season and pick up a delicate angel food cake or a half-dozen baking powder biscuits. They also sell an array of pies, bars, cookies, doughnuts, and muffins. The deli has salads and sandwiches. And one spring day I ate a slice of their rhubarb pie—pure sugar-tart bliss in a pastry crust. I never forgot it.

RED WING

Staghead
219 Bush Street • Phone: (651) 388-6581

This combination café-bar restaurant is set in a historic and beautifully restored building (worth a visit alone) smack dab in downtown Red Wing. Spacious and airy, it has a friendly and familiar ambience—and chef Greg Norton's cuisine sparkles with creativity and flair. (If only the tables were a little bigger!)

On my last visit, I was going to order the sirloin steak sandwich I'd heard so much about: a tender, juicy piece of beef, jazzed up with a molasses–hot pepper sauce and Roma tomato salsa. But I ended up with my regular fare: Staghead's fantastic chicken salad. Note: Don't expect your mother or aunt's typical chicken salad. This is a decorator-style version, an irresistible blend of grilled chicken breast tossed with fragrant roasted pineapple, red onion, and habanero-mint pesto, all lovingly arranged over a bed of fresh field greens. I also like their linguine. A tangle of pasta strands simply topped with fresh tomatoes, garlic, basil, and olive oil—the dish is a classic, and Staghead manages to deliver it beautifully.

Servers here wear T-shirts that read "No burgers and no ashtrays," but that doesn't mean no red meat. Dinner entrées include an incredibly fine ribeye served with gongonzola-stuffed portabella mushrooms, and a gem of a pork tenderloin with sun-dried cherries and applewood-smoked bacon. Fresh fish entrées include a Hawaiian ahi tuna, crusted with black and white sesame seeds, and a tasty Red King salmon with aromatic curry sauce and a spicy Thai cucumber sambal.

Desserts at Staghead are housemade, and an espresso machine buzzes up double lattes and mochas to sip with bagels flown in from New York City's H & H Bagels.

In the wintertime, the Staghead makes a nice spot for an afternoon break—perhaps with a cup of café au lait in an oversized blue ceramic cup and a decadent bite or two of that incredible white chocolate–cappuccino custard. In the summertime, I prefer a cold, frosty mug of the Sprecher root beer on tap.

A Range in the News

A gas range has been placed in the St. James hotel by the Red Wing Gas & Electric company. The range is eight feet long and has four ovens, two feet square. There are thirty burners on top. This stove was made to order in New York, and all cooking at the hotel is being done on the range, which proves most satisfactory. (From the *Red Wing Daily Republican*, June 23, 1899)

Port of Red Wing and Veranda Restaurants
St. James Hotel • 406 Main Street
Phone: (800) 252-1875 or (651) 388-2846

Built in 1875, the St. James Hotel was operated by the Lillyblad family for 72 years. During that time the hotel's restaurant was so renowned that trains would stop regularly so passengers could enjoy a meal at "Clara's."

Today, there are several dining options in the elegantly restored Victorian hotel. Port of Red Wing—on the lower level—only serves dinner. But although the meals are fine, they are a bit too expensive. I much prefer breakfast in the sunny Veranda restaurant. If you can find a window seat, you'll be able to watch the river traffic below as you dig into a golden, hot stack of Red Wing's own SturdiWheat pancakes.

And if you really adore the cakes, you can buy a package of SturdiWheat pancake mix to take home with you as well.

THE STURDIWHEAT STORY

In 1940, Arnold Kaehler was grinding wheat on a farm near Red Wing. When the casing on his portable grinding mill broke, some of the outer wheat layers sifted through by mistake. Curious, Mr. Kaehler tasted the stray wheat. "A particularly fine flavor," he thought. He began experimenting with the wheat in his kitchen at home. Before long he had a cereal, a pancake mix, a patent on a new process for grinding and screening wheat layers, and a name: SturdiWheat.

Through the years, SturdiWheat was eventually renamed V-10. It only recently returned to the SturdiWheat label—when Red Wing resident Suzanne Blue purchased the company in 1995.

Braschler's Bakery and Coffee Shop
410 West Third • Phone: (651) 388-1589

"This is GOOD New York rye with caraway," the clerk behind the counter is saying as she puts a loaf of the dark, scented bread into a bag for a customer. She's right. But she could as easily make the statement about any of the 150 breads baked at this always-bustling bakery.

Full-flavored breads offered here include onion sourdough rye, six grain, muesli (raisins, nuts, and a heavy dusting of ground oatmeal on top), and a beauteous round loaf of European cracked wheat. Then there are chewy sourdoughs: the popular Italian version is available on Fridays and Saturdays, and the San Francisco–style loaf is baked on Mondays. These are artisan breads—textured and flavorful. No frozen doughs here, says baker Bob Braschler, with pride.

"This is a totally scratch bakery," he adds, leaning against the glass display case, for a rare moment of conversation. "And we've never worried about ingredient cost." Bite into one of their Bavarian cream-filled long johns, and you'll understand his meaning as well. No canned metallic-tasting custard comes oozing out here. The filling is pure and simple: a creamy pudding consisting of vanilla, fresh eggs, milk, and butter. "That's also why I have to tell people to make sure they keep them refrigerated," says Braschler. Sample a lemon-filled Bismarck or their luscious lemon pie. Same thing.

Braschler has been interested in the bakery business since he was 10 years old and his 23-year-old brother bought a bakery in Michigan. "You know how you look up to your older brother," he says with a smile. "I always wanted to be in the bakery business just like him."

Braschler's Bakery, Red Wing

He and his wife, Nancy (he met her at his brother's bakery, where else?), bought the Red Wing bakery in 1972, "fresh out of college and married for a year." The sale included all of the recipes that were being made there at the time, including the long-time favorite: Swedish limpa bread. This sweet rye dough, made with lots of molasses, scents of licorice (the fennel), and a citrusy note of orange peel, is still available fresh on Fridays and Saturdays. And every holiday season for over 10 years, says Nancy, they always plan on baking extra: a customer from California orders some 20 loaves to be shipped to his mother in Arizona and another box full of the bread to be sent to himself in California.

Buchanan Grocery
512 Buchanan Street • Phone: (651) 388-5215

Nothing makes me feel more in touch with the past than to stroll into an old-fashioned grocery store like Buchanan's. Located high on a hill in Red Wing, this little neighborhood grocery has been operating since 1923.

Don't be surprised either, if when you walk in as I did, you catch owner Kevin Florine peeling a sink full of potatoes in back by the deli. This is a family operation, after all. In fact, Florine was making up more of his mom's recipe for the deli's potato salad—it wasn't even noon and they were sold out. ("We actually sell two and a half tons of my mom's potato salad in the summertime," he explained proudly.)

Florine, who owns the grocery with his wife, took over the business in 1991 from his parents, Don and Dolores. They bought the business from Kevin's grandfather, Elmer, in 1955.

Buchanan's no longer has the wood floors and pickle barrels depicted in the historic black-and-white photo by the front door. But reminiscent of days past, its shelves are still crammed in a pleasantly organized jumble: cans of tomato soup and sliced peaches, jars of pickles, boxes of Cheerios and Wheaties, and bags of chocolate chips and marshmallows. This is the kind of grocery store where boys still park their bikes out front with no locks and come in to buy Twizzlers and Mountain Dew.

What adds appeal to Buchanan's grocery is that besides the staples, Kevin's inventory includes a healthy selection of gourmet items, a fact that boaters, stopping in for supplies, have known for years. You'll see jars of jalapeño-stuffed olives, lingonberries (stirred with sugar), and bottles of apricot syrup snug against cans of cherry pie filling and boxes of Bisquick. Buchanan's also carries Red Wing's own SturdiWheat pancake mixes, imported jams, and bags of "real wild" wild rice, lake harvested by Native Americans.

The chalkboard hanging from the ceiling above the meat counter lists T-bones, tenderloin, New York strips, and lamb chops. Below and behind the glass, the offerings look as they are. Choice. Fresh. Natural casing wieners, brats, and sausages are lined up neatly. Jumbo shrimp, stuffed pork chops, and beautiful big pink slabs of fresh salmon. A small cooler case nearby holds cartons of that homemade potato salad as well as a fantastic homemade ham salad. Folks may like the gourmet selections on the shelves at Buchanan's, but it's the meat market and deli here that keep the hometown customers coming. Don't miss it.

A Braschler's Picnic by the River

First stop, Braschler's Bakery: get a bag of soft fresh cottage rolls—you know, the kind with a white dusting of flour on top. Then drive to Buchanan's. Pick up a carton of homemade ham salad for sandwiches and a container of Kevin's mom's potato salad. Need forks and napkins? You can get them here, too. Pickles. Root beer or maybe a bottle of Pepin Heights sparkling apple cider. For dessert: A handful of locally made, individually wrapped Knudsen's caramels (they're in a bowl by the cash register). Then get in the car and drive to Red Wing's Levee Park for a fine little feast by the river.

Knudsen's Caramels
219 West Third • Phone: (651) 385-0800

In an incredibly beautiful old building they saved and restored in downtown Red Wing, Ron and Peggy Knudsen moved their home caramel-making production in July 2000. This is good news to those of us who have fallen in love with their homemade, sensuously soft, sinfully rich chunks of butter, brown sugar, and condensed milk. Now the individually wrapped sweet treats, sold in specialty stores and coffeehouses, will be that much easier to find.

LAKE CITY

Chickadee Cottage Tea Room And Restaurant
317 North Lakeshore Drive (Highway 61)
Phone: (651) 345-5155 or (888) 321-5177

With a warmth and an air of well-being (not to mention an intoxicating scent of apple bread), this cheerful little home right along busy Highway 61 has been drawing in the neighbors and river-road trippers for meals since 1991.

To me, the house always looks like the inhabitants must be having a casual family gathering, with people coming and going up the sidewalk to the front door, sitting on the porch, or strolling through the backyard's tiny herb and flower garden.

Scones at Chickadee Cottage Tea Room and Restaurant, Lake City

Indeed, the restaurant really is about family. Owners Ron and Joan live upstairs. Daughter Shelly works as a waitress. "I have the nicest kitchen in town," Ron likes to say. The Schimbenos (both love to cook and have been in the food business all their lives) serve up a rich and homespun cuisine that ranges from the classic simplicity of an egg salad sandwich on homemade oatmeal sourdough bread to the more sophisticated pear and blue cheese crepes (creamed blue cheese spread on thin crepes, wrapped around a fresh sliced pear).

House specialties include such traditional tea favorites as sweet cream scones, strawberry jam and Devonshire cream, a spinach salad with a house-made raspberry dressing, and a "ploughman's lunch"—good bread, fine cheese, pâté, homemade rhubarb chutney, greens, tomato, and cucumber. In the autumn, one of the most popular entrées is a pork loin rubbed with a paste of pepper, salt, garlic, and fennel, then baked. After it comes out of the oven, a fragrant apple cider gravy is prepared from the juices.

Like any family, it's the little details that set this seasonal (open May through November) restaurant apart. Sit in the room overlooking the garden and you may catch one of the cooks snipping off a purple pansy that winds up garnishing your little crock of Devonshire cream later. They also serve only Taylors of Harrogate tea (the tea served at Betty's Tearooms of England and my favorite tea), and they have a small but nice wine and beer list.

In the tiny shop out front, tea lovers can browse amongst shelves full of bone china cups and saucers, lace doilies, books, and tea spoons with enamel flowered handles. Against the wall, a metal rack displays freshly baked cardamom braid bread ("we have to make that every day," says Joan), small loaves of sourdough (perfect for a picnic for two), square tins of pear cardamom coffee cake, and little rounds of a savory onion dill bread. All are wrapped in green-checked tissue. Or pick up a cellophane package of Chris's Snickery Doodles and Riley's Molasses cookies for a snack down the road. (Riley's 4H-winning recipe is included in the Chickadee's *The New Cottage Cookbook*—also for sale by the cash register.)

On glass shelves below the register, select from sweet cream muffins and scones, sugared triangles of almond shortbread, and my particular fancy, coconut angel macaroons.

Tip: If pie is on the menu, order it. No matter what the filling, you can't go wrong. (Joan used to roll out 100 pie crusts a day when she was working summers in a 3M kitchen during her college years.)

FROM THE CHICKADEE COTTAGE: SWEET CREAM SCONES

These are the scones we make every day, says Chickadee co-owner, Joan Schimbeno, in her cookbook *The New Cottage Cookbook* (for sale at the shop) from which this recipe is reprinted with her permission.

2 cups flour
1 tablespoon baking powder
3/4 teaspoon salt
2 tablespoons sugar
6 tablespoons cold, unsalted butter
1 egg
1/3 cup cream
1/3 cup milk
1/3 cup currants (Author's tip: I like to use dried
   cherries instead.)

Combine flour, baking powder, sugar, and salt. Cut butter into dry ingredients with a pastry cutter until the size of a dime. Add currants. Beat together egg, milk, and cream. Stir into dry ingredients just until blended. Turn onto a floured board and form into a soft ball, being careful not to work too much. Pat out to 3/4 inch high. Cut with a biscuit cutter and place on a sprayed cookie sheet. Bake at 375 for 12 minutes or until golden brown. Makes 12 2 1/2 inch round scones. Serve with jam and clotted cream.

Great River Vineyard
35680 Highway 61 Boulevard • Phone: (651) 345-3531

Pure, purple, and sweet, grape juice made from the freshly crushed fruit is the specialty at Great River Vineyard. Stop in when they're crushing the grapes in the back room here and the aroma wafts through to the small showroom like a sweet cloud. This is one of the few (if only) places in Minnesota where you'll find such old-fashioned honest-to-goodness grape juice. No additives, no pasteurization . . . just the real stuff.

Located out of Lake City, the purple grape cluster painted on the white garage door of this farm is a giveaway that grapes are the attraction here. But know that this is not a winery, owner John Marshall is quick to point out. Co-owner (and "chief grape stomper" according to their business card) Barb Marshall says they never were interested in the wine business even though John had been experimenting with grapes for several years before they moved to the sandy gravelly shores of Lake Pepin. Today, they grow about five acres of grapes, the main variety being the winter hardy Bluebell. Developed by the University of Minnesota, the Bluebell grape is bigger than the Concord variety, has an intense grape flavor, and—even though they have tiny seeds—are sweet and delicious eating grapes, too. They also grow Valiant grapes: tangy fruit that produce the rich red color in grape juice, says Barb. Besides making and selling grape juice, the Marshalls also offer the option of picking your own grapes. Just remember to return the clipper, as the sign in the window states. Jars of grape jelly and jam are available at the store as well, although

John and Barb Marshall at their Great River Road Vineyard, Lake City

the rich grape jelly made from the leftover juice of the crushed grapes usually sells out fast. On Saturdays during the summer season, you'll see Marshall's grape juice for sale at the Rochester Farmer's Market.

Pepin Heights Orchard

1753 South Highway 61 • Phone: (800) 652-3779 or (651) 345-2305
Web site: pepinheights.com

Most of the 80 varieties grown here, including the Haralson (the apple often considered Minnesota's favorite), can be found in major local grocery markets during the height of the harvest season. But it's much more fun on, say, a Sunday afternoon spin to stop in at the retail store near this Lake City orchard. Step through the bright red door and enter apple wonderland. The aroma of hot apple cider—it's dispensed from an old-fashioned red tin container—permeates the entire shop. Apples piled in bags sit on tables throughout the building. And folks stroll around, crunching a sample of Honeycrisp (the newest apple on the market) or cutting off a wedge of the spicy Sweet Sixteen from the tasting table.

Near the cash register, bottles of the orchard's signature Pepin Heights golden sparkling apple cider shine in the sun. This is good stuff. Don't leave without at least two bottles: one for the picnic you're going to have down the river road and one to have on hand at home for unexpected company.

Served icy cold, a glass of Pepin Heights sparkling cider is also wonderful with a few wedges of cheese—or even better, with some slices of freshly picked apples from the orchard.

Gil Courtier knew what he was doing when he chose this picturesque spot between the bluffs and along the shores of Lake Pepin for his apple orchard. The lakeshore area and its accompanying red clay soil are similar to that of Europe's finest wine-growing region. The same year he bought the land, 1949, he purchased 1,200 young apple trees, hauled them up the bluffs in a borrowed pickup truck, and planted them by hand. Today, the orchard is the largest in the state, and son Dennis and daughter-in-law Kirsten continue to preserve the spirit of this homegrown family business.

WABASHA

The Anderson House

333 West Main Street • Phone: (763) 565-4524 or (800) 862-9702
Web site: www.theandersonhouse.com

Down-home-style pot roast, double-smoked country ham, chicken and dumplings, sour cream raisin pie, and walnut icebox cookies. Who says you can't go home again? At The Anderson House, you may feel as if you are—that is, if your mom or grandma loved to cook like Grandma Anderson used to.

Opened in 1856, this is the oldest operating inn in Minnesota (it's listed on the National Register of Historic Places), run by the Anderson family. Although it's getting a bit rundown and ragged around the edges, it remains one of the friendliest country dining spots in the region. And with its old-fashioned wainscoting, smells of Sunday dinner coming from the kitchen, and sun streaming through windows framed in white ruffled curtains, the place does indeed look, smell, and feel like the Grandma's house everyone wished they'd had.

Sunday dinner here begins with soup and salad. The salad is dull, but the soup—homemade chicken noodle—is not to be missed; it's thick with chicken chunks, veggies, and lovely hunks of homemade noodles. Good eating continues when they bring around the tray of homemade breads; take a couple slices (make sure one is the chocolate bread). Then comes dinner.

"Chicken N Dumplings" is a hearty platter full of "seasoned butter-baked to a golden brown" chicken, all smothered with Grandma's own homemade Dutch dumplings. Although it's tasty, I don't think it's quite as good as it used to be (it bordered on greasy the last time I was there). It's accompanied by a warm-from-the-oven (but made from frozen dough) dill roll. I doubt kids will go for the sweet potato "country" vegetable or the cranberry relish, but they will, no doubt, love the double Dutch fudge pie for which the Anderson House is rightly famous.

Besides lunch and dinners, The Anderson House also serves breakfast. In fact, it was a breakfast that Grandma Anderson cooked the day after she and her husband bought the place that steady boarders never forgot: platters of perfectly

The Anderson House, Wabasha

fried ham, eggs baked with potatoes, rhubarb juice, and enormous cinnamon rolls with fruit doughnuts. By noon, the story goes, the word had spread through the little river town, and the dining room was packed.

Today, breakfasts are fairly standard. The best item on the menu is the Dutch apple pancakes. With a whisper of nutmeg and apple, they are crisp on the outside and not doughy on the inside. Although I'm not quite sure how authentic the recipe is, they are very, very tasty.

Two cookbooks filled with recipes that diners have requested over the years are available at the inn, and the cookie jar Grandma Anderson always liked to keep full still is. It's next to the cash register, and folks are welcome to help themselves. Everyday the samples change: molasses, chocolate chip, walnut icebox. These are fine cookies, too. Unfortunately, if you don't know about this little perk, the clerks at the desk rarely encourage people to enjoy one!

Rooms can be rented upstairs and are decorated with furnishings and antiques dating back to the inn's early days. You'll find homey handmade quilts (one time I noticed mine even had "Spider Web 11 by Phyllis Wiley Yetter. Wabasha Minnesota February 1997," stitched on the edge), radiators that hiss and creak on occasion (directions how to operate them are in each room), floors that tilt just a little, and window shades with those hand-crocheted "pulls." Guests who wish feline companionship during their stay can request one of their famous cats for the night (select from several lodged in the "cathouse" on the second floor).

Although the Anderson House is clearly in need of some extra attention and loving care, you must remember it IS old. But like Grandma, that doesn't mean it's not still a fun place to visit or have a meal.

Dumfries Tavern and Restaurant
Highway 60, Dumfries • Phone: (651) 565-3747

About seven miles west from Highway 61 out of Wabasha (on a bucolic, if rough, stretch of Highway 60) and lying along the picturesque banks of Trout Brook is Dumfries, population nine. The restaurant (originally the old general store) is the kind of place my dad loved to find on Sunday afternoon drives with the family. The old cliché "blink and you'll miss it" is the only way to describe this unassuming old building. Even so, don't be surprised to see cars with license plates from Wisconsin and South Dakota parked next to it. The place has a following.

Inside, the first thing you see is a huge old dark-paneled bar covering one wall. "That back bar is dated 1896," the waitress told me the first time she caught me admiring it while waiting to be seated. "Oh, and you can sit wherever you like," she said cheerfully as she bustled off to the kitchen. Know that the front room has more character than the back dining room, but it can also be smoky. It's not hard to order here: a quick glance at the silverware—steak knives (instead of butter knives) at each place setting provide a sharp clue: filet mignon, although Dad might have gone for the smoked pork chop.

BRACH AND BROCK

There's no salesroom and no seconds at Brach and Brock's candy factory in Winona. But did anyone know this place squirts out approximately 32 million gummi bears a day? Six colors, six flavors. They also make specific promotional molds for other companies, shaping the sugary, gelatinous sweet into numerous kid-popular Hot Wheels, worms, or tiny fruits. Next time, look at the detail on that soft, rubbery little piece of candy before popping it in your mouth. Pretty incredible. Made in Winona, Minnesota!

WINONA

Bloedow's Bakery
451 East Broadway • Phone: (507) 452-3682

Who could not love Bloedow's? This is one of my favorite places to visit in the state. It is doughnut dreamland. It's the shop every food and travel writer hopes to find. But even better, it's like books I loved when I was younger and believed behind every closet or wardrobe door, or in some mystical scented garden, I would magically step into another time zone.

Bloedow's Bakery, Winona

Step into Bloedow's today and you enter into an enchanting time capsule of a 1920s small-town bakery. Replete with the original dark wood glass display cases, pale yellow molding and walls, and huge elaborate antique cash register, this corner shop does indeed transport.

Happily, the doughnuts to which it transports you are real. Trays and trays of the sweet confections: chocolate-covered cake doughnuts, maple-glazed long johns, lemon-filled raised, and Bavarian creams. Icings on the treats here are not an afterthought: They're made from a candy base, lifting an apple doughnut to new heights with an apple cinnamon icing or snapping up a blueberry doughnut with real blueberries stirred in the icing. Plain, frosted, sugared, or glazed, they all beckon behind glass cases and on trays in the window of this small old building that originally had hitching posts in front of it. Late in the afternoon, locals driving along the street also know to keep a lookout for the DONUT SALE sign to go up in the window.

Ernie Bloedow, longtime owner and baker, is the third generation of his family at the fry kettle of Bloedow's, succeeding his father, who acquired this venerable operation from his father in 1924. The Bloedows, both Ernie and wife Darlene, are proud of their bakery and what they do here—and it shows. Several of their employees have been with them for 20 years or more. Grandkids, Emily, 5, and Caleb, 3, are in the shop daily.

Bloedow's has survived for so many years because everything is done the "same way, the old-fashioned way—the HARD way," says Ernie with a smile. This is a true "from scratch" bakery; all the dough is mixed here, and recipes are the same ones his grandfather used, "right to the ounce". There are no additives or preservatives mixed in. "These are just like the doughnuts my Grandma and aunt used to fry up at the farm," says Darlene, "and they're meant to be eaten the same day they're fried up." Yes, this means "you can throw them through a window the next day," she laughs. (They have no shelf life.) But who thinks about tomorrow anyway—especially when you're eating a doughnut in another time zone?

Folks come for some of the most beloved items in the repertory of a hometown bakery: Besides doughnuts, Bloedow's is known for its large loaves of white bread (slices are too big for a traditional toaster), cinnamon rolls, apple turnovers, brownies, cupcakes, cookies, and coffeecakes.

One specialty exclusive to the bakery is their peanut butter roll. It looks like a cinnamon roll, but instead of cinnamon, the sweet bread dough is coiled around a rich peanut butter filling and then frosted with a not-too-sweet peanut butter icing. This is a favorite of granddaughter Emily's—as well as my youngest son's. ("It's awesome," in his words.)

The staying power of Bloedow's clientele is incredible. They have faithful customers who return week after week, year after year, and generation after generation. The place is always busy. Parents bring kids for a Saturday-morning treat; years later, kids end up coming back with their kids. This is one of those shops where memories are made and endure. "It's a happy place," states Darlene, smiling. It's magic.

Lakeview Drive-Inn
610 East Sarnia • Phone: (507) 454-3723

The story goes like this: Lady Bird Johnson stopped here in a limo (she was touring on a riverboat that had docked in Winona) and ordered a mug of Lakeview's homemade root beer. Back on board the riverboat, she raved about how wonderful the stuff was. Ever after, says a local, the tour boats have been making arrangements for folks to take a side trip to this drive-in.

Reputedly the oldest eatery in town, Lakeview has been owned by only three owners in its over 62 years of existence. Directly across from the lake and park, the square, flat building is a throwback to pre-McDonald's drive-through days. Today, cheery carhops still bring food orders and mugs of root beer (in the summertime, they sell 100 gallons a day of the homemade brew) on trays that attach to your car window. And it remains a fun place to chow down a slightly greasy but tasty sloppy joe, washed down—of course—with a medium root beer. Tip: If you don't want your root beer in a plastic cup (trust me, you don't), order the medium size. For some reason, the large size only comes in plastic.

Stained glass over the entrance to the Watkins Vanilla administration building, Winona

WATKINS VANILLA

I can smell a wisp of vanilla from the wooden steps leading to the Watkins's factory bottling room in Winona. That exotic, sensual fragrance is like no other. But I'm a little disappointed to discover that the fascinating flavoring I've loved since I was a youngster is not being bottled today. I can only imagine the sweet aroma that might waft throughout the entire building if it were.

I grew up on cakes, cookies, puddings, and pies made with Watkins double-strength vanilla extract. Of course, our Watkins man also brought plenty more spices, flavorings, and fruit syrups to entice my mother into buying. Sometimes, along with concentrates for summer drinks of orange, grape, and cherry, he'd even throw in a free gift, perhaps an insulated pitcher or a place setting of dishes.

But it's the bottles of vanilla that I remember best. I've often thought since then that although the famous Mrs. Beeton in England wrote about vanilla's exciting and stimulating properties, and Frangipani used its intoxicating scent to perfume gloves, it was J.R. Watkins who truly introduced this essence of faraway lands to women in farmhouse kitchens across the Midwest.

Today, Watkins vanilla (about 104,000 bottles a year) as well as numerous other products are still being produced in downtown Winona. A visit here is well worth the detour. Factory tours are no longer available to the public, but the Heritage Museum (where the gift shop includes bottles of vanilla, spices, and flavorings for sale) provides a nostalgic peek into the past. Also be sure to stop in the now-famous Administration Building. Revered as one of the most beautiful private office spaces in the United States, it has four different varieties of Italian marble, unusual mahogany woodwork, and stained glass that includes an inspiring version of Sugar Loaf Mountain and graces the front of the building.

LA CRESCENT

Leidel's Apple Stand
2 blocks south of stoplights on Highway 16 • Phone: (507) 895-8221

From Leidel's apple orchard, almost a thousand feet above the Mississippi River on Apple Blossom Scenic Drive, you can gaze past the apple trees to Lock and Dam No. 7 and maybe even catch a glimpse of a barge—looking like a toy—from this height.

Leidel's Apples, one of the area's oldest and largest orchards, produces some 23 varieties of apples, many you won't find at the local supermarket: early August varieties such as Oriole and Viking and crab apples such as the Whitney and Chestnut. Originally begun in 1917 when Henry Leidel started planting apple trees on his family farm (where conventional crops wouldn't grow), the orchard has grown from 15 to 60 acres with approximately six thousand trees.

Since 1988, Bernie Buehler (who was employed at Leidel's for 25 years) and his wife Rosanne run the orchard and the shop located right on Highway 16.

At the store, you'll find not only bushel baskets of the fruit for sale but also top-quality jams, local honey, apple syrups, apple butter, and helpful advice (and recipes!) for cooking, baking, or eating. It's a must stop on the river road.

Apple Harvest Time in La Crescent

With more than eight hundred acres of orchards striping the hills surrounding La Crescent, it's apparent why this is the self-proclaimed apple capital of the state. Located on a half-moon-shaped crescent of land that narrows the river's channel, La Crescent apple growers insist it's this landscape and the rocky soil that gives the fruit here its richer flavor.

In mid-September, the whole area celebrates with La Crescent's annual four-day Applefest, admittedly the biggest apple celebration in the state. Nearly fifty thousand visitors come to enjoy events, orchard tours, pancake breakfasts, and food booths. There's also plenty of pie for tasting. Best to leave the calorie counter at home.

2. St. Croix Valley

Of all the regions in Minnesota, the St. Croix Valley has to be one of the most beloved. This is a place where everyone, it seems, knows how to have a good time. People picnic by the sparkling St. Croix River or lounge under umbrella-shaded tables at restaurants, sipping wine. Almost every village has an ice cream shop, and honey from the basswood trees that grow along the river is some of the best in the state.

Popular and pretty Stillwater, once an old logging town, has spun into something of a dining destination. Menus include wood-fired ahi tuna with foie gras at La Belle Vie or a cool Tuscan vegetable salad at Savories Bistro. At the Dock Café, you can sample the homemade roasted garlic and spinach soup while enjoying the river view from a flower-filled deck. Or forget dinner and simply indulge in a handmade chocolate-covered cherry from Barbara Ann's Fudge Shop on Main Street.

A few miles up river, the tiny hamlet of Marine on St. Croix includes the 1865 General Store, where you can pick up picnic fare, camp cuisine, and even freshly baked vanilla-frosted doughnuts (a bakery is in the basement). Behind the General Store is the town's ice cream stand—the Village Scoop. Or stop in at Voyageur Café nearby for Annie's breakfasts (or homemade chocolate or carrot cake). Don't be surprised at the number of bikers (the pedal-pushing kind) in town. The country roads nearby offer some of the best scenic bicycling in the area.

From Marine on St. Croix, Highway 95 dips and rolls away from the river and through lush woodland into Chisago County—where the lands become almost pastoral. Barns and silos dot the countryside; sheep and dairy cows graze by the road. Look for signs for Pleasant Valley Farm or Sugar Bush Trail and keep a look out for local honey, vegetables, goat cheese, and freshly picked sweet corn.

At the northern end of the riverside Highway 95/8, however, the road turns steep, and the precipitous descent into Taylors Falls is one of the most exhilarating in the state. As the road wraps around a sheer sandstone cliff, a dramatic vista of the St. Croix and its soaring bluffs opens up to the right. In the old-fashioned town of Taylors Falls, you'll find a tidy bakery, soda shop, numerous restaurants, antique shops, and even a vintage drive-in with homemade root beer sold by the quart, half-gallon, or gallon.

If you head west along Highway 8 and a bit beyond the valley, a cluster of large lakes awaits. The towns intertwined with these lakes—Forest Lake, Chis-

Announcing one of the town's specialties in Lindstrom

ago City, Lindstrom, and Center City—were founded primarily by Swedish immigrants and thus reflect their Scandinavian heritage. Besides sweet-smelling bakeries and small cafés offering Swedish pancakes on Thursdays, you'll also see signs enticing you with "Swedish Almond Cake baked here daily" or advertising lutefisk suppers at Christmas time. In fact, the town of Lindstrom's water tower even resembles a white enameled Swedish coffee pot with the words "Valkommen till Lindstrom" painted on.

Farther north up the valley on Highway 95 from Taylors Falls, travel smooth country roads and see more classic rural landscapes. Turn off into Almelund if you're in need of picnic supplies, soda, or groceries or perhaps even a new washing machine. Rod's Corner Country Store has a little bit of everything. I love places like this, with ice cream counters inside and another freezer full of Rod's homemade Swedish sausage (it's very tasty) next to an aisle of new kitchen appliances.

Keep driving through the town of Sunrise, over the Sunrise River, and eventually you end up in Rush City. A small town, its claim to fame is the slightly dilapidated but nonetheless historic Grant House, dated 1896 (it's noted on the peak of its roof line). The restaurant still serves standard meals amidst a run-down 1940s ambience—but with prices to match.

STILLWATER

Harvest Restaurant and Inn
114 East Chestnut Street • Phone: (651) 430-8111

When you are in Stillwater, don't limit yourself to the cafés along Main Street. Wander up a side street to find the Harvest Restaurant and Inn—a little B & B on Chestnut Street. Complete with ghost stories and three guest rooms upstairs, the house was built in 1848 and is the oldest wood-frame structure in town. Breakfast is for inn guests only, but lunch and dinners served in the Victorian dining room (don't let the fussy façade scare you off) are open to the public and are absolutely excellent. Chef and owner Mark Hanson is a Culinary Institute of America grad who cooked in New York and the Caribbean before settling in Stillwater. He serves up exquisite fare such as Newfoundland lobster and shrimp strudel (lovely flaky triangles filled with the rich seafood) and creamy polenta topped with mussels—all awash in an elaborate curry with hints of hot chilies and pungent garlic. Hanson turns out fantastic desserts as well. I love his dark-chocolate-and-coffee Charlotte, and his molten-center chocolate cake is a few steps above any I've eaten.

La Belle Vie
312 South Main Street • Phone: (651) 430-3545

This lovely, elegant little restaurant, on the corner of Stillwater's busy thoroughfare (and within walking distance of the St. Croix River), offers some of the best and most sophisticated cuisine you're likely to find in a small town . . . or a big city. And no wonder. Chefs and partners Tim McKee and Josh Thoma hail from one of the top tables in Minneapolis, D'Amico Cucina. While there, McKee, as executive chef, was also named one of America's best new chefs by *Food & Wine* magazine, and Thoma was his sous-chef. When the two decided they wanted a piece of the good life, away from the competition of the city, Stillwater (30 minutes away) seemed a perfect fit.

Serving lunch and dinner, La Belle Vie has two small dining rooms, nicely decorated with lots of wood and sheer gauzy curtains over the windows. The back room allows a glimpse of the chefs in the open kitchen; the front room is quieter and dominated by a wall-sized stained-glass piece.

Dining in this turn-of-the-century storefront, you'll find all the best elements of the French Mediterranean tastes that McKee adores. A chicken breast marinated in cumin and honey before grilling; roasted garlic and mashed ricotta added to potatoes. A perfect and pinkish tuna medallion surrounded by a rosemary-scented sweet pea puree. Entrees change with the seasons, with an emphasis on aromatic wood-grilling as well as sauces and garnishes that seduce and appeal. Desserts are as magical as they sound: warm apricot tart with rose-water gelato or raspberry and passionfruit bombe. The wine list is excellent; the service, attentive and knowledgeable. But know that the good life doesn't come cheap; dinner is expensive here.

Savories Bistro
108 N. Main Street • Phone: (651) 430-0702

Savories is always a treat for lunch, but the real reason I find it irresistible is Kristin Klemetsrud's dessert case. Chocolate raspberry linzer tart, Mexican lace cake with cinnamon buttercreme, double-chocolate drizzlecake, lemon curd and cream cake—these are just a few of dozens of sweet extravaganzas that Kristin whips up, and her flair for spectacular creations is obvious. "I grew up in the back of a bakery," says Kristin often with a laugh. She's the granddaughter of a German pastry chef, and her family owned the former Brick Oven Bakery in Stillwater for years.

Northern Vineyards
223 North Main Street • Phone: (651) 430-1032
Web site: www.northernvineyards.com

Owned and operated by the member grape growers of the Minnesota Winegrowers Cooperative throughout the state, Northern Vineyards Winery offers Minnesota-made wines with labels such as Columbine, Yellow Moccasin, Lady Slipper, Oktoberfest, Prairie Rose, St. Croix, and Rivertown Red. All can be swirled, smelled, and sipped at the salesroom in Stillwater.

ALFRESCO FARE

Herb-filled window boxes overflow with fragrance and subtle blooms outside Tasteful Thymes Company in Stillwater—and heavenly aromas drift over the sidewalk every time the screen door swings open. This is one of the best places in town to find picnic fixings. Some of my favorite alfresco fare here includes the seasoned potato salad, raspberry salsa, and thick brownies. Then for a sun-kissed lunch, head up the bluffs to Pioneer Park for a true feast with a view. From here, the vista showcases the sparkling St. Croix River between the cliffs and caves—and church spires pierce the summer blue sky over town.

Brine's
219 South Main Street • Phone: (651) 439-7556

If you're in the mood to throw caution and cholesterol to the winds, head over to Brine's, a Stillwater institution since 1958. Climb the extra long and wide wooden staircase to the second floor, sit in an old wooden booth, and

The Northern Vineyards Winery in Stillwater.

order the "pepper, pepper cheese steak sandwich" (tender, thinly sliced beef rib eye layered with melted cheese and sautéed green peppers). Afterwards, take a hike up the Myrtle Street hill (go left on Greeley) and order one of the biggest ice cream cones in town at Nelson's Dairy.

Aamodt's
6428 Manning Avenue • Phone: (651) 439-3127
Web site: www.aamodtsapplefarm.com

Aamodt's has always seemed to me the quintessential apple farm, with its cluster of historic buildings including two 1880s barns. Just driving into the place when apples hang heavy on the trees and the air is crisp with that tang of autumn gets me excited. And I love walking into the building where the just-picked fruit is stored—bags and bushel baskets overflowing, all labeled with mellifluous names like Honeygold, Keepsake, Sweet Sixteen, and Fireside. (Aamodt's grows 27 varieties on its 60 acres.)

Kids are fascinated by the bee display (under glass) and the clanking and clatterings of the on-site apple peeler as it "peels, cores, and slices over 35 apples a minute for use" in the bakery here.

In fact, at the height of the season, the place is packed with folks who visit as much for Aamodt's baked goods as its varieties of apples. Cinnamon and apple cider scents the building. Don't leave without a taste of fresh apple cake, a slice of steaming apple pie, or an apple oatmeal cookie. Better yet, take your treats to the "hayloft." Sit by the windows overlooking the orchards—and indulge on a true harvest scene.

For three generations the Aamodt family has been committed to their apple farm. Thor and Lucille Aamodt planted the orchard in 1948; Tom and JoAnn Aamodt expanded it to include more than six thousand trees. Today Chris Aamodt continues to improve the family homestead (and continues to make the apple pie according to the secret recipe passed on from JoAnn).

Aamodt's also produces some fairly good wine—approximately thirty-five thousand bottles a year—and is the only local winery to successfully grow Chardonnay grapes. The winery is located on the farmstead in a building next to the apple barn.

Besides red and white wines, their beautiful dessert wine, Raspberry Infusion, is a showstopping local favorite. A mix of freshly harvested raspberries coupled with fine red wine, it has a rich red color and deep fruit flavor—and makes a decadent little sip with, say, a slender slice of chocolate truffle tart.

Lowell Inn
102 North Second Street at Myrtle Street • Phone: (651) 439-1100

Ok, everybody pans the Lowell Inn for not changing anything—including its menu. But still, it's a grand old place and has been a venerable institution in Stillwater for decades. Truthfully, I feel that part of its charm these days is due to the fact that nothing *has* changed here. Opened in 1927 and built in the style of Mount Vernon, its columned front verandah is still lined with flying flags, and I can't tell you how many couples I have met who still return here for their anniversaries. The Matterhorn Room's five-course Swiss Fondue dinner, complete with wine, is one of those culinary legends. Although it's touted as this romantic sort of meal, I have never found the Matterhorn Room to be remotely romantic or even cozy—and it's noisy. I think it's much more fun to go with a group. For starters, the meal plus wine (no matter how much you eat or drink) is one price—which means no dickering over the bill later. Wine flows freely throughout the evening, and the service, as always, is impeccable and efficient. So the salad isn't designer greens; so what if the dessert is still those sweet cold grapes rolled in brown sugar? The shrimp for the fondue are plump and fresh; the beef tenderloin chunks, juicy and tender. And it's sort of fun to fondue again, spearing and dipping, eating and talking, drinking and reminiscing late into the night, and then simply going upstairs to bed.

MARINE ON ST. CROIX

Voyageur Café
51 Judd Street • Phone: (651) 433-2366

Tiny Voyageur Café is the original Chatterbox café (of Lake Wobegon fame) according to owner and cook, Annie Moore. "Yep," she says, "if you need to know anything, just come here, sit down, and pretend you're reading the paper." Author and public radio personality Garrison Keillor did indeed live in Marine on St. Croix for several years—and after a few breakfast and lunch visits to the Voyageur, I have no doubt this is a place you could find a million stories, true and otherwise.

The regulars' coffee mugs hang on hooks and cover the wall behind the cash register. Hand painted with names such as "Edna," "Norm," "Bike guy," "Mr. Serious," "Marvelous Marv," "OOGG" (out of gas guy), and "OOGGF" (out of gas guy's friend) tell it best about the clientele. And Annie, who bought the place 12 years ago (she saw it when she used to canoe on the St. Croix River behind it), treats them all with lighthearted style. If there's a lull in the minuscule kitchen, she often fills a frog-shaped cup with coffee (the café is filled with frog motif kitsch) and joins a table.

Even so, you don't have to be a regular to fit in here. The place is small. Folks are friendly. And Annie's humble homemade food is worth a trip.

Specials are noted on the dry erase board: apple cinnamon pancakes, veggie herbed cream cheese omelet. And don't leave without sampling Annie's famous Anadama Bread (the history of it is printed on the laminated menu; see the sidebar following). It's a heavy mahogany-colored loaf, molasses rich and dense. Warm thick toasted slices of it, slathered with melting butter, are an accompaniment to all platters of morning eggs and breakfast potatoes.

At lunchtime, sandwiches are also served on the bread, and salads feature fresh mixed gourmet greens from nearby Twin Pine Farm. Annie's carrot cake and chocolate cake are legendary, but so are any other homemade desserts you may happen on at the Voyageur. "I'm real moody," admits Annie, "so I never know what I'm going to bake each day."

The Voyageur is always open for breakfast and lunch. But during winter months, Annie also adds a Friday-night dinner. "Usually I do some kind of theme," she says, "maybe Mexican, or barbecue." And annually before Christmas she prepares a complete Scandinavian meal: Swedish meatballs, fruit soup, lefse, rice pudding, and Swedish sausage. "You know, all the white food," says Annie with a smile.

Do stop by the Voyageur if you're anywhere near the area—if only to pick up a loaf of the Anadama bread (loaves are for sale for $2.75). But don't be surprised if once here, you decide to pull up a chair (within earshot of another table, of course), get a bottomless cup of coffee, and um . . . read the newspaper.

THE ANADAMA BREAD STORY

Anna and Ole lived a miserly life. Anna baked bread daily to provide their only viable means of income. One day Ole came bursting into Anna's kitchen and proceeded to trip over a sack of flour and fall flat on his face. As he drove headlong to the floor, he screamed, "Anna, dammit!" and collapsed with a groan.

His screech startled Anna, who held a container of molasses in her hand preparing to add a smidgen to her bread dough. The smidgen became a bucket full, and the bread dough became a whole new concept for Anna's bread baking recipe repertoire.

It was delicious! The village people couldn't get enough of Anna's new bread, which she named "Anadama" after her husband's scream.

CENTER CITY

Eichten's Specialty Shop
16705 310th Street, P. O. Box 216
(2 miles east of Center City on Highway 8)
Phone: (651) 257-4752 (includes Twin Cities toll-free)
or (800) 657-6752; specialty retail shop, (651) 257-1566

This tidy, jam-packed cheese shop offers a little bit of everything ("a world of taste" is its motto), from the deli, with its imported Westphalian ham and ground buffalo meat (the herd of bison is out back), to the gourmet fancies such as lingonberries in syrup. But it's the cheese that overshadows all.

The Eichten's began cheese making in 1976, when Joe and Mary Eichten went to Holland to learn how to make European-style cheese. Since that time they have been making cheese in small batches with no artificial coloring, flavoring, or preservatives added. Besides an award-winning gouda cheese (which they make in many variations, dill, tomato basil, wild rice, chipotle pepper, and caraway), Mary has even earned a patent for her own Tilsit cheese recipe. "The flavor of my Tilsit is stronger than a Colby but milder than a cheddar," says Mary. It's a must buy, although I can't leave the shop without some of those Cajun Zesty cheese curds either. They're squeaky fresh and may be habit forming.

CHISAGO CITY

Dee's Bake Shoppe
29311 Main Street • Phone: (651) 257-6517

One of those slightly faded and aging little storefront bakeries, Dee's Bake Shoppe is the sort of authentic shop that every small town used to have—sadly, these little local havens have been disappearing slowly but surely. For over twenty years, Dee and her husband have been baking batches of Swedish cookies, warm chocolate chip banana muffins, and glazed doughnuts at their minuscule store. But it's Dee's soft bakery buns that remain the real draw. That's why the sign in the window says "Get your buns in here," and if you're smart, you do.

Old Towne Emporium

29346 Old Towne Road, P.O. Box 378 • Phone: (651) 257-4130

Old Towne Emporium in Chisago City is located in a beauty of a building in this quaint, antique shop–filled town. At this combination store/ice cream shop/café you can order lunch or a homemade lingonberry ice cream cone. You can purchase vintage linens, hot salsa, local maple syrup, or even the claw-foot dining room table you're eating at.

WineHaven Winery

9757 292nd Street • Phone: (651) 257-1017
Web site: www.winehaven.com

Just beyond the sign advertising "Sven's Quality Footwear" but before you get to Vilhelm Moberg Park in Chisago City, you 'll see the sign for WineHaven Winery. A turn onto a country road and a quarter-mile jaunt to this winery on the outskirts of town is worth the wander.

Serving up frozen treats at the Old Towne Emporium, Chisago City

In the land of wine and honey—the WineHaven Winery, Chisago City

Once here, visitors discover this place is as much about honey as it is about the fruits of the vine. Apiarist Kevin Peterson was collecting honey from the clover, wildflowers, and basswood trees that bloom along the St. Croix River Valley decades before he ever dreamed of growing grapes. And honey sampling in the Petersons' immaculate new retail building—with its knotty-pine walls, framed sets of State Fair blue ribbons, and welcoming ambience—is as much a part of the taste testing as the wine sipping and scenting.

In fact, the first wine the Peterson family produced was a honeywine, or mead. With such a plentiful supply of choice honey, batches of the sweet elixir were given away for years as Christmas gifts. Friends and family liked it so much they encouraged Kevin to enter it in the state fair. But it wasn't until 1995, upon the death of Kevin's father, Ellsworth, "and as a tribute to him," that he decided to follow his friends' advice. The bottle he chose to enter that year was a medium-dry honeywine. Made with basswood honey, it was awarded a blue ribbon, the first time a honeywine had ever taken top honors. Today, it remains WineHaven's most popular honeywine. (Try it served ice cold with a sizzling-hot plateful of fresh fried walleye, advises Kevin's wife, Cheri.)

Besides the medium-dry version, the Petersons also offer their bottled honeywine semisweet (made with wildflower honey) or dry (made with clover honey.) What makes this honeywine extra special is the fact that Peterson knows from the location of his 700 beehives, as well as the time of year in which certain flowers bloom, which honey is harvested for each wine.

Diversification followed the honeywine success, and today Kevin and Cheri Peterson's vineyard consists of about five acres of grapevines. In addition to producing grape wine (their Riesling has won the Bronze medal in international competition), the winery also makes wine from a number of fruit trees and berry bushes that are located adjacent to the vineyard.

The winery is a family operation—and their sons Troy and Kyle are also involved in the business located 20 feet from their kitchen door. ("That was always my dream location for a job," says Cheri.) In fact, happen by the farm around 5:30 A.M. on a July day and you may even catch Grandma ("she likes to go out in the patch early," says Kyle) handpicking raspberries for their incredibly delicious raspberry fruit wine. Over one and one-half pounds of the fresh berries go into this bottle of summer.

FROM WINEHAVEN WINERY: HONEY ORANGE DRESSING

Cheri Peterson varies the flavor of honey to subtly change the taste of this dressing. Use over fresh fruits or field greens.

> 1/4 cup nonfat mayonnaise
> 1/4 cup honey
> 3/4 teaspoon freshly grated orange peel
> 1/4 teaspoon dry mustard
> 3 tablespoons orange juice
> 1 1/2 teaspoons vinegar

Whisk together mayonnaise, honey, orange peel, and mustard in small bowl until blended. Gradually mix in orange juice and vinegar. For about 4 cups of fruit: Toss gently with dressing. Cover and refrigerate until ready to serve. For greens, toss a small amount immediately before serving.

LINDSTROM

Lindstrom Bakery
12830 Lake Boulevard • Phone: (651) 257-1374

In the shadow of the town's huge Swedish coffeepot (it's really the water tower), it seems only fitting I found the Scandinavian doughnut of my dreams. In fact, the sign out front of this ordinary-looking bakery actually claimed that this place was the HOME of the Scandinavian Doughnut. But who knew? Hometown bakeries make all sorts of claims.

What, friends ask, is a real Scandinavian doughnut? Well, it's similar to a regular sinker. But richer. Darker. Crisper. Sink your teeth into the thin crunchy surface, glazed to perfection (they're also available plain, cinnamon sugared, or chocolate frosted), and you'll discover a tender, cakelike consistency inside. A subtle difference to be sure, but definitely a delicious study.

Lindstrom Bakery is the kind of hometown bakery I adore—where hand-crocheted baby blankets and packages of personally embroidered tea towels (the sort with the days of the week stitched below teddy bears hanging wash on the line or ironing or baking) are stacked for sale on shelves next to bags of cinnamon toast. Ginger snaps are sold by the sack full and packaged by the dozens. Apparently, nobody buys only one of these spicy cookies in Lindstrom. (Even the clerk admitted she ate them like potato chips.) The shop also offers lovely Swedish white bread, caraway orange limpa bread, Lindstrom rye, raisin rye, caramel rings, and coffee cakes. According to a note on the wall, everything for sale is baked that day. Believe it.

Community Market
12825 Lake Boulevard • Phone: (651) 257-1128

Directly across the street from the Lindstrom Bakery is the Community Market. Outside, a banner on the building boasts "Homemade Corned Beef." Inside you'll discover a treasure chest of assorted sausages, beef cuts, and cheeses—and chewy, tasty teriyaki jerky. Look in the freezer and you'll find containers of frozen lingonberries stacked neatly next to Swedish meatball mix and potato sausage packages on a shelf above. On the wall, at least a dozen plaques from the Cured Meats Hall of Fame are proudly displayed.

"A Tradition of Excellence for over 50 years" states the market's label, and appropriately, "from the heart of Minnesota Scandinavia" is the last line in red. Is it any wonder the fellow in white cap and white apron behind the counter has a name like Peter Nelson—and that he's the mayor of Lindstrom to boot? "My father started the meat market business in 1936," says Peter proudly; he took it over in 1968.

Although everything in the shop is good solid butcher shop fare, it's the teriyaki jerky and homemade corned beef that makes this place special. The first time I bought a chunk of the corned beef, Peter recommended boiling it for "one and three-fourths hours" and then (after removing the meat from the water) adding a bunch of vegetables to the water. The flavorful broth permeates the vegetables, infusing them with extra flavor and creating a "boiled dinner" unlike any you've ever eaten, raved Peter. He was right. But he failed to mention that the process of boiling the meat scents the kitchen with a fantastic fragrant, spicy aroma for the entire time it cooks—and hours afterwards. Tip: The Reuben sandwiches you can put together the next day from the leftovers are the best.

Be forewarned: No plain processed grocery store corned beef will ever satisfy you after you've tasted the real homemade stuff.

Buying Local Cookbooks

I happen to love the regional spiral- and plastic-bound cookbooks (usually the result of some church fund raiser) that one often finds for sale by cash registers in small-town cafés and shops. I always find it oddly reassuring to read through recipes with names such as "Aunt Agnes's Scalloped Corn" (is it as good as my grandmother's?), "Kenny's Three-Bean Salad" (does it have red onion like my sister's?), or "Elsie's Original" (what in the world?). To be sure, some of these cookbooks are better than others. One of my all-time favorites I found at the Scandia Café in Scandia. I'd stopped for a piece of their coconut cream pie (it was okay), but the real discovery that afternoon was the *Elim 140th Anniversary Recipe Book*. Originally printed in May 1994, I got the copy (from a stack displayed on top of the bakery case) for $7.00—a steal. It has wonderful recipes and a great Scandinavian section. There's directions for making krumkake, rosettes, Grandma Allenson's korkaner cookies, Luverne's rye bread, Swedish almond toast, Swedish brown beans, Swedish meatballs, Swedish . . . etc.—and at least a half-dozen rice pudding recipes. (And how many cookbooks do you own that boast a recipe for eucharistic bread for holy communion?!) Although I often never get beyond much more than reading these cookbooks, occasionally I actually do make one of the recipes. The following is a good one to prepare on a wintery Saturday afternoon.

Perfect Custard Rice Pudding

This vanilla-scented recipe of Dolores Peterson's from Scandia's *Elim 140th Anniversary Recipe Book* is sweet and fine. Dolores says she always uses Minnesota's own Watkins vanilla for better flavor.

> 2 1/2 cups heated milk
> 3 eggs, beaten (4 eggs, if small)
> 1/2 cup sugar
> 1/2 cup cooked rice
> 2 teaspoons Watkins double strength
>   vanilla extract
> 1/4 teaspoon salt
> 1 tablespoon cornstarch*

In a saucepan, heat milk to scalding. In a medium-sized mixing bowl, mix sugar and cornstarch. Add beaten eggs, rice, vanilla, and salt, and slowly add warm milk to the sugar-egg-rice mixture. Pour into lightly greased (or sprayed with baking spray) casserole or baking dish. Dot with about 1 teaspoon butter. Sprinkle with nutmeg and cinnamon. Place casserole in pan of water that comes halfway up the side of casserole. Bake at 350 degrees for 1 1/2 hours or until pudding is creamy and most of the liquid is absorbed.

*Author's note: I add cornstarch although not called for in original recipe.

TAYLORS FALLS

Wild River Candy Shop and Schooney's Soda Fountain
384 Bench Street • No Phone (seasonal number)

"I actually dream about these Coney dogs in the winter," said the young woman (quite obviously pregnant) who was sitting next to me one day at the counter of Schooney's Soda Fountain in Taylors Falls.

I was sipping on a hand-pulled root beer at the time, but I remember looking at the delicacy of which she spoke, which had recently been placed in front of her. Steaming and smothered in chili, loaded with raw chopped onion, and oozing melted cheese, the ends of the hot dog curved out of the bun like a smile.

Who could resist such a statement accompanied by such a vision? So what if I'd just eaten breakfast two hours ago? "I want what she's got," I immediately shouted to the guy behind the counter, who was buzzing up a thick malt. "The Coney dog," I mouthed, pointing.

When my order arrived, the woman and her husband smiled at me in approval. "We drove here from Wisconsin just for these," said the husband. One mouthful of the delicious, properly greasy mess and I understood their compulsion. "This is great, " I managed to say. Then I realized it was the hot dog that lifted this Coney out of the ordinary. It was fabulous: the kind of dog with skin that snaps when you bite into it and then releases a tasty zinger of juicy flavor.

"Those are custom-made hot dogs," Jim, the owner, working behind the counter, told me later when I stopped in again. (I couldn't help it; I'd started dreaming about those Coney dogs.) "It took me a long time to find a guy who would make those the way I wanted them made."

With that kind of attention, it's no wonder the place has lines out the door come summertime. Good luck getting a red spinning stool at the old-fashioned soda fountain then. (The vintage soda fountain equipment, counter, and stools were brought from Balsam Lake, Wisconsin.) Jim also collects antique candy bar boxes and his collection of Oh! Henry, Mounds, Milky Way, Almond Joy, Jolly Jack, and more—all displayed behind another vintage counter—are almost worth a visit just for admiring.

Schooney's Soda Fountain in Taylors Falls

You should probably know that you can't get a cup of coffee here, but there's at least a half-dozen different kinds of bottled root beer to choose from. Even better, try the Richardson root beer on tap. Served in a cold mug, it tastes mighty fine on a hot August afternoon—along with that dream-inspiring Coney dog, of course.

Coffee Talk
479 Bench Street • Phone: (651) 465-6700

You can't get coffee at the Wild River Candy Shop, but you will find coffee (good coffee) at Coffee Talk, located just down the street. In an airy sunny building that belies its 1892 vintage, owner John Coffey (that's his real name, too) also serves up tempting baked goods.

The Drive-In
Bench Street on the north end of Taylors Falls • Phone: (651) 465-7831

Rich and smooth homemade root beer served in frosty mugs, chocolate malts topped with real whipped cream and a cherry, hand-packed burgers—all served by carhops in poodle skirts. This is vintage 1950s dining with a twenty-first century spin: At The Drive-In you can also order veggie sub sandwiches. You can take root beer home by the quart, half-gallon, or gallon. On "Cruzin' Thursdays," look for cool vintage vehicles: Customers with classic cruisers pulling in under the corrugated metal canopy that day get 10 percent off any menu item.

AFTON

Selma's Ice Cream Parlour
3419 St. Croix Trail S. • Phone: (651) 436-8067

Everyone loves Selma's Ice Cream Parlour, a real turn-of-the-century gem in tiny Afton. With a long oak bar, a mirrored backdrop, and that warm and sweet aroma of handmade waffle cones being pressed into shape, Selma's has been drawing tourists, boaters, bikers, and hikers for years and years. Named for Selma Swanson Holberg, an enterprising woman who once had slot machines in her shop, the place is now owned by Laine McGee. (She still remembers buying ice cream from Selma.)

Today, you'll find Brown's Velvet ice cream (made in Annandale, Minnesota) scooped up here. Sample a burgundy-hued Black Sweet Cherry studded with Bing cherries, or my passion, the dark but not bitter Zanzibar chocolate. Fresh off the bush, blueberry- or raspberry-flavored ice creams are made from flash-frozen fruits. Ice cream cone in hand, you need only cross Afton's main street to the village park for a perfect place to sit and savor your cool treat. But before heading over there, note the wavy blue-painted waterline on the door of Selma's, which shows how high the water reached here in the 1965 flood.

On summer weekend nights, crowds abound at Selma's, and the wait for an icy scoop can be 40 to 45 minutes. Even so, nobody here seems to mind. Folks while away the time looking at all the ice cream memorabilia displayed (it even hangs from the shop ceiling) or watching the stars pop out over this quaint (but not quiet) river town.

Lerk's Bar

3329 St. Croix Trail S. • No Phone

Walk up the steps and into Lerk's Bar and step into memory. But don't expect a typical dark and smoky tavern. Lerk's is sunny with windows and warmth, evoking spirits (all kinds) long past. The building has been here since 1920, when it was moved to its present location from the south end of the village and transformed into a confectionery store during Prohibition. In the early 1940s, Harold "Lerk" Lind turned the place into a hamburger and tavern business. The bar's signature item, the Lerkburger—juicy fresh and loaded with fried onions—is still sizzled and flipped on the grill behind the bar by Bonnie Lind, daughter of Lerk. How did the Lerkburger originate? Harold was called Lerk, which means "onion" in Swedish, because he had picked so many onions as a boy, the story goes. Besides a burger here, order a side of Bonnie's baked beans and potato salad. Don't even ask about French fries. Bonnie doesn't serve 'em.

THE WAY IT WAS

"The girls who worked for Mary Pennington . . . summoned guests from the parlor when dinner was ready and placed on the tables large platters of chicken, bowls of mashed potatoes with gravy, vegetables, corn on the cob, strawberry preserves, and relish. No meal ever lacked homemade white and brown bread. Dessert was usually Mary's homemade ice cream, apple or lemon meringue pie, or blitz tort." (Excerpt from *Afton Remembered* by Edwin G. Robb [Afton: Afton Historical Society Press, 1996])

The Historic Afton House Inn
3291 St. Croix Trail S. • Phone: (651) 436-8883

I really feel one must visit the Afton House Inn if only for a genuine piece of enchanting hometown culinary history. Originally the Cushing Hotel, the place has endured more than 125 years—and memories of Mary "Mother" Pennington (the hotel's owner from 1907 to 1945) still linger here. Actually, her spirit is also said to occasionally linger in this place—especially in the private Pennington Room, named for her. Pennington, a colorful character, was famous for her homemade ice cream and her fresh chicken dinners (so fresh, in fact, diners by the windows could watch their dinner scratching over the food in the yard.)

Things have changed somewhat since Mother Pennington worked her magic at the stove, but you can still get a decent meal and a room (these days, many come with a Jacuzzi) at the Afton House Inn. The windowed dining room, a casually elegant place for a memorable meal, is filled with distinctive woodcarvings by Afton native Elmo Erickson. I especially love to visit here in autumn, when the scent of applewood-smoked pork prime rib occasionally drifts through the building and onto the street. The entrée, accompanied with their signature Afton apple salad—mixed greens, tart apple slices, and gorgonzola cheese, all bathed in a honey vinaigrette—is one of my favorite things to order then. After such a meal, it's lovely walking by the river nearby—or just strolling along the old-fashioned street, golden leaves drifting down, knowing you're not the first . . . or the last . . . to enjoy such simple small-town pleasures.

3. The North Shore

One never needs an excuse to return to the North Shore, the region of the state that is probably my favorite. With its wooded hills, river canyons and waterfalls splashing down to Lake Superior, small rental cabins, smoked fish shops, fresh rhubarb pie, and fishermen's picnic celebrations, every season along its spectacular shoreline holds a memory.

In the summer, when the lake is sparkling sunshine and blue, visitors heading north from Duluth on Highway 61 can stop at places such as Russ Kendall's for his brown sugar–smoked trout or salmon and boxes of Swedish flatbrod crackers then pull over at any number of overlooks for an alfresco snack with Lake Superior as background. A friend in Duluth tipped me off to one perfect picnic spot: secluded Sugar Loaf Cove (15 miles after Split Rock; watch closely—and then turn right—after mile marker 73). Along the rocky shoreline here, she said the "rocks roll" and she's right.

"Homemade Pie" signs abound along the highway during the summer months, and ma-and-pa shops with maple syrup, local jellies and jams, and wild rice for sale are easy to find. Fish boils are popular weekend events along the shore, too, and at Emily's Deli in Knife River, they have been a Friday-night tradition for years.

When September blows in, I love to breakfast at Bennett's on the lake and then stroll near Fitger's Complex in Duluth, with the leaves drifting over the walkways and that coolness of autumn one can actually smell. September is also the time to drive up to Duluth's Hawk Ridge. Besides an inspiring vista of Lake Superior, you may also see the ridge fill with migrating hawks and eagles wheeling on the thermals rising from the uplands. It's an awesome sight.

If you head up the shore then, though, know that unless you've reserved months earlier, don't expect to rent any quaint cabins for the weekend. If you can escape and make the journey during the week, however, the highway is peaceful, lodging available, and folks friendly—with time to talk about the weather (of course) and the lake (as always). Hearty soups grace the menus, and places like the New Scenic Café serve up satisfying bowls of Mama Rita's pasta e fagioli—a hearty peasant minestrone-type soup, steaming fragrance and comfort. At other places you may discover roasted butternut squash or grilled lake trout as specials for the day.

In Lutsen, the Coho Bakery and Deli is a standard stop for me anytime. I love the breads, and this is one place by the shore where you're always assured a well-made espresso, mocha, or cappuccino. Dinner at the impressive Lutsen

Secluded Sugar Loaf Cove on the North Shore of Lake Superior

Resort nearby is lovely and fine: dining beneath the hand-hewed beams, near the huge stone fireplace, is a tradition for many. Bluefin Restaurant is another good stop; some consider the view with dinner here the best on the North Shore.

In the wintertime, dining while watching a moonrise over the frozen lake from the historic East Bay Hotel's restaurant in Grand Marais always makes me appreciate the simple beauty of white. Stay overnight at the hotel, and in the morning the sunlit dining room is scented with that fine mingle of breakfast smells: pancakes, syrup, and coffee.

When spring arrives, the mood along the North Shore sings yet another tune. Sap is running, maple syrup kettles bubble, and amongst the wildflowers, herbs start poking up and fresh asparagus begins appearing on plates again. Rivers gush from melting snow, waterfalls roar, and—as always—appetites are aroused in every way.

DULUTH

Blue Max Restaurant
6139 LaVaque Road • Phone: (218) 721-4235

When the sun sets over Fish Lake on a Friday night, its rays scatter into the Blue Max restaurant and shine over a crowd of locals and resorters alike. Outside the place, cars are parked everywhere, spilling out of the gravel parking lot and onto the highway bridge leading to the restaurant.

The place is noisy and somewhat smoky from the large open bar room, but it's always packed like this for the Friday-night all-you-can-eat fish fry, according to the big guy (a local football player) who is wiping down our table before we're seated. My friend Chel, an area resident as well, agrees. In fact, before moving here last year, she lived in Wisconsin—and prided herself on knowing where the best fish fries in that state were located.

"This fish fry beats out any I've had in Wisconsin," she had told me in anticipation of taking me to the Blue Max. Not to mention the cost: At $6.95 ($7.95 with the all-you-can-eat salad bar), it surely has to be one of the best deals in Minnesota *or* Wisconsin.

Popovers—homemade and warm from the oven—are the first thing brought to the table. Then they start you out with two cod fillets, fried perfectly crisp and arriving hot, hot, hot. When that beauteous golden crust is cut into, the steam escapes in a misty heated rush. You can order salad or French fries to go with, but those in the know order a mess of cheesy hash browns with onions instead.

And honestly, that's all you need. Oh, and maybe a good cold beer to wash it all down with. You don't find many such simple, basic, and purely regional meals like this anymore. It's worth the drive.

THE END OF THE DROUGHT

In 1933, on the day Prohibition was repealed, Pickwick's owner Joe Wisocki drew the last stein of near beer from the tap, tasted it, and threw it into the fireplace in the Dutch Room. The Pickwick remained open 24 hours that day and served between eight and nine thousand people. A stein of beer, at that time, was a nickel.

Pickwick
508 East Superior Street • Phone: (218) 727-8901

"The pleasure is ours, the experience is yours" is the first thing you see printed on the historic Pickwick restaurant's oversized laminated menu. It's also no doubt the only menu where you're going to find appetizers that include such enticements as "charcoal broiled filet mignon tidbits, " "Polish sausage with saltines (enough for two)," and "Lake Superior Smoked White Fish with creamy horseradish."

Although the food is good here and the service friendly, efficient, and fast, everybody knows the real reason you go to the Pickwick is for the atmosphere. The building (originally a saloon in 1888) was moved to its present site in 1914.

Overlooking Lake Superior, the place has a long and intriguing history. (You can read all about it on the Pickwick's menu.)

The exterior belies the bustling activity and dark old European-style rooms that visitors step into when they open the door here. There's lots of rich white-oak woodwork, and many of the heavy tables and chairs, also white oak, were imported from Vienna and brought from the original "Old Saloon." On the walls, shadowy colored paintings of images brushed on in 1893 (at the time of the grasshopper plague) are intriguing studies. (For instance, why *does* the monk have five fingers and a thumb on his left hand?)

German beer steins are displayed everywhere, mounted trophy fish hang on the walls, and glass-enclosed stuffed wildlife is arranged atop shelves and moldings, including two owls that flank the bar.

The menu is heavy with supper club–type fare: charcoal-grilled specialties, barbecued pork ribs, and walleye, deep fried or broiled. But you can also get great sandwiches. The best? I can't resist their famous super-spicy, breaded, and deep-fried "pepper cheeseburger."

There are several different rooms in the Pickwick to dine in, and the Dutch Room, the Broiler Room, or Joe's Room are all perfectly fine spaces. But whenever I go to the Pickwick, it's the old dark bar room I choose. Laughter booms through, beer mugs clink, and it's terrifically LOUD. Still, in here, I sometimes crazily like to think you can almost feel eons of atoms from folks long gone mingling in the air or bubbling above the frothy brews.

CANAL PARK

Most visitors flock to the waterfront and trendy Canal Park in Duluth to watch the ships, shop, and eat. Several food-worthy spots in this area include At Sarah's Table (a combination bookstore/coffeehouse), Amazing Grace Bakery and Café (excellent homemade breads and soups), and the Blue Note (good made-to-order sandwiches). For dinner, try Little Angie's Cantina & Grill for salsa and spicy entrées or Bellisio's Italian Restaurant, which offers a nice selection of pastas and a good wine list.

European Bakery
109 West First Street • Phone: (218) 722–2120

This downtown Duluth bakery is sunny and bright and well worth a stop. Especially if it's June, when they sell fresh rhubarb muffins: moist, sugary crusted, and studded with big pieces of rhubarb. Yum. The bakery also offers an excellent, full-flavored caraway rye bread, just one of many delectable specialties they've been baking here for several generations.

Fichtner's
134 West First Street • Phone: (218) 722–2661

About a block from the bakery is Fichtner's, one of those long-standing old-fashioned meat markets "where wurst is best," sawdust once covered the floor, and it wasn't uncommon to have 400 customers a day come through the place. These days, it's eerily quiet in downtown Duluth. Everyone goes to the malls, says the woman waiting on me; "We're a dying breed." It would be a shame to lose such a wonderful landmark as Fichtner's. The homemade sausages are fresh, aromatic, and excellent, made from generations-old recipes. The home-smoked jerky is good, the help is friendly, and service is personal. Stop in. These are the places we're going to miss if they close.

Bennett's on the Lake
600 East Superior Street (in Fitger's Complex)
Phone: (218) 722–2829

A visit to Duluth isn't complete without sampling at least one of Bob Bennett's distinctive and made-from-scratch meals—especially when they're served in one of the prettiest rooms overlooking Lake Superior.

Check out breakfast here and you'll see that Bennett's manages to take bread and jam to new heights. Little crocks of fresh homemade raspberry jam ("it might be blackberry or blueberry tomorrow," a waitress told me, "the pastry chef makes all of our jams and jellies with whatever is in season") accompany their signature Tuscan bread. A not-too-chewy and tasty bread, it's first lightly brushed with olive oil and then grilled. Although I could make a meal out of the bread/jam combo, their hash brown omelet with bacon is incredibly good, too—expertly crafted eggs swirled, flipped, and wrapped around big chunks of perfectly fried bacon and good cheese.

Lunches and dinners reflect a bit of chef-owner Bob Bennett's varied culinary background, including executive chef stints in California and Phoenix—which he says inspired his passion for the southwestern touch. Appetizers include Arizona egg rolls with an ancho chili sauce and a grilled achiote chicken breast with a good salsa. But be aware: The menu does change "due to creativity and product availability," which is part of the reason folks keep coming back.

A Perfect Picnic

In late July, the place to picnic in Duluth is the Rose Garden. Uniquely landscaped over the freeway tunnel systems near London Road and 12th Avenue East, it's hard to believe such a serene spot exists here.

Walking paths overlook the lake in the distance. There are arbors and lovely donated "memory" benches. Then there's that faint smell of roses on the lake breeze. Who would guess? Folks picnic, take photos, sketch, read, and write amidst more than three thousand rose bushes bursting in blooms: crimson edged, pink tinged, blood red, pale yellow, and dusty coral.

If you need fortifications, I suggest stopping at the nearby Lakeview Coffee Emporium in Fitger's Complex. Pick up a chicken Caesar wrap, treat yourself to a malt at the historic Portland Square Malt shop next door, and then drive over to the rose garden and find yourself an empty bench. My personal favorite is the one inscribed on the back with the words "Eric Carl Peterson, 1924–1998. He always took the scenic route." (That sounds so much better than "He always took the short cut.")

New Scenic Café
5461 North Shore Drive (8 miles northeast of Duluth)
Phone (218) 525-6274 • Web site: www.sceniccafé.com

What's not to like about a place where Mason jars of locally harvested maple syrup sit on the counter for sale and breakfasts include such lyrical sounding entrees as a "Singing Waters Omelette" (a rich combo of goat cheese, cream cheese, red onion, and spinach leaves stuffed into eggs and topped with blackberry peach salsa) or the "Scenic Sunrise" (two tender whole wheat buttermilk pancakes with eggs)?

The New Scenic Café, near Duluth

Although its North Shore location alone is reason enough to stop (look out the dining room windows and you may see an iron-ore ship out on Lake Superior), the New Scenic has some of the best and most innovative fare you're likely to find in such an unpretentious-looking joint.

The building—at one time called the Scenic Drive-In, complete with carhop service—has been moved, added on, remodeled, and renovated. It's still not much to look at from the outside, but walk in from a fog-scattered day along the shore and you face cheery, bright warm rooms filled with a fiesta of colorful painted sculptures on the walls. (I like the wooden moose head decorated in a patchwork mosaic of bright colors.)

It's also highly probable that when you walk in, Rita B. will be near the door to greet you. She's the co-owner, along with her nephew and the restaurant's chef, Scott Graden. They took over the restaurant on April 1, 1999—and since then, these two unlikely partners with a passion for wonderful food have been the driving forces behind New Scenic's ambitious menu. Everything is well thought out here, from the homemade "bumble bluesberry" jam and good granola (it's packaged for sale) to the handmade butternut squash ravioli ("People mourned it when we took it off the menu," says Rita.) But the menu is ever changing, says Scott, who worked 10 years in corporate restaurants and loves being able to break "ethnicity rules" now in his own kitchen.

Even the sandwiches are sparked with creative flair. A French baguette is layered with tender, thin slices of roasted pork tenderloin and then topped with a confit of sweet caramelized onions and dripped with savory ginger sauce. The pistachio-crusted goat cheese sandwich is like "an adult grilled cheese," says Scott.

Many of the desserts, and especially the New Scenic's pies, are Rita's domain. And whenever she happens to be standing in the kitchen, rolling out pastry, gazing out the window at the sky and lake view, she says she still feels that owning the New Scenic is a dream come true. I think maybe her happiness gets absorbed into those pies too, because after tasting the triple-berry pie and sampling a slice of the blackberry peach one afternoon, I have to say I left the New Scenic a very happy woman indeed.

KNIFE RIVER

Russ Kendall's Smoked Fish House
P.O. Box 146, 149 Scenic Drive • Phone: (218) 834-5995

This small shop, one of many smoked fish shops along the North Shore, is probably one of the oldest and best known. And even though he's getting on in years, don't be surprised to see Kendall himself, swathed in a bright red apron, behind the fish case, offering up samples of his brown sugar–smoked salmon to taste. If the place is quiet (rarely), encourage him and he may even tell you how his dad started the place in 1925 after the truck in which he was hauling fish broke down. To avoid a complete financial disaster, the elder

Russ Kendall serving them up at his fish house, Knife River

Kendall sold all the fish he was carrying off the back of the truck. Inspired by his success, he stayed on and eventually opened the market.

The shop is crammed with plenty of picnic fixings, boxes of crackers, pickles, cheeses, and good homemade beef jerky. But the attraction is clearly his barbecued smoked lake trout, salmon, ciscoes, herring, and whitefish. Personally, I think it's the maple wood he uses exclusively in his smokehouse that produces the addictive and superb flavor.

Our family always stops here on our way up the shore for a fix of smoked fish and again on our way back home to the Twin Cities. Always. To me, the little shop, with its savory, smoky smell, epitomizes the whole North Shore scene and experience. Eating the tasty fish simply seals the memory.

Emily's Eatery and Inn
P.O. Box 174, 218 Scenic Highway 12 • Phone: (218) 834-5922

Another all-time favorite fixture on the North Shore is Emily's. Situated in a great old (1929) picturesque building, it's complete with country creaky wood floors and a little front porch. Dine in (the smoked-trout salad is always fine) or order take-out sandwiches for a picnic farther up the shore. From February to October, there's a fun Friday-night fish boil. Upstairs, three homespun rooms (sharing a bath) can be rented out.

TWO HARBORS

Betty's Pies
1633 Highway 61 • P.O. Box 12
Phone: (218) 834–3367 or (877) 269-7494

No one can mention the North Shore without saying something about Betty's Pies. It's a long-standing summer tradition for travelers to make a stop at the little shack with its charming blue/white décor that has been turning out fantastic pies for years. But sad to say, Betty's Pies (it has changed ownership several times in the past few years) has gone from quaint little old place along the lake to slick new restaurant by the shore. The last time I visited, I actually got in a traffic jam in the huge new parking lot next to the huge new building.

Inside, teenage help hustled madly around, short tempered. The girl at the cash register couldn't keep up with the crowd—and didn't bother to look up or say thank you when she handed me my receipt and a piece of pie to go. The place was packed, though. And the cars kept turning into the parking lot, and the pies kept popping out of the ovens at regular intervals. The pies are still good enough, although last time I found nary a wild, tiny blueberry in the blueberry pie). I know times change. Even so, it's kind of heartbreaking to see the little original pie shack vacant out front. It looks lost.

Rustic Inn Café
2773 Highway 61 (2 miles south of Gooseberry Falls State Park)
Phone: (218) 834-2488

Built in 1930, the Rustic is yet another of the treasured old cafés remaining on the North Shore. And even when highway work a few years ago required the café to be moved three blocks, the original log structure was saved, although a new addition was added on. The new section offers the same menu of plain and simple fare and a long list of pies, but old-timers know the best reason to eat (and stop) here is for a chance to sit once again in the original section of the building, with its log interior, cheerful red and white–checked curtains, and memory-filled ambience.

BEAVER BAY

Northern Lights Roadhouse
Highway 61 • Phone: (218) 226-3012

This is one of those misleading places where the exterior totally belies the interior. Located on the same property as the authentic double-decker English bus (transformed into an ice cream shop, serving Brown's Velvet ice cream), the Northern Lights Roadhouse appears to be an A-frame, rather 1960s sort

Northern Lights Roadhouse, Beaver Bay

of generic spot. But inside, it's North Woods quaint, funky, and filled with merchandise.

Beyond the shop shelves, you can dine in the pleasant screened-in porch or out back on the absolutely lovely landscaped garden overlooking the lake. The menu includes burgers and baskets of fish and chips but also features an interesting raspberry-sauced walleye (when available) and something called the North Country Brunch Pie, which the menu describes like this: "Beyond ordinary Quiche, this dish features wild rice, bacon, Swiss cheese in a Dijon mustard crust." You can also get a decent bowl of wild rice soup, touted by loyal fans as the best on the North Shore. The soup is good, but in all honesty, I can't say it's the *best* on the shore.

TOFTE

Coho Bakery and Deli
Highway 61 • Phone: (218) 663-8032

A bread lover's paradise awaits at the Coho, although you do need to get here early in the day to take advantage. Breads baked daily include spinach parmesan, onion river dill (used for the deli's popular Reuben sandwich), and chewy baguettes. If I'm here when the whole wheat variety for the day is the roasted pepper (a slightly spicy and wonderful boule), I always buy it.

There's also a revolving list of daily specials. Fridays, their signature French bread dough gets mixed with fragrant herbs and wild rice. Sundays, don't leave without the Norwegian cardamom bread, a sweet, cinnamony Scandinavian treat. Thursdays, it's sun-dried tomato basil. And if there's pesto bread, it must be Monday.

All breads are baked on brick hearths and made using a sourdough starter and a small amount of yeast. A two-day process to allow the dough to develop is what gives the Coho loaves their thick hearty crust and chewy texture.

And don't leave without at least a lustful peek at the absolutely gorgeous tarts and cakes that tantalize behind glass display cases on the dining-in side of the room.

In fact, if you are here around lunchtime, do take time to eat here. Besides several tables indoors, there are umbrella-shaded tables on a flower-filled patio outside, too. Tasty soups, salads, sandwiches, and pastas fill the menu. Try one of the calzones; the "sawbill spinach" is a fragrant medley of caramelized onions, five Italian cheeses, spinach, garlic, and herbs all baked within a wonderful crust. Or sample the award-winning pizzas. The "call of the wild" variation is sprinkled with a locally made Italian wild rice sausage and then loaded with all sorts of mushrooms and cheeses.

GRAND MARAIS

East Bay Hotel Restaurant
1 Wisconsin Street • Phone: (218) 387-2800

The first time I walked in to the East Bay Hotel, I still remember stepping by a honey-colored lab who was sleeping in a patch of sunlight in the lobby. "Belle" (I found out later) glanced sleepily up at me and then went back to her afternoon nap in the sun. I was, I admit it, completely charmed. By a dog.

I fell in love with the place immediately. Maybe it was because Belle reminded me of my pet lab from childhood. More likely, it was simply because Belle epitomized the whole slowed-down pace of the place. At any rate, it was also even more pleasantly rewarding to discover that the windowed dining room and summer patio—overlooking a curve of the lake—also serve some fairly fine food. Raspberry pancakes for breakfast, broiled Lake Superior trout for lunch. As if that weren't good enough, the view with dinner (in wintertime at least) occasionally includes a full moon slipping heavenward over an icy and snow-frosted expanse of water.

If you want the specialty Scandinavian fish cakes, though, you'll have to visit in the warm season. And even then, they're not always available. Time it right, however, and your server may say, "You're in luck; we just got them in a half hour ago." In truth, Scandinavian fish cakes are better than they sound. Prepared with fresh Lake Superior herring (they make them with whitefish too, but they're not as good), these delicacies are an airy, fluffy concoction (similar in texture to a soufflé). The fresh ground herring is mixed with eggs, milk, onions, and a hint of nutmeg and then spooned onto a grill and cooked into light oval clouds.

The other thing you'll want to order, if it's on the menu, is East Bay's rhubarb pie. "It just came out of the oven, and it's too hot to cut yet," I was told the first time I ordered a slice, "but if you want, you can wait."

I wanted. I waited. It was worth it.

World's Best Donuts

10 East Wisconsin Street • Phone: (218) 387-1345

On summer Sundays at the World's Best Donuts, the line is out the door and down the half-dozen steps to the sidewalk and street. Although doughnuts and "roly poly's" are the draw, the specialty not to miss here is "skizzle," something that reminds me of the leftover bread dough my mom deep-fried in small stretched shapes and then sprinkled with sugar while still hot. Heavenly stuff. There really is nothing to compare it to.

Besides the sweet offerings, regulars come into World's Best Donuts with their own coffee mugs, and the girls behind the counter know who wants the real thing and who needs the decaf. The cozy low-ceilinged building has tables in a room off to the side. Or you can sit at a table outside in the tiny courtyard, sip hot coffee, nibble a chocolate-covered doughnut, and watch people photograph each other with their faces stuck into the life-size wood cutouts of a Viking guy and his lady. Always entertaining.

The Angry Trout

P.O. Box 973, 416 West Highway 61
Phone: (218) 387-1265 (seasonal number)

This little restaurant smack dab next to the lake is light, bright, airy—and as locals and tourists always want to tell you—so trendy. But oh, what food. It's the place to find fresh, never frozen, fish. And it's the best that Lake Superior anglers have to offer: lake trout, herring, whitefish, and menomonie.

The sign says it all, Grand Marais

Besides the freshest fish, you'll also see that at the Angry Trout, *everything* matters. Just take a gaze at one entire page of the menu labeled "For Your Information." Credits go everywhere: Wild rice harvested nearby in Finland, Minnesota. Organically raised chicken. Even the gorgeous flowers on the tables are "from Libby Wilkes' garden in Lutsen." Tables and chairs are "made from the wood of 15 different local species of trees." Serving dishes are "pottery, hand thrown, wood fired by Dick Cooter of Two Harbors." "Teeny tiny napkins" (small to conserve energy in washing) are made from organic cotton.

You can sit inside at tables under a sunny atrium-windowed area. (Look outwards and see the lighthouse in the distance or look up and see seagulls swooping over.) But if the weather is nice, nothing beats a table outside, within touching distance of the water. The kids can skip stones on the shoreline while you're waiting to be served. If the trout chowder is noted on the chalkboard outside (detailing the day's specials), it's a must. Added bonus: It's served with two thick slices of wonderful herb bread. If "Steve Aberle's wild Alaskan salmon" (flown in occasionally) is on the menu, you don't want to miss it.

Another good choice: the Fish & Chips—the Trout's "meanest meal," according to the menu. Select cuts of Alaskan cod or Lake Superior herring (choose the herring) is breaded, deep fried, and arrives not a bit greasy, along with a small metal container of creamy dill mayo and a generous amount of hand-cut potato fries.

On my last visit, I think I had my best meal yet: the grilled fish-of-the-day salad, a beautiful concoction of greens (an edible purple pansy peeked from the plate edge) topped with perfectly prepared Lake Superior whitefish. The whole fragrant artistic medley included a couple season-fresh cherries on the stem and was tossed with the Trout's homemade maple mustard dressing.

For dessert, I skipped the intriguing shot of local maple syrup "served warm—just like a visit to the sugar house in spring." (I tried this once and it was way too sweet for me.) Instead, I opted for Angry Trout's vanilla ice cream, drowned in a whipped smooth syrup of espresso and sugar. I wasn't disappointed. It was a nice racy hit of caffeine and cold, and seemed the perfect ending to an already Superior meal.

Naniboujou Lodge and Restaurant

20 Naniboujou Trail • Phone: (218) 387-2688
Web site: www.naniboujou.com

It wasn't until recently that I read that the Naniboujou takes its name from an impish outdoor-loving Indian spirit who was also "a trickster and a man-god who taught by experience." Perhaps that (and not the below-zero temperature) explains the fact that my car wouldn't start one winter morning when I was ready to leave this historic place for home. "Same thing happened a few weeks ago," I remember the mechanic who came out from Grand Marais telling me at the time. "A red car, just like yours," he says, "parked in the exact same spot. Wouldn't start either."

Even so, that won't deter me from another midwinter escape up the North Shore to Naniboujou. (I'll park the car facing the morning sun next time.) But I must admit, it's still the summer season when I most love to visit this beautiful lodge, with its history, food, and incredibly stunning Cree Indian painting in its great hall.

Opened in 1929 as a retreat for the wealthy (Jack Dempsey, Babe Ruth, and Ring Lardner were reported to be investors), this Jazz Age motor lodge sits about fifteen miles north of Grand Marais and just east of the Brule River's mouth—on land that juts out into Lake Superior. While the stock market crash put an end to the most ambitious of plans here, including the riding stables, tennis courts, and cottages, the lodge and some of the original furniture remains. (Check out that ten-sided faded coral velvet gossip seat and the carved chandeliers of balsam pine and parchment.)

The massive fireplace at one end of the room is formed from two hundred tons of wave-rounded stone gathered from the beach. And when the fire flickers here, the colorful geometric Cree patterns painted on the ceiling and walls fairly glow.

In the morning sunlight, however, the room—with its curved ceiling (shaped to resemble the bottom of a canoe)—is bright and warm. Breakfast is a cheery and leisurely event. Try the silky made-with-milk porridge. Topped with a brown-sugar mixture, caramelized and crunchy, it's comfort food with a sweet spin. The waffle, served with a tin pitcher full of warm orange rum syrup, is airy and tender; the blueberry pancakes, loaded with ripe fresh blueberries. I love the old heavy restaurant china that the food is served on as well, even if it doesn't match the Cree motif in the least.

Afterwards, you can linger in the old-fashioned solarium, where several half-assembled puzzles beckon on tables, or you can take a stroll outside by the lake. If you're really ambitious, head nearby for a hike to Devil's Kettle.

Dinner at the lodge is an entirely different experience. It's dark, shadowy, and sensual, with a haunting ambience you can almost feel. To be truthful, I have had both very good and also very mediocre meals then. One time, the chicken was underdone and dessert was fairly tasteless; another time the meat was perfect and tender and a cheesecake was luxurious.

FROM THE NANIBOUJOU: ORANGE RUM SYRUP

This is a favorite at Naniboujou's Sunday Brunch; the restaurant continually gets asked for the recipe. Although the kitchen crew is not too keen on grating all the orange zest needed for the gallons of syrup, at home the task is not so daunting—especially if you halve the recipe (which still makes plenty of syrup for even a company breakfast).

     2 cups sugar
     1 1/2 cups orange juice

2 oranges zest** (grated peel)
1/4 cup dark rum

In a medium saucepan combine the sugar, orange juice, and orange zest. Stir over low heat until the sugar is dissolved. Bring to a simmer. Remove from the heat. Add the rum and serve. Makes 2 1/2 cups.

**Avoid grating any of the white pith next to the skin, as it has a bitter taste.

Reprinted with permission from *Dining in the Spirit of Naniboujou*, compiled and edited by Bonnie Jean Swanson (Grand Marais: 1999).

GUNFLINT TRAIL

Black Bear Bar and Restaurant and Trail Center
7611 Gunflint Trail, Grand Marais • Phone: (218) 388-2214

A writer friend once told me that if you're looking for the heart of the Gunflint Trail, stop by the Black Bear. She was right. This combination grocery store/restaurant/resort and local gathering place goes back to the 1930s and is filled with North Woods antiques and lots and lots of atmosphere. Gunflint Lodge chef Ron Berg, down the road, advised me not to miss the place as well. His words: "It's the quintessential North Woods hang out, revered by locals and visitors alike."

You can buy a handmade quilt, an animal pelt, a fishing license, or bait here. Mostly, though, it's a great spot to stop in, sit on a log barstool by the bar (where a pitcher of wildflowers usually graces one corner), and order Smitty's Tenderloin, a breaded pork tenderloin sandwich served with a big ole slice of raw onion. You'll also find burgers such as Dale's Jalapeño ("for the brave at heart"), and steak lovers can get an eight-ounce Jack Daniels Filet.

Don't forget dessert here either: Order an apple dumpling or bread pudding if it's on the menu.

Gunflint Lodge
143 South Gunflint Lake • Phone: (800) 328-3325 or (218) 388-2294
Web site: www.gunflint.com

Sitting in the dining room at the Gunflint Lodge, gazing out at a pristine lake, and expectantly awaiting a meal cooked by chef Ron Berg is my idea of true wilderness bliss.

But the gourmet meals served here at the Gunflint, 45 miles north of Grand Marais on the Gunflint Trail, are anything but wilderness cuisine. In his book

A common sign along the North Shore

Northwoods Fish Cookery (Minneapolis: University of Minnesota Press, 2000), Berg writes that his up-north cooking philosophy is much like an old woods-man's who once told him, "Roughin' it's for them that don't know no better."

And boy, does Berg know better. Each day the Gun-flint's menu is different. Breads change from wild rice and honey to butter-milk to black onion rye. Soups might be tomato, scented with fresh basil, or stracciatella (a wonderful Italian-style Parmesan cheese and egg-drop soup) or a rich salmon and wild rice chowder. Entrees vary from a perfectly roasted breast of duck with sun-dried cherries to tender chicken wrapped around a savory sage and onion-bread filling to an even more incredible bacon-hazelnut–stuffed rainbow trout. And I do believe the appetizer of salmon rubbed with cracked peppercorns, glazed with local maple syrup, and then slowly smoked over applewood is a lesson in love.

Dessert? Well, that ranges from a cream puff filled with homemade maple ice cream and served in a pool of blackberry sauce to a bourbon-spiked choco-late bread pudding. Berg likes to say, "To me, the perfect meal is from bread basket to dessert." Happily, you can always expect such a meal from his kitchen.

FROM GUNFLINT LODGE: BEER BATTER–FRIED WALLEYE WITH MANGO SWEET-AND-SOUR SAUCE

This golden-fried walleye with an Asian-style sweet-and-sour sauce has become one of the most popular walleye entrées at Gunflint Lodge, says the lodge's executive chef, Ron Berg. Indeed, "people have fits when we try to take it off the menu," says the lodge's owner, Bruce Kerfoot, who admits that when Berg first told him about the recipe, he was skeptical it would sell.

Sweet-and-Sour Sauce

1 cup sugar
2 teaspoons minced garlic
1 1/2 cup rice wine vinegar
2 teaspoons chili paste with garlic
2 tablespoons Asian fish sauce
Cornstarch slurry, as needed (Author's note: Use 3 teaspoons cornstarch to 1/3 cup water; adjust as necessary)
1/2 mango cut into 1/4-inch dice (other fruits such as fresh peaches, raspberries, wild blueberries, or strawberries or a combination of fruits may be substituted).

Garnish

1/2 red pepper, finely diced (or a combination of colored sweet peppers)
4 green onions, green part only, finely sliced on the diagonal

Beer Batter

10 ounces all-purpose flour
3 tablespoons paprika
2 tablespoons kosher salt
1 tablespoon ground black pepper
2 or 3 twelve-ounce cans of beer
All-purpose flour (to dredge walleye in before battering)
6 (8–10 ounce) boneless, skinless walleye fillets, whole or cut into finger-sized strips

Make sweet-and-sour sauce. Combine sugar, garlic, rice wine vinegar, chili paste, and fish sauce in a heavy-bottomed saucepan over medium heat. Bring to a boil and simmer for 4 to 5 minutes until reduced and flavor reaches desired intensity. Thicken with cornstarch slurry. Refrigerate until needed. Serve warm. Makes about 2 cups of sauce.

Prepare garnishes and refrigerate until needed.

Make beer batter. Whisk the flour, paprika, salt, and pepper together until well combined. Whisk in beer to make a thin batter, not much thicker than buttermilk or very heavy cream.

To serve: Dredge walleye in flour and shake off excess. Dip into beer batter and deep fry until golden brown and crisp. Remove and drain. (Author's note: You can also sauté filets in canola oil or corn oil until golden brown and crisp.)

Cover the bottom of 6 heated plates with 1 1/2 to 2 ounces of the sauce mixed with 1 to 2 tablespoons of the chopped mango. Sprinkle the red peppers and green onion tops over sauce. Place walleye on top and serve. Serves 6.

Tip: Stored in a covered container, leftover sweet-and-sour sauce keeps almost indefinitely in the refrigerator.

Reprinted with permission from *The Gunflint Lodge Cookbook* by Ron Berg and Sue Kerfoot (Minneapolis: University of Minnesota Press, 1997).

4. The Iron Range

I once read about a restaurant that described its food as very much a kind of country cooking . . . roughly assembled but incredibly delicious and intense—its own kind of art form.

That's how I think about Minnesota's Iron Range country. It's a rough country, this northeastern part of the state—with its pit lakes and mini-canyons created by a century of intensive mining. But it's also a region rich in ethnic heritage and strong traditions. With its tall pine trees lining the highways and manmade lakes and hills slowly being reclaimed by nature, it truly is its own kind of art form.

Historic sites in the area include plenty of glimpses into the mining life that once thrived here. A tour of the Soudan Underground Mine near Tower is a trip no one should miss. This is the real thing . . . and when you step into the cage that takes you almost a half-mile below the surface of the earth, you're experiencing the same elevator ride that hundreds of miners once took every day to work. After the tour, you can stop in Tower at Erica's Bakery and lunch on a hot meat pie, called a Cornish pasty (pronounced *past*-tee). One of many ethnic specialties you'll find on the "Range," the pasty is similar to what many of the immigrant miners once ate on the job.

It's these immigrants—from more than forty countries—who came to work the mines here and created the Range's varied cultural landscape. Gastronomically, that's also why you'll still find delicacies here such as the southern Slavic potica (pronounced po-teet-za—a walnut-filled sweet bread) or Italian porketta (a fennel-flavored pork) or Finnish sarmas (cabbage leaves stuffed with meat, then layered in a pan with sauerkraut and baked).

At one time, these ethnic specialties were concentrated in specific regions on the Iron Range as well, but today the boundaries have blurred somewhat owing to intermarriage and movement in and out of the area.

What exactly constitutes the Iron Range's boundaries? In fact, there are really three so-called iron ranges in Minnesota. To the south is the Cuyuna Range near Crosby and Aitken. The Soudan—the first mine in the Vermilion Range—lies between the present towns of Tower and Ely. Once considered the capital of the Vermilion Range, today Ely is known more for its popular Chocolate Moose restaurant, mukluk manufacturing, canoe building, and dozens of Boundary Waters outfitters. Trendy spots that seem more metro than North Woods include the Northern Grounds coffeehouse in town, where you can get a cappuccino, mocha, or an organically correct sandwich sporting fresh bean sprouts. Two Ely restaurants are located in big attractive old houses: At the

Mantel House, a French chef prepares classic cuisine and even offers cooking classes during the winter. At Minglewood's, you'll find solid homemade fare, vegetarian offerings, and a relaxed, laid-back atmosphere. (Make sure you taste their homemade bread-and- butter pickles, too.)

Still, it's the Mesabi Range that most people in the state are referring to when they talk about "the Range." This includes the towns of Hibbing on the western edge to Hoyt Lakes on the east—a distance that can be driven in less than an hour. Start at Hibbing, where Bob Dylan grew up, and stop in at the Hibbing High School for a tour. This vintage showplace, completed in 1923 (at the cost of nearly $4 million dollars), includes an auditorium with cut-glass chandeliers and seats upholstered in gold velveteen.

From Hibbing, take a jaunt up to Chisholm and Ironworld Discovery Center, where you can lunch on cabbage rolls and Cornish pasties. Then, in Virginia, make time to drive downtown and visit Canelake's candy shop, where the old-fashioned "hot air" candy is still being made by hand.

A polka step away from Virginia is Eveleth; see the large hockey stick and tour the U.S. Hockey Hall of Fame. Gilbert has gotten its culinary name on the map with its Jamaican-inspired restaurant, The Whistling Bird. Next town over is the Bavarian-themed Biwabek, a pretty little village with colorful murals of alpine meadows adorning the façade of buildings in town and host of one of the most charming holiday festivals in the state: Weihnachtsfest. Daytime festivities throughout town then include a bake sale at the Park Pavilion, where you can pick up fantastic homemade cardamom bread, potica prepared from heirloom family recipes, and dozens of cookies. Then you can dance a polka after lunching on sarmas, pasties, or Italian beef sandwiches—and finally, meet at the Park Gazebo for the tree-lighting ceremony and fireworks (in the cold air, they're doubly bright!).

If you make a detour through Aurora (and you should), a stop at historic Hank's Bar 'n Grill is a must. Pick up some of their broasted chicken to go and then drive north to Tower for a picnic at Vermilion Lake, called "Lake of the Sunset Glow" by the Ojibwa. The best way to get to Vermilion Lake from here is to turn left on St. Louis County 697. The road winds its way through woods and meadows to Hoo Doo Point on Pike Bay. It's a grand setting and lovely view.

CLOQUET

Gordy's Hi-Hat
415 Sunnyside Drive • Phone: (218) 879-6125

When you're driving from the Twin Cities and nearing Cloquet, the freeway sign proclaims "Range Cities" ahead. Following the signs leads vacationers through Cloquet, where folks have been summertime stopping at Gordy's Hi-Hat for years.

Gordy's is a joyful place with "famous" juicy hamburgers and merry eaters chowing down wherever they can find a table or a booth, inside or out. In fact,

Emerging happier—and fuller—from Gordy's Hi-Hat in Cloquet.

sometimes it's almost fun not even bothering with finding a seat but simply wandering around the place, looking at the old black-and-white photos of the way it was at Gordy's in the 1960s: Dressed-up moms at the walk-up window ordering a 19 cent egg salad sandwich, perhaps, or a 39 cent fishburger and a chocolate malt.

Today, the fishburger is $3.99, and it's still one sweet deal—five pieces of hand-battered Alaskan fish sandwiched in a steamy bun. The total package is unwieldy in the extreme. But it's worth every messy bite: The batter is heavenly, and the hot fish inside done perfectly.

Burgers at Gordy's are fresh and personally hand-pattied (no mass machine-shaped beef rounds here), and the onion rings are excellent. If you order a fresh strawberry or raspberry malt to go with your meal, know that you'll need a spoon. These rich beauties are too thick for a straw. Finally, forget the calorie and cholesterol police for the day. Heck, you're probably on vacation, anyway.

HIBBING

Sunrise Bakery
1813 Third Avenue East • Phone: (218) 263-9647

When you're in the area, do make a little detour to visit this charming regional bakery that offers a wide selection of fantastic bakery as well as deli items and gourmet sweets and savories. Apple strudel, Italian bread, romano cheese bread, and chocolate-covered fruitcake (I love it!) are among the offerings. But like the Italian Bakery in Virginia, Sunrise is also famous for its potica.

A labor-intensive pastry, potica is made with flour, butter, eggs, honey, vanilla, and walnuts. The dough is rolled or pulled extremely thin and then covered with a walnut mixture, rolled up jelly-roll style, and baked in long bread pans. It has been said that it wouldn't be a wedding on the Iron Range if you didn't serve potica. Happily, both the Sunrise Bakery and the Italian Bakery in Virginia still prepare this time-consuming delicacy—should you not have an aunt or grandmother who remembers how to prepare the specialty.

Besides the south Slavic potica, Sunrise's sweet repertoire represents many of the more than forty countries with roots in this part of the state. I'm a big fan of the Scandinavian dipping cookies, made with whole toasted almonds, butter and sour cream, and that irresistible spice: cardamom. The biscotti-like cookies are stacked by sixes and tied up in a cellophane bag with a bright blue ribbon. Sunrise also makes Scandinavian yule kaage, stollen, and kolaches— a filled pastry of Czech origin that has as many variations as spellings. Sunrise's version uses a strudel-like (not yeast) dough and comes with apricot, prune, or cream cheese fillings. As for bread, the Italian bread here was the original item in the bakery and has been made for over eighty years. Bakery owner Ginny Forti says this is still the best bread in town. (I agree.)

It was Ginny Forti's grandfather, Julius Forti, who opened this bakery in 1913; today she's the one you're most likely to find at the shop. Ginny is the type of friendly person I have seen keep the store open long after closing hours on a Saturday—just because someone knocked on the door and explained they had made a special trip here from out of town. One time it was a couple who had grown up on the Range and remembered the bakery from their younger days, and another time it was me, peering in the window. She was still in the store, and she simply opened the door and invited me in.

CORNISH PASTIES

Eleanor Ostman, food columnist for the *St. Paul Pioneer Press* newspaper for 30 years, grew up in Hibbing, on the Iron Range—and ate her share of the popular Range specialty known as the pasty. In her cookbook *Always on Sunday* (St. Paul: Sunday Press, 1998), she writes "variations on pasties are rife" on the Range. Some sauté their meat cubes and onion before adding raw vegetables. Others scoff at that idea, while still others use hamburger instead of cubed raw meat. Then there are the vegetables: Potatoes are a must. So are onions. Use lots, advises Eleanor, because "nothing is more lackluster than a bland pasty." Eleanor grew up with carrots in pasties, but some bakers insist on rutabagas. You can use both, grating them if you like. But never grate the potatoes in pasties. They should be tiny diced so they'll cook through but retain their shape. Finally, Eleanor advises tossing all the vegetables in a bowl, adding salt and pepper, and mixing everything well before combining with the meat and pastry. The following is her mother's recipe for the pasty. It's the real one.

The Real Ellen Ostman's Pasty

Pastry for 2 large crusts
2 cups peeled and finely diced potatoes
1/2 cup peeled and finely diced carrots
1/2 cup finely diced onion
1 cup peeled and finely diced rutabaga (optional)
1 tsp. salt
1/2 teaspoon freshly ground pepper, or to taste
1/4 pound round steak, cut into small cubes
butter

Make pastry. Chill for 1 hour. Peel and finely dice vegetables (adjust proportions as you wish). Toss with salt and pepper. Roll half of pastry into large round. Place half of vegetables (drained first, if necessary) on 1 side of pastry. Top with cubed meat. Sprinkle with salt and pepper. Add a few bits of butter. Fold over other half of pastry. Tightly crimp edges so filling stays put. Carefully lift pasty onto lightly greased baking sheet. Cut 2 or 3 small slits in top for steam to escape. Repeat with remaining pastry and filling ingredients. Bake in 375 degree oven for 50 to 60 minutes or until pastry is nicely browned. Serve hot, with ketchup, if desired. Makes 2 large pasties.

VIRGINIA

Canelake's Candy

414 Chestnut Street • Phone: (218) 741-1557
Web site: www. canelakes.com

There is nothing like walking into Canelake's candy shop in the autumn, when the seductive, buttery smell of caramel—as in caramel apples—scents the shop. These are the old-fashioned treats, with crisp apples dipped in the real handmade and butter-rich caramel stuff. There is no comparison. I have made special trips here for them.

Stepping into Canelake's candy shop in Virginia anytime of year, however, is like entering one of the many candy kitchens that were open on the Iron Range during the early 1900s. "That's when all the little towns had their own candy kitchens: Hibbing, Eveleth, Chisholm . . . ," says John Canelake, whose father, Gust, founded Canelake's in 1905.

Today, Canelake's is one of a handful of old-fashioned candy and ice cream parlors that have stayed true to their roots. Vintage display cases are filled with dozens of hand-dipped and monogrammed dark and milk chocolate delights as well as cashew clusters, hand-cut caramel, and brittles.

In the back of the shop, you can sometimes peek in and watch a lone worker hand-dipping butter almond toffees at one of the original marble-topped tables. Or glance in the kitchen and catch sole candymaker Jim Cina stirring together a bubbling brew of sugar and syrup that will eventually bloom into a batch of Canelake's uniquely light and crisp confection called "hot air." Cina is one of few who knows the secret recipe for this Canelake specialty—an airy (and addictive) brown sugar–like sponge interior (it's crunchy!) that gets dipped in dark or milk chocolate. But the old recipe from Gust Canelake didn't come cheap.

In 1982, when brothers John and Leo Canelake were considering retiring, Cina arrived in their kitchen, an Aurora native from down the road who wanted to learn the candy business. But it was only after the persistent Cina apprenticed for nine months with no pay that the brothers concluded he was serious. Shortly thereafter, they sold him the business and the prized sweet recipes.

Ever since, Cina has been making candy in the same open-fire copper kettles, using ingredients that built Canelake's reputation: Grade AA butter, real chocolate, whipping cream, and no preservatives. The signs posted on the candy display cases say it all: "We're very proud of the great candy formulas developed by Mr. Canelake and we always follow them to the letter."

The Royal Café
217 Chestnut Street • Phone: (218) 741-6282

"Mean Jean" runs this old-time restaurant in downtown Virginia. "Just a greasy spoon," she says—and that's the way she wants to keep it. The place has a small counter with a few stools, generally occupied by some old-timers in suspenders and flannel shirts. Mean Jean knows them all. "You're late, Clyde," she scolded one customer. "Your buddy was here at 6."

The floor is that big old-fashioned celadon green and cream–checked pattern. (I actually thought of Martha Stewart colors.) The blood-red booths along the wall are comfy and clean, if a little moveable and worn—and the room is usually decorated for the season. (One October I visited, I sat next to two mechanized and dressed-up skeletons who occasionally burst into song.)

Breakfast here is good . . . and cheap. "Tony's Special: two eggs, two sausage, toast. No exceptions. $2.25." The toast that comes with your meal is from the

Italian Bakery up the street—and you get four thickly cut and buttered slices with your eggs or omelets. (The toast alone is worth $2.25.) Hash browns are homemade and marvelous, too, if a bit greasy.

If you go to the restroom here (and you should), the route will take you through the next door bar (it's part of the restaurant). Make sure you get a look at the actual bar counter in here. Inlaid with pennies, it stretches all the way across the narrow room. When I couldn't help admiring it, the bartender informed me with some pride, "This is the longest bar on the Iron Range." I didn't doubt her.

Italian Bakery

205 First Street South • Phone: (218) 741-3464 or (800) 238-8830

The Italian Bakery, founded in 1910, is a lively bakeshop, and its potica has drawn customers for years.

Although the potica is popular at the bakery, the "ranch style" whole wheat bread is another reason to make a stop here. (It's marvelous toasted, too.) This is also one of few bakeries where you'll find baked bismarks (rather like a bread dough with jelly filling) and occasionally homemade "snowballs" (you know, the kind you usually see at convenience stores, packaged in twosomes labeled with an arm's-length list of preservatives). The marshmallow-covered cakes

The Italian Bakery in Virginia

here are the way snowballs are meant to taste. And don't leave without at least one of their lemon-filled deep-fried pastry pie pockets. At the cookie counter, even the sugarless treats look good, but as the clerk said, "Oh, you don't want those, they're for people who can't have sugar." Go for a couple of those caramel-filled truffle cookies (with sugar) instead.

EVELETH

K & B Drive-In
Highway 53 • Phone: (218) 744-2772

Just a mile and a half out of Eveleth, you can't miss this local favorite. A checkerboard beacon of red and white, it's tucked beside the highway in a park-like setting of tall pines. Pull your car under the awning here, and you can still get old-fashioned car-hop service. Or go indoors to the sparkling clean, red-and-white dining room. If you don't want to stay inside (the car *or* the building), there are picnic tables scattered under the beautiful trees a short distance away.

But the main thing: Don't even think of stopping at the K & B and not ordering at least one pasty. Originally, these were considered a good, solid meal for miners, consisting of a mixture of beef, pork, and garden vegetables (rutabagas, potatoes, and onions), all stuffed and sealed within a hearty pastry crust, then baked and served warm. To eat it, no fork was necessary. Pasties were meant to be eaten out of hand. Today, the recipe is pretty much the same, although you don't have to be a miner to enjoy one of these juicy, hot meat pies for lunch or dinner.

The fresh pasties at K & B are made for the week on Monday, so you'd be wise to call ahead (it's not uncommon for people to do so) if you know you're coming through later in the week and plan to stop. They often run out of the pasties by the weekend, and trust me, you don't want to be disappointed when you get here. Of course, you can also buy frozen pasties to take home (or to the cabin). They're no good microwaved, but heated in the oven, they make for a toasty warm meal on a rainy day. Pasties are often offered with gravy, but everybody knows the best way to eat a pasty is to simply dip them in a little ketchup.

The K & B has been serving up pasties and plenty of other drive-in food fare for years. Exactly how long? Well, when I asked the young woman who was taking my order how old the place is, she answered thoughtfully, "Gee, I don't know exactly how many years it's been open." Then she added brightly, "But my mom waitressed here, and now I am."

Besides pasties, the K & B makes a good burger and serves up hot dogs, shrimp baskets, root beer floats, hot fudge banana sundaes, and a fine porketta sandwich. All the meat comes from Fraboni's meat shop in Hibbing. And in this region of broasted everything, their Minnesota Grown Gold-n Plump "Genuine Broasted Chicken" is darn good too. "You'll taste the difference," states the menu, and you will.

GILBERT

The Whistling Bird
101 Broadway Street North • Phone: (218) 741-7544

Here in the tiny town of Gilbert, across from Big Al's bar, a funeral home, and Jim's Bait, sits a little oasis of color, hot neon, and Jamaican jerk sauce: The Whistling Bird Café & Bar.

It's hardly the type of restaurant you'd expect to find on the Iron Range and certainly not one you'd expect to last in this land of prime rib and Cornish pasties. So why is the place jam-packed almost every Saturday night? (You need to call for reservations.) Even weekdays, the café can get crowded. Get a glimpse of their guest book and you'll discover that customers who have eaten here hail from everywhere, including Texas, Canada, Florida, and even Germany.

Step inside and find out the attraction. The spirit here is pure Jamaican: welcoming and warm: pink walls, lime green accents, ornate mirrors—even fancy fruit rum drinks garnished with the little paper umbrellas. Servers are busy, but the place still evokes that laid-back, time-is-no-problem Jamaican soul and feeling. "My customers come first," says co-owner Toney Curtis, who visits with diners whenever he can. "We don't have a closing hour. We close when our customers are done. Then we follow them out the door."

Toney, a friendly and gentle Jamaican guy (dreadlocks and all), opened this adventurous café with his wife, JoPat, in 1998. JoPat, a cook for over twenty years in area country clubs and hotels, met Toney while on vacation in Jamaica and later married him. When the chance to open the restaurant came along, she was all for it. Named after a guest house in Jamaica, the Whistling Bird's menu includes pastas, steaks, and seafood items. But it's the four Jamaican entrées, all based on Toney's mom's recipes ("she used to cook at a place between Montego Bay and Negril," says Toney, who grew up a stone's throw from the ocean), that are the most requested.

Sample the flame-grilled Jamaican jerked mahi mahi and you get the picture here. An 8-ounce filet of fish, it's spiced and served with a side of jerk sauce that is nothing short of perfect: hot but not burning, with a spicy, addictive flavor. The sauce is a fragrant concoction of taste and scent and heat: minced onions, allspice, fresh thyme, cinnamon, peppers.

Or try the Caribbean Coconut Shrimp—another popular item on the menu: four jumbo shrimp, battered and dipped in coconut and served with a hot wasabi orange marmalade. Sweet potato fries are delicate and pencil skinny pieces, and a shocking tiny taste of sweetness takes them over the top: They're rolled in sugar!

Jamaican jerked pork tenderloin is smeared with the aromatic signature paste and oven roasted, arriving as tender bites of bliss. The "rasta pasta" is another winner—chicken sautéed with peppers, red onions, mushrooms, and spinach, finished in a splendid, aromatic coconut-lime cilantro broth. (Ask for hot red curry to go with.) Yum.

AURORA

Hank's Bar 'n Grill
111 North Main • Phone: (218) 229-2024

It seems like there is a tavern on every corner in Aurora, but only at Hank's Bar 'n Grill will you find Abbie, the most famous and popular dog and model in town. The darling basset hound (although Abbie's getting on in years) has appeared in all sorts of the hometown newspaper's ads. One year she was photographed as the Wisconsin and Minnesota post office dog of the year (well, at least in this town's post office). The year she ran for mayor, her photos were accompanied by campaign promises of a bone in every pot—and a fire hydrant on every corner. (She wanted to please her constituents as much as the local fire fighters, it was said.) But still, it's at Hank's where you'll find the old gal between the campaign trail and modeling assignments. She may lift her head when you walk in, and then again she may just gaze soulfully up at you as you walk by. (Being a famous model is hard work, after all.)

As for Hank's bar, there's a separate room beyond the bar room, where they

Hank's Bar 'n Grill, Aurora

serve meals. This is the " 'n Grill" part of the name—and their broasted chicken and Jo Jo potatoes (a good-size potato that has been sliced end-to-end in thick wedges, then seasoned and fried so that they develop a light crisp skin and creamy insides) are some of the top sellers. Although most people choose to have their meal at a table in this casual dining area, it's much more picturesque to eat at the old bar. Perch on a stool, your foot on the built-in ledge—but at some point, be sure to turn around and admire the mural of Chisholm that runs parallel on the opposite wall. It was painted in the 1950s by a former Chisholm resident.

This is one of the oldest bars on the Iron Range, a

relic of Aurora's boom days as a mining town. Its bar is not the longest on the Iron Range (the Royal in Virginia takes those honors), but even so, the room—with its clean, old wood floors and high ceilings (plus the wall mural)—evokes a rich sense of history. It's fairly quiet these days, says owner Dave Grivette. (He and his wife, Vyna, have owned the place for 20 years; Vyna is the wit behind Abbie's antics.) But when mining was at its peak, on a Friday night here, the bar room would be jammed with guys, five and six deep trying to get a beer. For now, munching on a hunk of crisp juicy chicken in such a historic taproom setting (with a famous model lying on the floor nearby, no less) simply makes for a memorable meal.

EMBARRASS

Four Corners Café
Highway 135 and Highway 21 • Phone: (218) 984-2055

A fine little out-of-the-way dining treasure, the red-lettered Four Corners Café seems located out in the middle of nowhere—although its address is Embarrass, Minnesota. At first glance, the Four Corners complex appears to be a big gas station with a small café attached. The only indication that this might not be the case is the fact that the huge pothole-filled parking area out front is filled with cars and trucks.

Inside, it's a casual, almost cutesy eatery (who would have thought?), with knotty pine paneling and perky sky-blue curtains. It's also much bigger than you'd expect. Extended families are gathered at tables, digging into pizza burgers, patty melts, and onion rings. A few single men sit at the tiny counter, sipping bottomless cups of coffee, eating pie, and reading the newspaper. A group of hunters is in another booth over by the window, chowing down steak and eggs. You may wonder where they've all come from, but you won't wonder why they're eating here.

The place has been serving substantial and decently delicious fare for over twenty-five years. It's all pretty flawlessly American, and it's good. (Tip: Order the grilled steak hoagie with pepper cheese, onions, and peppers.) Skip the desserts. They sound good, but they're made elsewhere and they don't measure up to the homemade entrées here.

TOWER

Erica's Bakery
509 Main Street • Phone: (218) 753-4705 or 888-801-3233

A small storefront on Highway 169, Erica's Bakery is known for its bread. (Even the folks from Ely drive here for it.) Wild rice, limpa, sourdough, pumpernickel, French, Swedish rye—and a wonderful hearty loaf, full of grains and honey, called Synoda.

Get here early in the morning, and you'll find the small horseshoe-shaped counter next to the display case crowded as well. This is a great stop for travelers up early (6 A.M.) wanting a cup of hot coffee and toast (it's made with the wonderful Synoda bread) or maybe a bear paw or long john. For a picnic lunch for two, you might want to pick up a couple of the bakery's homemade precooked pasties, and something called a "purse"—a small free-form pastry shaped around a raspberry filling—perfect for two.

ELY

Mantel House

323 E. Sheridan Street • Phone: (218) 365-2960
Web site: www.themantelhouse.com

If there's one reason to spend an extra day in Ely (especially for those who may be readying for a rustic retreat into the Boundary Waters Canoe Area), that reason is the Mantel House. The locals love it and want to keep it their secret. I can understand why. But the truth must be told. This is an excep-

Long Island duckling elegantly presented at the Mantel House, Ely

tionally fine and classic dining experience, complete with a third-generation French chef—but minus all the attitude and stuffiness.

The restaurant, located on the ground floor of a two-story house right on Ely's main street, is decorated simply with nature photos and vases of silk flowers. The lighting seems way too bright for the sensual and elegant meals that arrive "at table"—and the pink plastic tablecloths are rather gauche. But these are minor quibbles—especially when you're talking about some of the best food I've tasted this far north of the Twin Cities.

The menu is small, and it changes every few weeks. On the night I visited, we started with the housemade pâté; three rich slices, accompanied by fantastic rolls and the traditional cornichons, those tiny picnic pickles the French so love. Next, the petite pois/pea soup arrived. Lush and velvety, it had a scattering of whole peas with a few tiny cubes of smooth vegetable mousse spooned in—soothing and satisfying.

Then the roasted Long Island duckling was presented. Encircled with sliced oranges, a twizzle of candied zest, and a decadent Grand Marnier sauce, the duck was crisp on the outside, flavorful and tender (not a bit greasy) on the inside. My friend's chicken breast was top heavy with portabella mushrooms— sautéed in an incredible rich red wine sauce. Both entrees included rice ter-rine, a carrot-pea mousse (a slice of smooth and intense flavor), and two stuffed cherry tomatoes, hinting at herbs of summer—and proving once again that less is often more on a plate.

Chef Bernard Herrmann keeps his recipes "locked in his heart," our wait-ress told us when we asked if he ever shared any of his menu offerings. In fact, she said, he'll only make the chocolate truffle cake when he's alone in the kitchen.

I don't deny that his chocolate truffle cake sounded good the evening we were there, but it was the pumpkin, pecan, and rum crème brûlée that won my heart for the night. An exquisite tiny shatter of crust led into a silky, barely per-fumed custard. Ooo la la. When I tasted it, the earth moved.

Britton's Café
5 East Chapman Street • Phone: (218) 365-3195

Sometimes you learn about good local eateries the easy way. And some-times you learn the hard way. Britton's was one I discovered in the latter fashion.

I had a flat tire around midnight the night before I arrived in Ely—out on a lonely stretch of road about ten miles from town. Luckily, St. Louis County deputy sheriff Joe Zebro just happened by my vehicle on his way home. When my friend, Angie, and I offered to take him to breakfast the next day as a thank-you, he suggested we meet at Britton's, where they serve great blueberry pan-cakes.

Unfortunately, we missed breakfast (our tire wasn't done at the local sta-tion), so we headed over to Britton's for Sunday dinner with Joe. We ended up ordering the "special"—turkey, gravy, mashed potatoes, and dressing, ac-companied by a little paper cup of cranberry sauce. It was good, hearty, and homespun fare . . . nothing fancy, simply a tasty hot meal. You won't find espresso here or stuffed bagels. And we didn't see any customers in mukluks accompanied by a Husky dog or scanning BWCA maps. This is definitely a Local Spot. Good stuff. (Thanks again, Joe.)

Blueberry Streusel Muffins

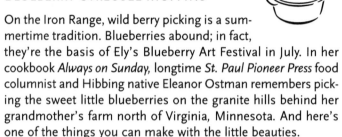

On the Iron Range, wild berry picking is a summertime tradition. Blueberries abound; in fact, they're the basis of Ely's Blueberry Art Festival in July. In her cookbook *Always on Sunday*, longtime *St. Paul Pioneer Press* food columnist and Hibbing native Eleanor Ostman remembers picking the sweet little blueberries on the granite hills behind her grandmother's farm north of Virginia, Minnesota. And here's one of the things you can make with the little beauties.

Muffins

1 1/2 cups all-purpose flour
2 teaspoons baking powder
1/2 teaspoon salt
4 tablespoons butter or margarine
1/2 cup sugar
1 egg
1 teaspoon vanilla
1/2 cup milk
1 1/2 cups fresh or dry-pack frozen blueberries,
    rinsed and drained

Streusel-walnut topping

2 tablespoons butter or margarine
2 tablespoons brown sugar
1/4 to 1/2 teaspoon cinnamon, to taste
1/4 cup finely chopped walnuts

To make muffins: Sift flour, baking powder, and salt onto wax paper. In large bowl, cream butter with sugar until fluffy. Beat in egg and vanilla. Stir in flour mixture alternately with milk. Fold in blueberries. Place paper baking cups in each of 12 large muffin pan cups. Spoon batter into cups, filling each two-thirds full.

To make streusel-walnut topping: In small saucepan, melt butter. Remove from heat. Stir in brown sugar, cinnamon, and walnuts. Sprinkle over muffins.

To bake muffins: Bake in 400 degree oven for 20 minutes or until tops spring back when lightly pressed with fingertip. (Note: If blueberries are juicy, add another 5 minutes.) Remove from pan. Cool on wire rack. Makes 12 large muffins. This recipe and the one on pages 60–61 are taken from Eleanor's book and used with her permission.

5. Up North to the Lake

In Minnesota, the whole idea of going "Up North"—families getting away from the stress of everyday, metro life—has long had a certain sand-in-your-shoes appeal. And for many, the sand inferred was synonymous with the popular Brainerd Lakes region in the north central part of the state.

This is a land of log cabins and lakes, home to former lumberjacks and the mythical stomping grounds of Paul Bunyan and Babe, his blue ox. This is the place where the Mississippi River begins. Signs reading "u pick blueberries" dot the region's backcountry roads, and "All you can eat" nightly specials are advertised in the local papers. Many of the grand old lodges, built around grand old lakes, are listed on the National Register of Historic Places: Breezy Point, Madden's, Cragun's, Kavanaugh's, Grand View, and Ruttger's—all well known for exceptional North Woods dining options, too. (Guests not staying at the resorts are usually welcome to dine in the historic settings, although it's a good idea to phone first to see if reservations are needed.)

Old institutions like Iven's on the Bay are standard Friday-night stops for weekend resorters. (Iven's serves Bloody Mary's that are spicy and spectacular, by the way.) Bar Harbor, another longtime supper club favorite is always crowded with business—and a steak sandwich, or a basket of their addictive garlic bread, tastes mighty fine on the deck overlooking the lake on a Friday night here. In fact, expect steaks and walleye and barbecued something-or-other on just about any menu in the area, and you won't be disappointed.

Right off the main thoroughfare (Highway 371), there are also still plenty of homespun spots where you can get a decent Reuben sandwich, rent a movie for the kids, and buy a fishing license for grandma, all in one fell swoop. These are personalized places, like the A-Pine family restaurant out of Jenkins, where owner Rick Beyer's great-great-grandfather's old accordion ("he brought it here from Germany in 1897") is proudly displayed near the cash register—and a slightly worn wooden bear has been posing outside the restaurant for years of summer vacation photos.

Get off the beaten track even slightly and you'll pass bakeries with window boxes out front. Or drive through a small-town main street (where they still park in the middle of the wide avenue) and find a vintage theater (with original marquee, showing first-run movies, too) steps away from an authentic soda fountain where they remember how to make an old-fashioned Green River phosphate.

No doubt about it, you'll also drive by a good share of miniature golf courses, go-cart tracks, and restaurant chains that are sprouting up all along the highway here. But everybody knows it's the old favorites that make the best memories.

Lake cabins Up North

BRAINERD

Morey's Market and Grille

1650 Highway 371 North • P.O. Box 2508
Phone: (218) 829-8248 • Web site: www.moreysmarkets.com

It's true: There are two other Morey's (the newest is in Nisswa; the original is in Motley), so the service here isn't quite as personal and doting as it once was. But this is still the cheapest place to personally point out the fish (from the market's display case) that you would like for dinner—and then choose how you'd prefer it prepared: blackened, pan fried, grilled, or broiled. (Tip: Regulars request "cheesy potatoes" to accompany their fish.) People also stop here and order Morey's famous walleye sandwich, which is good enough, but I think their fresh crab cakes, served with corn salsa, are more deserving of praise.

A family-owned business, Morey's began in 1937, when Ed Morey perfected his special fish-smoking procedure in a four-by-six-foot smokehouse. Today, Morey's is one of the premier fish and seafood companies in the country. I love the location in Brainerd because you can shop while eating your meal . . . jars of gourmet jams, sauces, cans of Irish oatmeal, aprons, cooking utensils, birthday cards, flannel shirts, and fishing knickknacks and supplies line the walls near the tables you're sitting at if you decide to eat in.

If you just want to pick up some cheese and herring for the cabin, though, stroll around the glass display cases first, and don't be afraid to ask for a sample. An accommodating staff is happy to oblige if they haven't already offered. Eleven kinds of herring include a horseradish version and a Cajun cream variation. Morey's smoked fish products are many: trout, carp, whiting, mackerel, ciscoes, and, of course, salmon—classic, Cajun, dill, and peppered!

The refrigerated deli chest is loaded with regional cheeses as well as others from around the world: Irish cheddar, Vodka currant, German Tilsit, and one of my favorites, Amber Valley "double Gloucester"—creamy English Gloucester cheese layered with robust Stilton. Condiments such as mustards, olives, and pickles can also be found, along with boxes of crackers, packaged cookies, and bags of chips. Best of all, Morey's has kept up with the times: it also buzzes up a great cappuccino.

FROM MOREY'S MARKET AND GRILLE: SUMMER SALMON SALAD

Combine these ingredients in a bowl:

8 ounces Morey's Smoked Salmon, flaked
1/2 cup chopped celery
1/4 cup minced green onions

Whisk these ingredients together:

2 tablespoons minced fresh parsley
1 teaspoon lemon juice
1 teaspoon tarragon vinegar
1 teaspoon Dijon mustard
1/4 teaspoon dried tarragon
2 tablespoons plain low-fat yogurt
2 tablespoons light mayonnaise

Add dressing to salmon mixture, toss gently to coat, cover, and chill. Serve on lettuce-lined plates. Serves 4.

Coco Moon

601 Laurel • Phone: (218) 825-7955

Even though the highway bypasses downtown Brainerd, it's still worth the detour to visit Coco Moon. This little coffeehouse with the carving of a life-size wooden bear doing a handstand in front is fun, friendly, and funky. The coffee is excellent; there's even a "hyper hour" between four and six o'clock (featuring discounted coffee drinks), and there's a few well-chosen gift items, including beautiful handmade jewelry. But the real reason to stop here is to see the artwork of local artist Cindy Jackson, who has carved and painted cool images on the tabletops of three wooden booths by the windows. "World of Coffee" is my favorite. There is no way to describe these, but if you are a coffee lover, you will definitely want to stop and check them out—just for the fun of it. Even better, stay for a double latte and chat with Rod, the amicable guy who owns the place.

LAKESHORE

Lost Lake Lodge
7965 Lost Lake Road (on the Gull Lake Narrows)
Phone: (218) 963-2681

If you want a sophisticated dining experience on an early summer's eve, with food prepared with thoughtfulness and attention (and you're willing to pay a little more for it), Lost Lake Lodge is for you.

Tucked back into tall pines and situated between its private Lost Lake and the Gull Lake Narrows, the dining room lodge is the epitome of North Woods authenticity and locale. Take the steps up to the little terrace, flanked with hanging baskets of blooms and numerous bird feeders, and then step inside the knotty pine interior. The first seating at Lost Lake Lodge is mainly for guests staying at the resort, but visitors are welcome, by reservation only, for the second seating.

Chef and owner Kieran Moore prepares four multicourse nightly specials (all fixed price), which typically include fish, poultry, a vegetarian dish, and a red meat entrée. (A 12-ounce char-grilled sirloin steak is always on the menu.)

One of the times I visited, the menu featured a marvelous fish creation: mahi mahi marinated in lemon, lime juice, and olive oil; dusted with a hint of

Morey's Market and Grille, Brainerd

Jamaican spices; and then char-grilled and served with a fresh strawberry salsa. Another superb entrée was a rich chicken cacciatore. Tender chunks of chicken were set in a lush tomato and red wine sauce, thick with salty green olives and artichoke hearts and fragrant with fresh herbs scattered about. If pork is on the menu, it could be sliced into medallions and finished with a roasted red pepper sauce. And steak—occasionally topped with a Gorgonzola sauce—is prepared exactly as you request.

A bread basket includes offerings made with the stone-ground Minnesota spring wheat from the Lodge's own grist mill: heavy warm dill rolls or savory garlic cheese biscuits, if you're lucky. With the meal, sample a bottle of wine (there's a nice wine list) and do save room for dessert (which also varies nightly). If it's on the menu, try the sublime fresh peach shortcake. If none of the three dessert choices appeals to you, you should know that ice cream topped with Lost Lake's simple and incredible homemade butterscotch syrup is always available. In fact, the lodge gets so many requests for the recipe sauce that they have it printed up on Lost Lake Lodge stationery.

From Lost Lake Lodge: Butterscotch Syrup

1 1/2 cups sugar
1 cup white corn syrup
1/2 teaspoon salt
1/2 cup butter
1 cup heavy cream
plus 1 more cup heavy cream

In a small saucepan, combine the sugar, corn syrup, salt, butter, and 1 cup of the heavy cream. Cook over low heat, stirring often, and gradually bringing the mixture to 226 degrees. Then stir in the additional 1 cup of cream and cook to 220 degrees. Remove from heat and stir in 1 teaspoon vanilla. Allow sauce to cool, stirring occasionally. Store in a covered container in the refrigerator.

NISSWA

Sherwood Forest
Phone: (218) 963-3146 or (800) 432-3788

Historic and romantic, if one were building a stage set for a North Woods love story setting, Sherwood Forest would make a fantastic model. Located between Lake Margaret and Gull Lake, the lodge was where Sinclair Lewis once spent a summer working on a novel, and rumor has it that Ma Barker and her boys hid out here at one time as well—although the classy setting hardly seems like Ma's kind of place.

In 1980, the building was designated as one of Minnesota's Historic Places, and it's worth a visit, even if you only sit at the bar in the front and admire the room from a distance. A huge stone fireplace, old wood rafters glowing with that patina of age, windows looking out into deep woods, and sparkling white lights really do seem to give the place an enchanted forest feeling.

Signature menu items here are the roasted pork prime rib, salmon, and halibut. Appetizers such as the grilled shrimp are dazzling, strange, and delicious—but pricey . . . almost $11 for three small shrimp wrapped with prosciutto ham and supposedly stuffed with . . . banana? I never tasted any, but maybe the chili oil drizzled over all disguised it.

No question, the place is expensive (it's also part of the Grand View Lodge properties), but the food is fine and the atmosphere bespeaks romance. Ask to dine by the windows in the side room. (Don't bring the kids.)

PEQUOT LAKES

Sibley Station
309 Government Drive • Phone: (218) 568-4177

If you're looking for a spot on a rainy day for a steamy bowl of hot soup and a slice of homemade pie in Pequot Lakes, Sibley Station is it. The welcome here is nonexistent, but other than that, the food is tasty and offerings many. Their Hungarian soup gets raves, but I found it oily and not exactly appealing to the eye. I'll take the chili, made with molasses, dark beer, and seven varieties of chili peppers. The grilled turkey and pesto sandwich is grand, too, homemade fresh basil pesto is slathered on hot turkey, topped with provolone cheese and tomato. Don't leave without a slice of "Mary Etta's" pie. Raspberry rhubarb? Peach? (You can also purchase whole pies to go.) The décor is paper paraphernalia: old maps and New Yorker magazine covers. If it's sunny, sit outside on the popular patio, with an herb garden and a fountain. This place is always crowded—and for good reason.

Smokey Hollow Fish Company
Located on the frontage road off Highway 371 in downtown
Pequot Lakes • Phone: (218) 568-FISH

"What better place to put a fish shop than under a bobber?" asks Mark Forsberg, chief of police in Pequot Lakes and co-owner (with his wife, Lynn) of this town's friendly little smoked fish and gourmet shop. Located beneath (well, not directly) the Pequot Lakes water tower (yes, the tower is painted to resemble a huge fish bobber), Smokey Hollow Fish Company sounds as cool

Smokey Hollow Fish Company, Pequot Lakes

as it is. The exterior sports old outboard fishing motors and other kitschy fish stuff, but it's clever and quaint, not junky. Inside, the store is classy and fine, with barbecue sauces and fancy foods surrounding its showcased smoked fish.

Forsberg has long been interested in the food business, and his fish reflects his passion for good taste. He steeps fresh Atlantic salmon in a special brine for three days and then moves it into a "brown sugar cure" before it's finally smoked with sugar maple wood. Besides smoking approximately two hundred pounds of salmon a week, Forsberg's smokehouse is also used for about a hundred pounds of whitefish. I've sampled a good share of smoked fish, and Forsberg's is one of my favorites.

Timberjack Smokehouse and Saloon
Highway 371 two miles south of Pequot Lakes
Phone: (218) 568-6070

Diners in search of an authentic smokehouse meal should stop in at Timberjack's. If you score a table by the window in the dining room at lunchtime, your view actually includes the little smokehouse shack in back, shadowed by tall pines. Don't be surprised to see the cooks carrying trays of meat out to the building or bringing meat back in to the restaurant kitchen. The door to the cabin is usually propped shut with a garden hoe, but when opened, smoky billows curl out—and imagining the meat slow-smoking to succulence out there is a certain appetite booster.

The welcome is warm in this restaurant, too; the menu, basic and traditional. It's a casually rustic place, decorated simply with old saws and historic black-and-white photos of loggers and logging days. Besides barbecued ribs, you can order smoked chicken, smoked pork loin, smoked Cornish game hen, and even smoked jumbo shrimp. Recipes handed down from the Duoos family (the previous owners) have been prepared here for 20 years—and the combination of woods used in the smoking, along with secret seasonings, are what make the magic. No barbecue sauce is slathered on the meat, either; it's served on the side.

If you're here at high hot noon and looking for something besides a plateful of ribs, I suggest Timberjack's BLT. Three slices of smoked bacon are done to chewy-crisp perfection and then layered with lettuce and circles of tomato between slices of warm Texas toast.

Before leaving, check out the cooler, conveniently located near the cash register. If you're on your way home, you can pick up a couple extra packages of bacon or a whole smoked chicken for a late-night dinner when you get there.

Bean Hole Days
First Wednesday after the Fourth of July

"People plan their vacations around the Bean Hole Festival," a woman told me in July as we were standing around waiting for the lowering of the bean pots on Bean Hole Eve in Pequot Lakes. I probably wouldn't have believed her except I'd just talked to a husband and wife (while I was listening to the 3 Bobs in the gazebo playing the "Bean Barrel Polka") who said they hadn't missed the festival in many years.

If not so long ago someone had told me I'd drive all the way to the middle of the state for a bowl of free beans, I'd have said, "I don't think so!" But a very tasty bowl of beans later, I can honestly say that the experience of Bean Hole Days is worth a detour.

Everything about the festival, held on the first Wednesday after the Fourth of July, is refreshingly small-town fun. There's royalty: A King Bean is crowned. There's even a collectible Bean Hole Day postal cancellation. Then there's the whole ritual of preparing those irresistible beans: the lowering of the bean pots, the raising of the bean pots, the taste testing of the beans, even the secrecy surrounding the bean recipe. (Sealed in a vault, never to be shared, it was "handed down" to Jim Oraskovich on a hot summer night in a room with the shades drawn.) It all seems somehow weirdly appropriate for this event that draws upwards of twenty-five hundred people!

Historically, this "fascinating free feed" event (with its roots in logging camp tradition) commenced in 1938. That September, a group of Pequot Lakes businessmen got together and prepared the first bean feed as a thank-you to area

Stirring things up at the Bean Hole Days festival, Pequot Lakes

farmers for their support of local stores. The first year, only one cast-iron pot of beans was lowered into the hole where fires had burned to heat the rocks lining the pit.

Today, the date has been changed to serve area tourists, but the tradition continues—nowadays, with five cast-iron pots. The beans (400 pounds of dried navy beans, raised nearby in Waubun) are presoaked in water overnight on Monday. On Tuesday, the beans are put in kettles, along with 200 pounds of cut-up raw bacon, molasses, onion, salt, and . . . "secret" seasonings that have been premeasured. The pots are stirred up with canoe paddles and preheated with propane heaters for a couple hours before being lowered on Tuesday night (known as Bean Hole Eve) into the preheated pits where fires have burned for hours. The lids are checked, and then the pots are covered with six inches of dirt.

On Wednesday at noon, the buried, smoky cauldrons are carefully lifted out of the holes with the aid of a backhoe (strong lumberjacks being a thing of the past), uncovered, stirred up again with canoe paddles, and taste-tested (again) before being served to long lines of folks who know just how good these beans are. Yes, they really are exceptionally fine. (And on a personal note: Jim Oraskovich, keeper of the sacred recipe, I'd still like to know what the secret ingredient is.)

BARS FROM BEANS

A Bean Hole Days recipe contest began in 1988—with the first winner also being the only entrant. Dee Dee Buckley won for her Bean Bars. She devised the bars from a rhubarb recipe and won a bean pot for her efforts. Through the years, recipes created for the contest included Pinto Bean Rice Krispie Bars, Pork and Bean Bread, and Pinto Bean Pie.

PINE RIVER

Al's Bakery
215 Barclay Avenue • Phone: (218) 587-2545

Window boxes outside the bakery spill over with colorful blooms at this welcoming little bakery in Pine River. And since Al Klocke, the owner, is "only in his 40s," this bakery should be around for a long time, one of the clerks informed me happily.

Breads, doughnuts, lovely looking caramel pecan loaves, and cookies and pastries line the shelves and fill the display case here. But it's the "sugar pies" I fell in love with. These small, half moon–shaped pastries are fruit filled with rhubarb (in season) or cherry, apple, or blueberry. They are perfect picnic fare. The pastry is light and flakes like butterfly wings when you take a bite, and the rhubarb filling that I tasted was rich and intense. As far as I'm concerned, these sugar pies alone make Al's Bakery worth a stop. But Al also prepares something called "jelly balls." He fries up the holes cut from doughnuts and then injects the rounds with a seedless raspberry jelly. These make for bite sized and indulgent snacks. Everybody loves them, so don't expect to find any late in the day; they sell out early.

Shamp's Meat Market
Highway 371 South • Phone: (218) 587–2228

Shamp's Meat Market is one of a kind. Founded in 1965 by Archie Shamp, his "on the farm" meat market then consisted of some coolers and display cases in a two-car garage building. Today, Shamp's is housed in a fancy new building, but they still have their own way of doing things. What other meat market have you walked into and found an old model pickup truck—à la Bonnie and Clyde (with running boards)—parked in the middle of the store? Gourmet jams and jellies are displayed on the back trailer part, along with bottles of barbecue sauce and all sorts of other sweets and savories.

Don't be put off by Shamp's somewhat goofy Western town front façade either. And if you miss the place coming from the south (amazingly easy to do because it's tucked back behind trees), do stop further down the road and turn around, even if it means waiting for traffic. You'll be glad you did, especially if you're on your way to your cabin for the weekend, or even better, if you're camping. A stop at Shamp's will fill your cooler with the freshest and best cuts of meat, including buffalo and elk, that you've had the pleasure to taste (and eventually throw on the grill) in a long time.

Families on bikes along the Paul Bunyan Trail often make a stop at the clean, busy market for the makings of a sandwich— Shamp's is well known for its homemade sausages. The wild rice summer sausage is unusual and popular, but the garlic summer sausage is the biggest seller— and for good reason: It's spicy and seasoned perfectly. I love it, sliced ultra thin for a hoagie or even scattered on a pizza crust.

An entire display case is devoted to over a dozen different kinds of jerky here—all with intriguing sounding labels: "Rattlesnake Pete" (old-fashioned), "Slim Pickin's (teriyaki old-fashioned), "Craven Raven" (turkey), "Ye Old Buzzard" (teriyaki turkey), and other variations such as "Sidewinder Sam" and "Wild Bill."

Archie's son, Mike, now runs the market, along with his daughter Melissa Anderson, as the third generation in the business. They still raise their own beef and pork—and since 1980 have been making sausage, processing deer, and selling gift box assortments.

Eyeing up some unusual treats at the Ethnic Fest in Walker

If you stop in Shamp's, you'll see at least a half-dozen workers in back cutting and packaging meat—and friendly help in the front may tell you if you ask how long they've worked at Shamp's, "Gee, I don't remember how many years. . . ." Now there's a testimonial.

WALKER

Ethnic Fest
Second Weekend in September

This is a great little festival and one I'd gladly choose to attend again. Walker is a clean, busy town, retaining enough of its history to still be interesting, even if expensive designer-type shops (catering to the area's cabin clientele) seem to have taken over a good share of the old storefronts.

During Ethnic Fest, food stands are set up on the courthouse lawn, and vendors serve hot American Indian fry bread doused with sugar, juicy steaming bratwurst, egg rolls, pasties, walleye cheeks, and gyros. The smells are sensual and intoxicating, the crisp air is invigorating, and afterwards there's even an old-fashioned Saturday-night street dance. I loved it all. It's held the second weekend in September.

BEMIDJI

Tutto Bene
300 Beltrami Avenue N.W. • Phone: (218) 751-1100

The first night I dined here on this humble sidewalk patio, it felt like a dream. Maybe it was because the summer evening was so perfect and the restaurant lighting so enchanting. A cool breeze, the sun setting through green vines wrapped around lacy ironwork, wine smooth and mellow, pasta homemade and rich.

Lucky for us my sister and I had stopped in the restaurant earlier in the day to check out the menu. We had no idea we might need reservations—but we were advised to make them, and we did. The best part of the deal, though, was that after we saw the outdoor courtyard, we also requested to be seated there for dinner. And we were obliged. (Sometimes planning ahead is worth it!)

Billed as an "Italian Ristorante and Espresso Bar," Tutto Bene looks like it belongs in one of the trendier neighborhoods of the Twin Cities. Outside, pale lemon-yellow stucco walls with windows trimmed in bright white paint. Inside, artwork and sleek tables. To be honest, the corner café and sidewalk terrace *is* near a main downtown Bemidji street intersection. But face it, in this small town, what is considered "traffic" is nothing to a person who has lunched at sidewalk cafés along busy Minneapolis's Lyndale Avenue.

The current menu offers some soothing Italian favorites, such as cheese ravioli and manicotti. Or try the tagliatelle—wide noodles tossed with spicy slices of sausage (I would have liked them a little spicier), a handful of "forest" mushrooms, scattered sun-dried tomatoes, and garlic. Even the spaghetti sauce was inspiring: thick with big chunks of fresh tomatoes. And the meatballs that accompanied it were fragrant with basil and garden herbs. Or sample the handmade rotolo—large sheets of fresh pasta layered with spinach, minced ham, and ricotta cheese, rolled, sliced, and served with an incredibly lush but not overwhelming alfredo sauce.

For starters, there's a marvelous minestrone soup. Rich and flavorful, it's served in a white restaurant coffee cup atop a saucer. Bread is good and chewy, served with oil for dipping and a touch of balsamic vinegar ($1 extra) if you're so inclined. Salads are fresh mixed greens with Caesar dressing. Desserts? The kids entrées included mixed frozen-fruit granita (kiwi/strawberry), but adults would do well to order a little refreshing dishfull, too. Still, don't forget this is an espresso bar. The Gelato Affogato—vanilla ice cream "drowned" in espresso—is served in a demitasse cup. It's a sundae all grown up. Definitely worthwhile.

Raphael's Bakery & Café
319 Minnesota Avenue • Phone: (218) 759-2015

I could make a meal out of bread and butter at Raphael's Bakery and Café. This is one of those downtown fixtures (it's been around over forty years) in Bemidji—and a real find in a touristy town mostly famous for Paul B. and his blue ox.

Come in this clean, spacious shop for their special "Frontier" bread—a hearty, dense multigrain loaf—or the best-selling wild rice bread. (Developed in 1973 by Raphael Sweeney Sr., a slice of the wild rice is excellent toasted, too.) Raphael's also makes a magnificent New York onion rye, "great for ham sandwiches," advised a friendly customer waiting in line behind me. I also like the tangy sourdoughs, and the potato bread (soft and delicate) reminded me of my mom's homemade bread, warm from the oven. Raphael's makes the standard bakery items, but you should know that the glazed homemade angel food cakes go fast and so do the chocolate macaroon haystacks.

At lunchtime, the bakery/café (half the huge room is filled with tables) serves sandwiches and homemade soups, with a different one featured each day. On Mondays, the locals rave about the awesome chicken wild rice soup, but on the Friday I was there, I loved the creamy potato. Meals come with baskets of potato bread or Raphael's premium white bread. Along with a spread of real butter on your slice, you may find yourself finishing off the basket of bread before your soup arrives. Afterwards, pay for your meal at the bakery counter, and then head down to the lake for your photo session with Paul Bunyan and Babe the Blue Ox.

NEVIS

Goose Crossing
East of Nevis on Highway 34 at County Road 82
Phone: (218) 652-2366

If you were driving by Goose Crossing at twilight, saw all the cars, knew nothing about it, and decided to stop in, you'd no doubt feel you had stumbled into a wonderfully serendipitous discovery . . . or at least walked into some big family's happy holiday gathering.

Wreaths and garlands and white icicle strings of sparkling lights hang from the rafters inside; lace curtains are on the windows, and country collectibles fill the walls. Somebody may be playing "Oh Lonesome Me" on an Electone piano—and folks are lined up on a bench waiting for a table. Reservations? Who knew you would need them out here? But they're advised.

The reason? The food, of course. The menu reads like a book, and then your server recites another half-dozen offerings. Specialties of the house are the rotisserie-cooked meats, prepared in smokers (which you walked by on your way into the restaurant) and then finished in the kitchen. Basics include prime rib, steaks, breast of chicken, or mallard. Seafood is flown in twice weekly—all fresh, not frozen. Mixing and matching is encouraged, too; maybe the mesquite medallions of tenderloin sound good, but so does a fillet of walleye—if so, you're encouraged to combine them for a personal entrée. (However, you should know that this isn't exactly cheap!) Sauces are what chef and owner Steve Erickson is known for, and his lingonberry-enhanced sauce for quail one night certainly didn't disappoint.

Desserts here are somewhat standard—Snickers torte, Irish cream pie—but they are often jazzed up by being flamed quietly at your table . . . a rather glamorous touch to end an already memorable meal. Later, when the screen door slams behind you and you're standing outside in the dark country night, look up. Talk about glamour. The stars out here are incredible.

DORSET

La Pasta Italian Eatery
Phone: (218) 732–0275 (seasonal number)
Web site: www.dorset-lapasta.com

When it's windy, one almost expects to see a tumbleweed roll across the highway through Dorset, a tiny village of fewer than twenty permanent residents. Of course, that's not during the town's "Taste of Dorset" (the first Sunday in August) when thousands descend on this self-styled "Restaurant Capital of the World."

If you like fun-loving crowds and want a sample of Dorset's four restaurants' fare, go during the festival. Otherwise, a quiet drive on a summer day gets you into any of the eateries easily and without a wait. I particularly like the charming little one called La Pasta. Open seasonally, the windowed porch in the back (overlooking birdfeeders and open country) is a choice place for lunch or dinner. The menu here is bigger than you'd expect, and everything sounds good. The food is simple (spaghetti, fettuccine alfredo, lasagne) but certainly satisfying. Although it's a bit salty, I've still enjoyed the house favorite, cannelloni—pasta tubes filled with minced chicken and cheeses—as well as a homemade meatball sub sandwich, served with a side of great housemade potato salad.

After dinner, you can stroll the boardwalks in town and check out Sister Wolf Bookstore across the street. Do peek in the Dorset House Restaurant & Soda Fountain, housed in a cool 100-year-old building with pressed-tin ceiling, original wood floors, and a vintage counter with a few kid-friendly twirl-around stools. If you're craving a decent enchilada, Compañeros nearby is a good bet.

The MinneSoda Fountain in Park Rapids

PARK RAPIDS

The MinneSoda Fountain
205 South Main Avenue • Phone: (218) 732-3240

If I had the time to linger at just one ice cream shop in all of Minnesota, I think I'd choose the MinneSoda Fountain. This is a big, old-fashioned, authentic soda fountain with 17 stools at the counter and several old wood booths. Here they still serve huge ice cream sundaes (in fluted stemmed glasses) loaded with whipped cream and topped with a cherry. Go on a sultry summer afternoon and absorb the atmosphere while spooning up some cold comfort. Forget a book. It's more fun reading the menu, aptly titled "The Sundae Times," certainly a sensual and all-consuming read: *Mega Malts & Shakes. Sundaes: i.e. "Lady Slipper Sundae: pink and pretty like our state flower. Made with strawberry ice cream, gently covered with marshmallow and strawberry topping . . . "Turtle Sundae: . . . two scoops of creamy vanilla ice cream, topped with slow moving hot fudge. Smooth caramel and pecans drowning in real whipped cream . . . !" Banana Splits* [there's more than one kind?] *i.e. Hot Caramel Split, Hot Fudge Split. Ice cream sodas. Daring Delights: i.e. "Butterscotch Royal . . . a buttery blend of butterscotch topping, vanilla ice cream, marshmallow and pecans . . ."*

Here, you can also treat yourself to that favorite drink of long ago, the Green River: a refreshing, icy lemon-lime phosphate. Later, catch a flick at the Park Theater, a vintage movie house (original marquee out front) only a few steps down the block. This is fun. (Remember *Back to the Future?*)

HISTORY OF THE MINNESODA FOUNTAIN

The MinneSoda Fountain was originally established as Schmider's Confectionery in 1922 by brothers, John and Otto Schmider. For years, it was a popular candy and ice cream shop—even making it through World War II, when good sweets were scarce and sugar rationed (they used honey).

In 1952, following the Korean War, Don Schmider (Otto's nephew) became co-manager of Schmider's. Otto was in the soda fountain business 51 years prior to his death in 1973. Don and Joanne Schmider took over the business at this time and sold it 20 years later to "soda jerks" Todd and Gina Williams.

From the Coca-Cola memorabilia to the soda fountain equipment, most everything here is the real thing. It's a find.

6. Western Lakes Country

With its many lakes tucked into rolling hills and farmland like sparkling secrets, this west central part of the state is also a region where you don't have to go far to find a Sunday-afternoon smorgasbord or an old-fashioned supper club. And although fast-food chains have certainly moved into the busy lake resort areas, you can also still discover fun, independent drive-ins with names such as Dash Inn or ice cream shops such as The Little Dipper and Tip Top Dairy Bar scattered along streets in old buildings that close up soon after Labor Day.

In the region's small-town bakeries, it's not unusual to find packages of homemade lefse or boxes of rosettes for sale as well. And don't be surprised to see that a few Main Street cafés—where coffee and pie totals a whopping 99 cents—actually exist, many because of the huge influx of seasonal resorters who visit lake cabins during the warm season.

In fact, when Minnesotans say they're heading "to the lake," you can bet this area is one of the areas they're heading toward. Otter Tail County, which contains the town of Fergus Falls, claims 1,048 lakes—more than any other county in the state, while nearby and much smaller Douglas County, with Alexandria as its hub, has a mere 300 lakes. Roughly bounded by these two fair-sized towns and Detroit Lakes and Perham to the north, the region is aptly touted and often referred to as "Lakes Country."

Scenic byways curve around itsy-bitsy bodies of water as well as huge expanses of blue—and prime picnic spots are abundant. One of my favorites is just outside the tiny town of Vergas. Stop in town at Big Jim's Drive-In for sandwiches and then drive out of Vergas on Highway 228 until you see a giant loon monument. The spot is actually called the Long Lake Wayside. A green jewel of a tidy and cared-for park, it has sheltered picnic tables, a romantic swing for two overlooking the water, and a long fishing dock that juts out into the pristine blue lake. Another lovely little spot for a picnic is at Phelps Mill County Park. The picturesque mill is the backdrop for many weddings and is listed on the National Register of Historic Places. Located on the Otter Tail River, there are picnic facilities, too. A huge craft show here in the summer features numerous food booths, but I prefer this tranquil secret place when we have it to ourselves.

In the autumn, traffic (and life) slows considerably in the lakes region, and a drive through Maplewood State Park blazes with tree leaves turned to rich burgundies and gold. Buy some fresh apple cider or fill a thermos with homemade hot soup and then stop at a picnic table near Lake Lida (one of

30 lakes within the park) and enjoy.

For a different view of the state's autumn hues, head over to Inspiration Peak, where a short morning hike is rewarded with a panoramic vista of the season's color. Long ago, native-to-the-state novelist Sinclair Lewis (not particularly known for his complimentary thoughts on Minnesota country life) waxed poetic about the view here 400 feet up: "A glorious 20-mile circle of some fifty lakes scattered among fields and pastures, like sequins fallen on an old Paisley shawl."

The setting sun over Leaf Lake

DETROIT LAKES

Main Street Restaurant
900 Washington Avenue
Phone: (218) 847-3344

Detroit Lakes is another one of those towns edged with the franchises where you can wait 45 minutes in line to be seated for Sunday breakfast or take a spin down Washington Avenue to the Main Street Restaurant and walk right in. (Look for the sign jutting out high over the sidewalk. Like a movie marquee, the signboard below entices: "Through Xmas Pie & Coffee 99 cents.")

Inside, you can seat yourself at a cushy but seen-better-days burgundy booth or circle the family around one of several large round tables. Longtime waitresses greet customers with salutations like "Hi, Eddy. You want ice cream with that cherry pie?" and juggle three huge platters of bacon and eggs in one arm while pouring coffee with the other hand.

Behind the cash register in the middle of the spacious room, folks at the counter are in sight of the cook reading the order slips as they come to his little window, clipped on the metal spin-around holder. This is heartwarming Midwestern small-town life at its most appealing.

The pie is homemade and fine here—at least a dozen varieties are listed on the dry erase board on the wall. Do try the buttermilk variation, a custardy smooth pie filling topped with crunchy nuts. But it's the breakfasts I find exceptional. Eggs are prepared the way they should be: soft and seasoned nicely, flipped by someone who knows what he's doing—and they arrive with a smooth glisten, that secret of country flavor. Order a side of perfectly spiced Polish sausage—or just one, and have it split and grilled. Coffee is free when you order a breakfast and costs a quarter if you have part of an order. If you have room, don't leave without one of their huge cinnamon rolls, lavished on top with a wonderful glob of powdered sugar frosting, melting into the warm bread. These are the kind of cinnamon rolls I love untwisting, savoring each soft, cinnamony bite of bread, melting butter and spice . . . the best.

A retro sign—and retro prices—at the Main Street Restaurant, Detroit Lakes

Lake Country Bakery
921 Washington Avenue
Phone: (218) 847-7361

One rainy summer morning, a Thursday, I stopped into this longtime neighborhood shop (across the street and down the block from the Main Street Restaurant) and was immediately greeted by a cheery woman who informed me that today was bun day. Buy any package of buns at regular price and get another—any kind, "mix and match," she advised, for a penny.

Before I strolled out of the bakery that day—with my two packages of buns, some bread, and sugared cake doughnuts—I also picked out a "blueberry flip." "Oh, these are won . . . der . . . ful," said the woman, stretching out each syllable as she tucked my sweet, glazed purchase into a waxed bag. And she was right, of course.

Lakeside 1891
200 West Lake Drive • Phone: (218) 847-7887

This friendly, casual family restaurant across the street from the lake is named for its century-old history as an institution in Detroit Lakes. Though there have been additions, the original structure, built on the shore of Detroit Lake, is intact and filled with memorabilia that even includes old prom dresses displayed on the walls. The menu is a newspaper, and packed between area ads are offerings such as tender, marinated pork chops or their "so popular we couldn't take it off our menu" chicken Amaretto. There's also a good share of burgers and pasta, steaks, and shrimp. But the best items on the menu are its old-fashioned entrées and desserts prepared tableside. Order Steak Diane (remember that classic?), and your waiter rolls out his portable stove, prepares the dish, and then flambés the whole thing with brandy before plating and serving it to you—truly made to order.

For dessert, you can order ice cream drinks you haven't thought about in years. Remember the Grasshopper? Pink Squirrel? Golden Cadillac? Or if you didn't indulge in a flaming entrée, do order the tableside-prepared Pecans Praline for your finale. The smell alone is intoxicating: Butter sizzles in the sauté pan; brown sugar gets tossed in and then pecans. Finally, the server ignites the whole fragrant mixture with bourbon—and when the flames die down, he spoons the warm and buttery caramel sweetness over vanilla ice cream.

Hotel Shoreham
Six miles south of Detroit Lakes on Highway 59, then west 1 mile on County 22 in Shoreham on Lake Sallie • Phone: (218) 847-9913

Visit here in late August when the crowds have thinned out and you're in for a treat. This historic place, a stone's throw from lakes Sallie and Melissa (it sits on the channel), goes way back. Arrive at dusk when the lights are just winking on Hotel Shoreham's sign out front, and you'd swear you landed somewhere back in time.

Inside, skip the porch dining area and choose the bar room for dinner or a drink ($2.50 for a vodka tonic!). This is the original room (circa 1910), where a mural of a younger Hotel Shoreham, done by Chuck Merry, a local art teacher, fills one wall. The rest of the room's décor includes an eclectic collection of college memorabilia, while a huge moose head, big black bear, and numerous mounted trophy fish adorn higher up. On the ceiling you'll see dollar bills, shot up there in a method that the owner might explain if you part with a bill yourself. (At the end of the season—the place closes after Labor Day—the bills are pulled down and used for the staff good-bye party.)

The menu cover itself is a nostalgic peek at the past as well, with black-and-white historic photos of the place on both the front and back of this *Life*-magazine-size folder. "Welcome to the Hotel Shoreham Bar and Bistro—alive with history, food and spirits," it says. Locals will tell you to arrive early (5

P.M. is when the restaurant opens) if you don't want to wait in line for dinner during the peak of summer. Otherwise, show up anytime, enjoy the camaraderie and free-for-all atmosphere, and be prepared to wait.

The place is known for its homemade pizza, and "people drive miles for our walleye," a server informed me one night. "The other evening, I had twelve people at one table and they ALL ordered walleye." The walleye *is* exceptional, dusted and seasoned and camp fried in an old-fashioned black iron skillet that always imparts its own marvelous flavor to the fish.

A woman at the next table also informed me that the next best entrée is the Shoreham Dip. "Not French Dip" according to the menu, this hunk of an entrée is slow roasted beef, shredded and "served with Swiss, Au Jus and chips." The woman should know the menu; she and her husband come here five nights a week during the summer, she told me. "We love the place."

FERGUS FALLS

Viking Café
203 West Lincoln Avenue • Phone: (218) 736-6660

I've always believed that freeway travelers who pull off exit interchanges and eat at the franchise nearest their on ramp are missing the whole purpose of road travel. By simply taking an extra five or six minutes and driving to the heart of the small town they're bypassing, they might get lucky and find a wonderful hometown café.

Doing just that, I discovered in Fergus Falls not only the Viking Café but Lucky, too. Lucky Shol (his photo hangs by the cash register up front) was the owner of this bustling restaurant for over thirty years until he died in 1998. Today his wife, Blanche, and nine kids (as well as fifteen-plus grandkids) are still running the place. In fact, at breakfast one busy November day, Blanche informed me that three daughters, two granddaughters, and a grandson were all working in one capacity or another.

At first glance, the stark brick-fronted Viking, with its round porthole windows, looks like it could be home to a brandy-scented nightclub. But once you step inside, there's no mistake; this place is obviously the town's bustling daylong local favorite for breakfast, lunch, and dinner. Bright lights, high ceilings, the clatter of coffee cups and spoons clinking, the scent of frying bacon and hash browns—not to mention the noise level of folks catching up on town news—fills it with that elusive, homey spirit no franchise can ever capture.

At the Viking, it figures that everything is homemade—and when you order coffee, they bring a thick white cup, saucer and spoon, and a little pitcher of cream. No coffeepot sits on these tables; there's no need. Some member of the family is constantly swinging by, refilling your cup on his or her trip back to the kitchen. (We counted my dad's cup refilled at least five times during breakfast one morning.) You can sit in old dark wood booths (look closely and see declarations such as "I dig Jim C." and "Carol + Rick" scratched in) or sit on a stool at the counter overlooking the malt machine and shelves of old-fashioned ice cream glasses reflecting in the mirror. Get there early enough, and pans of fresh, warm (and huge) cinnamon rolls tempt nearby. For breakfast, a side order of bacon is a must: Three chewy, salty, and thick-cut strips arrive on their own platter.

When you're done eating, you pay at the cash register, which sits atop an old-fashioned glass display case filled with a dozen or so boxes of cigars. During hunting season, the Viking is also the kind of place that prints up special business cards (on bright orange cardstock) with the café's earlier opening hours—as well as the sunrise and sunset hours from September through December charted on the back.

NEW YORK MILLS

Eagles Café
31 North Main Street • Phone: (218) 385-2469

The original reason I stopped in this tiny town on Highway 10 midway between Detroit Lakes and Brainerd was to visit its cultural center. Home to the Great American Think-Off, the New York Mills Regional Cultural Center is housed in the town's oldest building. The place always has wonderful (and sometimes quirky) gallery exhibits (one time the rooms were filled with hand-carved and painted fishing lures that were unusual and exquisite) as well as local art, sculpture, and jewelry.

The summer day I visited the center, it was already getting near dinnertime—and while I was closing the place up (buying hand-beaded jewelry), I started talking with the two women working there. It just so happened their 10-year-old daughters scampered in at the same time, bringing pie from across the street—and it wasn't long before I was informed that "Jean Gerber at the Eagles Café makes the best pies in the world."

By the time I left, I had two little girls accompanying me across the street to the Eagles Café to introduce me to Jean and show me the place. "Where should I sit?" I asked as we walked into the small restaurant with several booths and a half-dozen wobbly wooden chair stools at the counter. "Oh, right here," the girls said as they directed me to the counter and onto a spinney chair. And then, one on either side of me, they proceeded to help me order. The soup is homemade and good, they stated, and a cup is plenty. "Just look how big the bowl size is!" exclaimed one of the girls, pointing. So I had a cup of the day's broccoli cheese soup and it *was* very, very good. "Oh, and you should have this French dip sandwich, too." No, not the plain one, this one, the "supreme," they showed me on the menu—with the melted cheese and onions on it. So I ordered as directed—and was impressed with the flavorful sandwich as well as the girls' young and quite well-developed palates.

After the sandwich, the big decision arrived as to which kind of pie I should order. The apple was really good, said the girls, the strawberry rhubarb, too.

They weren't crazy about the banana cream, but the lemon was super delicious. Finally, the two decided I should have the coconut cream pie, with its four-inch billow of meringue. ("The meringue's the best!" I was informed.) "Oh, and there's Jean, the lady with the curly hair and apron on, over there," the girls advised me, barely taking their eyes off the pie.

Later, after my young dining partners left (first making sure that I agreed the pie was heavenly), I found out that Jean, along with her husband, Orv; their son, Tom; and his wife, Julie, have been operating this hometown café since 1984. Don't miss it.

WATERMELON DAYS IN VINING

Before I visited Vining's Watermelon Days, I believed that they must grow watermelons in the area (i.e., vining, watermelon) and that the celebration had something to do with their melon harvest. I was wrong. The celebration commenced when the local businessmen decided they wanted to do something for the farmers who supported their businesses.

Today, after many years, the festival is still going strong. Watermelons are trucked in to tiny Vining, and shifts of local men

The Watermelon Days festival in Vining

93

cut, slice, and serve the juicy wedges free to everyone, all day long. Kids, old farmers in overalls, young moms in sundresses, and teenagers all dig in to this classic summer treat—oblivious to juice dripping off their chins while they're spitting watermelon seeds uninhibitedly on the grass.

Later, you can wander the town—there's a craft fair going on in the streets during Watermelon Days—but even more fun, take a tour of the town's unusual collection of painted steel sculptures. Created by Ken Nyberg of Vining, these sculptures of ordinary things made large are created from scrap left over from Nyberg's job erecting farm elevators. They include a big square knot, a clothespin, a cup supported by the coffee streaming out, and a pair of pliers holding a cockroach. One of the most popular is a huge foot—and kids (of all ages) love to climb up on the toe for a photo.

While you're in Vining, you also really should not miss a stop at the Vining Palace. The truth is, you *literally* CANNOT miss this bar/restaurant—unless you're color blind. It's known to everyone for miles around as the Purple Palace, and for a reason: The building is painted eye-shocking purple. The place has been here over thirty years. It's smoky, the acoustics are awful, but it's small-town fun. Families feast on chicken and burgers and onion rings. You can get a pork chop for $2.50 or a fish dinner (served with broasted potatoes or French fries) for $3.75. It's decent fare and it's tasty, too.

LEAF LAKES

Doug and Mary's
Highway 108 (Edgewater Drive) "at beautiful Leaf Lakes"
Phone: (218) 583-2141

For those passionate about the quintessential lakeside eatery, this place is pure serendipity (although it was my brother, Curt, who tipped me off). If you arrive by car at Doug and Mary's (a few miles south of New York Mills), you'll walk up a couple steps to a back deck; go in the back door; stroll past card tables and chairs, beer posters, and TV—and then step a few feet through the tiny kitchen (if you're lucky, Doug will be sautéing some fresh vegetables for a stir fry) and into the main dining room.

Here, a TV is on near the ice cream freezer (above, a sign advertises Luigi's Italian Ice), and the rest of the space is filled with tables and a few small wooden window booths . . . the kind where your knees touch the person's across from you. The floor lists a little toward the lake, and you can see the dock where those arriving by water can tie up their boats. Get here at twilight and your reward is to watch a Midwestern sunset sweep across the lake as well.

Mary's usually in this main dining room, ringing up the cash register, helping at the bar, or serving food to diners. She's as energetic, lively, and personal as the food here. So are the rest of the waitresses, teasing and cajoling: "What? You didn't clean your plate" one might say. Or "I saw you taking that off your wife's plate; are you still hungry?!" They wander by, chat, and tease, keeping your water glasses filled along with the friendly banter.

But besides the happy family ambience (it's catching), the food makes the magic here. In Doug's

One-half of the Doug and Mary team showing off his culinary artistry, Leaf Lakes

tiny kitchen, he manages to prepare really fine, beautifully seasoned dishes. The Cajun spiced chicken pasta primavera was heavenly, hot, and perfect. I wake up in the city on winter nights and crave a bowl of it. A simple pork chop was moist and tender, and a plate full of "Texas toothpicks" (itsy jalapeño and onion slices, breaded and fried and served steaming) provided a hot hit of flavor.

Doug grew up nearby and has been in the restaurant kitchen since he was a youngster. "My grandparents had this place for ten years, and my parents for thirty," says Doug proudly. "I'm the third generation."

ALEXANDRIA

Traveler's Inn
511 Broadway • Phone: (320) 763-4000

I spent my teenage years in Alexandria and many hours sipping cokes and dipping French fries in ketchup at both Traveler's Inn (still going strong) and Osterberg's Café (long gone). So how can I not mention "Trav's," even though it looks much different nowadays (so do I). Then there's that matter of graduating from high school with one of the family owners. Actually, this mainstay of my hometown turns out good and decent fare—and happily, even still serves my long ago favorite: the hot gravy plate.

The place has been in business for more than seventy years and has evolved with the times, certainly helping to ensure its continued success. And if they had offered cappuccino and latte when I was a teenager, who knows? I might never have left for the big city.

Carlos Creek Winery
6693 County Road 34 N.W. • Phone: (320) 846-5443;
fax: (320) 846-7191 • Web site: www.carloscreekwinery.com

This is a breathtaking and romantic spot, and it certainly deserves the award for the chic-est winery in the state: freshly painted white fences surround the acreage, which includes an apple tree orchard blossoming across the road and sleek horses grazing in fields beyond. (This is one of Minnesota's largest pure-bred Arabian horse facilities, too, and visitors are welcome to wander the grounds.)

Stop in some afternoon on a sunny day, sample a few wines, and then settle on the terrace with a glass of the wine you like best and gaze out on the blissful and bucolic scene in front of you. Don't forget to select a few bottles of wine to take home.

The winery is owned by Robert Johnson, an Alexandria businessman, but the winery's winemaker is Santiago Martinez, an Argentine-trained enologist with experience in France, Italy, and California. They make an award-winning and velvety Merlot, and their Chardonnay was an award winner in the International Eastern Wine Competition too. They also make a sparkling hard apple cider that's not bad. Still, I like the winery's medium-sweet Riesling the best, award or no.

TERRACE

The Terrace Store Co.
27162 Old Mill Pond Road (just off Highway 104 on the Mill Pond)
Phone: (320) 278-2233

On a summer afternoon, it's hard to beat sitting out on the screened porch here, sipping a glass of iced sugared rhubarb tea, and listening to the wind rustling through the treetops over the mill pond.

This really is the sort of spot to go to enjoy the quiet of the country. Terrace, with a population of 26 ("on a good day") is a long way from anywhere. I loved it the moment I drove into the tiny town and saw a street sign reading "Dreaming River Drive." Heading down the hill to the restaurant, perched above the pond that runs into the Chippewa River, the whole scene seems vaguely Brigadoon-like.

At least it does until one enters the Terrace Store Co. and takes a peek at the menu. Linguini and clam sauce, chicken cacciatore, eggplant parmesan. An Italian restaurant, housed in a once-upon-a-time pharmacy (the restored 1883 building is listed in the National Registry of Historic Places), owned and operated by two ex–New Yorkers!

However, it's not quite so preposterous as it appears. Owner Robert Greenfield grew up in Terrace, and both he and co-owner Richard Grella (most of the Italian sauce recipes come from Dick's grandmother) have been restoring homes in the area for many summers. When they retired from teaching jobs in New York, they ended up staying in Terrace, and the coffeehouse they first envisioned here "sort of evolved" into the seasonal restaurant.

It's obvious they both love good food and good wine. Try the garden lasagne—served at both lunch and dinner, it's a rich layering of ingredients between sheets of pasta: fresh zucchini, spinach, peppers, broccoli, carrots, and mushrooms, finished off with a creamy marinara sauce. The Penne Abruzzi is another winner, with its flavor-packed sauce sparked with sausage, pepper, and onions. Jumbo cheese ravioli—generous pasta pockets—are stuffed with rich ricotta, parmesan, and romano cheeses. Desserts include an ultra rich bread pudding with maple cream, the standard "chocolate decadence," a creamy rhubarb Bavarian custard pie, a traditional tiramisu, and a lovely, light "Lemon Breeze Pie." Save room.

The screened porch at the Terrace Store Co. in Terrace

FROM THE TERRACE STORE CO.: ICED RHUBARB "TEA"

For something truly different, try this tangy, pink, and pretty rhubarb drink. It's certain to become a summer tradition.

> 3 pounds rhubarb, diced
> 1 quart water
> 2 1/3 cups sugar

In a large saucepan, simmer the rhubarb in the water until soft. Strain the juice into another large pot. (Discard the rhubarb.) Then add enough water to the strained juice to make two quarts of juice. Add the sugar to the warm mixture and stir until dissolved. Chill, covered, in the refrigerator. Just before serving, dilute with 1 quart ice water. If serving 1, fill glass with ice, pour glass half full with undiluted sweetened juice, and then add ice water to the top. Makes about 30 glasses of iced "tea."

BATTLE LAKE

Ament's Bakery
Phone: (218) 864-5636

I love Krispy Kreme doughnuts, those glazed fixations that movie stars and truck drivers drool over and lust after. But I have to say, the raised, glazed doughnuts here at Ament's Bakery in Battle Lake come pretty close, especially if you happen in early in the morning, when the warm aroma scents the room and the glaze on the doughnuts shimmers in the sun.

Don't be put off by Ament's rather austere storefront, either. (Ament's is housed in another of those small-town main street boxes of a building, totally ugly and easily passed by.) But locals know, and resorters in the area have discovered, that beyond the door here you'll find first-rate breads, cakes, cookies, baking powder biscuits, cookies and bars, and foccacia for pizza.

The décor is funky flea market: antique coffeepots hanging from hooks on the wall behind the counter and cash register. A collection of old tin layer cake carriers and antique cookie jars are displayed above the wooden shelves labeled and filled with loaves of bread. There are even a few tables for reading the morning paper and drinking a cup of coffee. One of the preteenage boys stocking the shelves and doing odd jobs is available to help carry your purchases to the car. (Especially nice if you splurged on a whole cherry pie; several of the foot-long, soft, garlic bread sticks; and a dozen glazed doughnuts.)

Ament's Bakery, Battle Lake

PERHAM

Kenny's Candies
609 Pinewood Lane • Phone: (218) 346-2340

Housed in a big concrete rectangle of a building on the edge of town, Kenny's Candies spurts orange and turquoise and purple and lime green inside. Oh, not on the walls. Colors here spill out of different spouts and funnels into numerous tubs and kettles. "It's sort of like a giant Play-Doh factory," the general manager told me the day I visited. And it's one of the only such factories in the Midwest. If you haven't heard about it, don't be surprised.

Licorice making, it seems, is very secret business. Licorice makers guard their techniques with zeal. In fact, when Kenny's Candies' owner, Ken Nelson, decided to go into the flavored laces, ropes, and twists business in 1986, no licorice factory in this country (there are only three major licorice producers in the United States) would let him tour. The same reluctance at factories occurred when Nelson tried to visit in England. But while he was overseas, Nelson met a consultant who was knowledgeable about licorice and knew where the appropriate used equipment could be bought. By the end of the trip, Nelson had still never seen a licorice plant, but he was well on his way to owning one. What started as an 18-employee storefront operation in Perham has since grown to a business employing 100 workers.

The main factory today brims with colors and flavors being squished and shaped through all sorts of slowly spinning tubes, giving the licorice its familiar twist. Different colors mean different tastes, and Kenny's produces 18 flavors of the stuff, including root beer, apple cider, blue raspberry, and, of course, the traditional black, a mixture of organic molasses and organic wheat flour. The licorice is sold throughout the United States, Canada, and in Europe. You'll also find it for sale in Perham's grocery stores and at the Pines Gift shop in town.

Unfortunately, the licorice factory is not open for tours. No secrets; it's strictly due to health and building codes.

Place in the Country &
The Gathering Grounds Coffee Shoppe
134 First Avenue S. • Phone: (218) 346-7969

On the corner down from the old-fashioned Comet Theater (complete with marquee out front, it's still showing first-run movies) is this combination gift store/coffeehouse/café. You can get a curried chicken pita sandwich, an unusual "nutty bird" (turkey and cream cheese, with sunflower seeds and sprouts) or a warming bowl of homemade soup with cornbread and honey—and you can wash it all down with an Italian cream soda.

The Lakes Café
136 West Main Street • Phone: (218) 346-5920

At the Lakes, the locals and resorters mingle—especially on summer weekends, when the place bustles at a fast and furious pace. Food is a notch above homespun, and dinner prices include a small ice cream sundae. Although some folks rave about the pies here, my mother and I were less than impressed. Stick with the homemade rolls or muffins. And always order the mashed potatoes. Complete with a few tiny bumps, they're real and they're good.

7. Prairie and Valleys

Prairie

Windswept ridges and fertile valleys thick with corn, soybeans, and remnants of the tall grass prairie—this is southwestern Minnesota. Considered a part of the western plains, the landscape out here is dotted with towns few and far apart: places like Pipestone, Tyler, and stone-built Luverne.

In July, look for fresh corn on the cob sold at small produce stands near tidy farms. If you're lucky, you might even happen into a town celebrating the corn season with a free corn feed. Come harvest moon time, the region is similar to many others in the state: Markets overflow with tomatoes and cucumbers, squash and zucchini.

The roads are quiet and traffic often nonexistent in this wide-open-to-the-wind way. That's one of the reasons I find it so appealing, I think. When you can see land, unbroken, all the way to the horizon, it tends to soothe the soul. Add to that birdsong and solitude—and a good hometown café for coffee and pie. The appeal is simple, and the joys are plentiful. Like the prairie wildflowers out here, you just have to look a little harder to find them.

PIPESTONE

Lange's Café
110 Eighth Avenue S.E. • Phone: (507) 825-4488

Hometown and heartland come to mind when you walk into Lange's Café—a Pipestone culinary landmark that has been here more than forty years—open 24 hours a day, 365 days a year. The story is told that the day the late Les Lange opened the doors to Lange's, he declared it would always be open—and in a pledge to that promise, he buried the key beneath the concrete.

Today, son Steve runs this 24/7 business, which still sports the slogan "Where old friends meet" and where homemade pie comes in over a dozen different varieties. You name it, Lange's has probably baked it: banana cream, coconut cream, cherry, peach, blueberry, sour cream raisin, lemon. Besides the pie here, which is very good, by the way, Lange's offers cakes, cookies, and excellent caramel and cinnamon rolls. Everything is baked from scratch. In fact, I think I heard once that Lange's even makes its own premium ice cream.

There's a four-page menu of choices for breakfast, lunch, and dinner—but if you're here in the morning, go for some kind of eggs and that thick hand-sliced bacon. Maybe a caramel roll, too. If you're a glutton for gastronomy, go for a slice of pie while you're at it.

TYLER

Aebleskiver Days

On a sunshiny bright morning, with the smell of pancakes and syrup float-ing in the air, I found the Tyler Fire Department—where I was told they were making, serving, and selling the Danish delicacy called aebleskivers.

I'd heard of these Danish "apple pancake balls," and actually even tried to make them once in a fit of younger gourmet fancy, but never had I eaten any prepared by someone who actually knew how to make the sweet treats. I figured attending Aebleskiver Days would give me the opportunity to not only taste the pancake balls but hopefully also give me some tips on how to prepare them.

So before I got in the line waiting to be served the hot, golden, tennis ball–looking treats, I wandered over to watch the women at the aebleskiver pans. Inside the fire hall, two rows of six women each stood before the pans with the traditional seven deep, round indentations. Poised with wooden skew-ers, they patiently turned the golden sweet delights, shaping the aebleskivers as they did so. Lucky me, I happened to ask Ines Peter a question about the procedure. In her Danish outfit, with her sparkling blue eyes, expertly turn-ing the pancake delights, I had an idea she would know.

A fiberglass prairie chicken in Rothsay welcomes visitors to the area.

Oh, she told me, aebleskivers are a "Danish adventure to make." She'd been making them for over forty years, and she'd learned the technique from her mother, who was "100 per cent Danish." Yes, she said, many women use the wooden skewers to turn their pancakes, but "my mother used a wood-handled fork, so that's what I use." Basically, the trick to these luscious numbers is that after you've poured the batter into the pan, you need to watch closely, turning the ball approximately three times, making sure it doesn't burn—and even more important, making sure that the inside is cooked and not pudding, said Ines.

Believe it or not, they make thousands of these pancakes during this annual festival. In fact, more than ten thousand ae-bleskivers were served on September

Serving up a panful of Danish "apple pancake balls" at Aebleskiver Days in Tyler

21, 1963, when Tyler celebrated its Danish heritage with the very first Aebleskiver Day. Today, nobody can even guess the numbers.

Folks walk out of here with paper baskets piled with the pancakes; others sit down and eat their three for $1.50 at a table in the hall. You can buy as many as you want—and Ines points out that many people buy a heaping basket or two, with plans to freeze them. They reheat beautifully, she said.

After the pancake breakfast, make sure you make a visit to the Danebod Historic Complex in town. This historic site runs cultural camps and folk-arts workshops throughout the year. The group of buildings in a parklike setting includes a church with a sailing ship suspended from the ceiling, a stone hall on the National Register of Historic Places, the folk school, and the gym. During Aebleskiver Days, if you've planned accordingly, you'll want to have lunch here as well. Served in the basement of the Danebod school, a $3.50 plate lunch is an authentic Danish meal. It's pretty as a picture and tastes even better. Afterwards, stop upstairs at the bake and craft sale. This is a find. Cream wafers ("they're nicknamed 'Danish Oreos,'" the woman who baked them told me), cinnamon sticks, rosettes, kisses, and something wonderful called finsk brod.

Later, you can sit outside, savoring your bake sale buys and perhaps sipping a cup of "holy water"—that's what the Danes call coffee, Ines told me.

SOUR CREAM COFFEE CAKE

This tender cake from the recipes compiled by Danebod English Ladies Aid, Tyler, Minnesota, is layered with a crunchy sprinkling of cinnamon-scented nuts. It's perfect for the coffee hour.

1 cup butter or margarine
1 1/2 cups granulated sugar
3 eggs
2 teaspoons baking powder
1 teaspoon baking soda
1 teaspoon lemon juice
1 cup sour cream
2 1/2 cups all-purpose flour
1/2 teaspoon salt
1 teaspoon vanilla

Filling: 1/3 cup brown sugar, 1 cup chopped nutmeats (your choice), 2 teaspoons cinnamon.

In a large bowl, cream butter and sugar. Add the sour cream and eggs. Beat well. Add dry ingredients, vanilla, and lemon juice.

Spread half of the dough in a greased 9-by-13-inch baking pan. Sprinkle half of the filling over this. Repeat one more time. Bake at 350 degrees for 40 minutes.

LUVERNE

Coffey Haus

111 East Main • Phone: (507) 283-8676

Bright, friendly, and casual, a stop at the Coffey Haus is worth a trip for anyone who loves a well-made sandwich, a cool glass of ginger peach iced tea, and a slice of pecan pie, hot out of the oven.

The small storefront, across the street from the Palace Theatre, belies the spacious step-back-in-time room that awaits: black and white–checked floor, high tin ceiling, and shelves with a collection of tea kettles and teapots. Glass jar lamps filled with coffee beans sit atop the green-tableclothed tables.

The shop is the dream of Susan Gruis, who opened it several years ago. On a milestone birthday, she gave her resignation at a long-standing job she'd held in town, walked outside, and saw the building she'd eventually open as the Coffey Haus. If you go outside and look up near the roof, you'll see the words in stone that she saw on the building where her shop is: Coffey Block. The rest, as they say, is history.

Any of the breads Susan makes are exemplary: onion dill, walnut rye, sourdough. Sandwich filling choices include crab salad, a tasty cashew chicken, and old-fashioned ham salad. The chicken wild rice soup is well seasoned, and the French onion soup is aromatic and fine. If you're here for morning coffee, there are fresh black walnut scones and a coffee cake topped with browned coconut that may still be warm in the pan. I've been here when macadamia white chocolate cookies were cooling on the parchment paper on which they came out of the oven. There's amaretto cheesecake and raspberry pie. Gazing at the dessert options, you may just want to skip soup and a sandwich all together.

Celebrating Corn

"People have tried and tried, but sex is not better than sweet corn"—heard on *A Prairie Home Companion*.

Corn has long been a favorite Minnesota food to fete—witness Sleepy Eye's Buttered Corn Day and Plainview's Corn on the Cob Festival. Ortonville's Cornfest is going on near sixty years, with twelve 55-gallon drums full of corn prepared using a huge, old steam-engine boiler. Olivia, the self-proclaimed Corn Capital of the state, not only celebrates the vegetable at its Corn Capital Days but also boasts a 35-foot-high ear of corn at its own Memorial Park.

Minnesota River Valley

Looking at a map of Minnesota, the Minnesota River looks like a giant backwards check mark. From the Twin Cities, it slants down to Mankato and then slashes at an angle back up to Granite Falls and Ortonville.

Belle Plaine, Le Sueur, and St. Peter mark Highway 169 along the river from the Twin Cities. Driving along here, you'll pass pumpkin patches, a few u-pick berry places, and a farm market or two. At Mankato, the Blue Earth River joins the elbow of the Minnesota River. If you've packed a picnic or stopped for doughnuts at the Starlight Bakery in Belle Plaine, you can take your treats and drive just west of Mankato to Minneopa State Park. Located on the bluffs overlooking the Minnesota River, the park surrounds a picturesque rush of waterfalls on Minneopa Creek.

From here, New Ulm, city of sausages, schnitzel, and strudel, is on the upward slash of the river. If you time things right when you arrive in New Ulm, you might just see the Glockenspiel, a 45-foot-tall musical clock tower with animated characters (on the corner of Fourth and Minnesota streets) when it makes its music. (It plays three times a day.) Northwest from New Ulm lies Granite Falls, whose rather harsh name belies a pretty soft secret of a town. In the summertime, it's fun to pick up an ice cream cone at the Grinder, a coffeehouse/café on busy Highway 212, and then drive downtown by the river and the Granite Falls dam. Here you can stroll the walking bridge. Or bring a loaf of day-old bread and you can feed the ducks in adjacent Rice Park.

BELLE PLAINE

Starlight Bakery
137 North Meridian • Phone: (952) 873-2726

I love the name of this little bakery. I think it sounds like it should be in a novel. In truth, the name came about after Tom and Valerie Peterson bought the bakery some 12 years ago. At that time, "it was called Don's Bakery," says Val. And people told us, 'Well now, you can't call the bakery "Petersons" in this Irish community.'" So they came up with the Starlight.

Stop in here on a Saturday morning, and the place is buzzing with people. They all seem to know Val personally. Some are picking up boxes of buns for a graduation party; others are simply selecting their Saturday-morning doughnut fixes. This is one of the old "from scratch" bakeries, and the pastries are admirable. Sample the "butterfly"—a fried cinnamon roll with a stripe of chocolate frosting down the middle. Or the blueberry-filled croissant. Or the plain cake doughnuts. There's nothing like them in a box at the supermarket.

Located in downtown Belle Plaine, the bakery itself has been here for over forty years. The Petersons gave it a face-lift a year ago, though, removing the pink and white candy striping above the windows and the seafoam green below. Now, look for a wooden storefront with a bright blue awning above. In the window the sign reads "Starlight Bakery."

ST. PETER

Ooodles Café
402 South Third Street • Phone: (507) 931-4455

Turn off the main street in St. Peter onto Grace, drive a block, and you'll find Ooodles. Ooodles, the restaurant, that is. It's right on the corner, a couple doors down from an antiques shop and an intriguing artistic shop called Eye Tattoo Impulse Piercing.

The Saturday morning I stopped in this clean, sunny hometown café, the guys were rolling dice in the daily loser's game of who pays, and the room was busy with locals; one woman was having her birthday breakfast. I always like these kinds of places where when you sit down, the waitress comes over immediately with a menu and a smile and says, "What can I do for you, hon?"

Daily specials are on the dry erase board: for example, steak and eggs with hash browns and toast, $4.79. Oooodles nightly "all you can eat" specials are listed above it: Monday, broasted chops; Tuesday, broasted chicken; Wednesday, spaghetti; Thursday, Ooodles's famous BBQ ribs; Friday, fish; every night, hamburger steak.

The book-sized menu is packed with other offerings. Breakfasts include Texas-size French toast. Eggs are cooked to order and arrive hot and fast. If you order home fries, they're the real, skin-on chunky kind, perfectly seasoned and cooked. Cinnamon rolls are homemade and served warm—with a big goop of melty frosting. If you sit at the small counter, you won't be able to resist the pans of warm caramel rolls that just came out of the oven.

German food and German goods on display at Domeiers, New Ulm

NICOLLET

Schmidts Meat Market
319 Pine Street • Phone: (507) 232-3438

A nicely seasoned homemade sausage is a beauty to behold and a joy to savor. And at Schmidts Meat Market, you'll find racks and racks of these deep scarlet cylindrical beauties. In fact, there are over thirty varieties of award-winning sausage and bacon! Not to mention hundreds of other meat, deli, cheese, and food items. Heck, they even have smoked beef bones for dogs and suet for birds in their deli here.

This is "Southern Minnesota's 'Meating' Place" (according to the business card), and what a meeting place it is—virtually out in the middle of nowhere. Drive through Nicollet, and the town looks empty. But turn off the main street and you'll see where the action is in this town. Schmidts Meat Market stretches along almost half a block. Window boxes brighten up the stucco exterior, and over the door the word *Willkommen* beckons.

The shop—started in 1947—has gone way beyond its humble beginnings, says Betty Schmidt, whose husband, Bruce, and brother, Gary, bought the business from their father. His small shop was mostly all sausages, says Betty. In 1975, the brothers expanded the building and business to what it is today. A huge smokehouse in the back is used to prepare the homemade recipes of their father's, all still smoked with select woods. But the brothers also do custom butchering, curing, and wild game processing for the many deer hunters in the area.

On a Saturday, the clerks (including Betty) in their red and white–striped shirts are kept busy. I never did find out where all their customers come from, but it's apparent the Schmidts are known far and wide. Taste the sausage, however, and "word of mouth" comes to mind.

NEW ULM

Veigel's Kaiserhoff
221 North Minnesota • Phone: (507) 359-2071

Back in 1938, the Kaiserhoff—it was located next to the New Ulm Theater then—sold their first order of barbecue ribs for 45 cents and beer for a dime.

Octoberfest at the Schell Brewery, New Ulm

Since that time, they've relocated, expanded the restaurant, and probably cooked up about three million pounds of ribs, says owner, Don Veigel.

Today, the rack of ribs couldn't be more gorgeous (even if the cost has gone up a tad)—covering the platter, cooked until the meat is ready to slip off the bone, and then slathered with sauce. You still can't go wrong with an order. On the other hand, don't let it deter you from the Kaiserhoff's fine offerings of bratwurst, wiener schnitzel, or landjaeger (old German-style pork and beef smoked sausage). Served with the Kaiserhoff's warm, bacony German potato salad (yummy) or homemade beans, these grand and hearty dishes are at their finest here. Even the accompaniments are delights: spaetzles and gravy, red cabbage, old-fashioned brown baked beans, and fresh rye bread.

The maze of dining rooms is continually packed with people here, and Don and Jan Veigel are always around to greet, seat, and chat. Do stop in the kitschy-cool bar before you leave. Dark gnome murals cover the walls as well as the "Boulevard of Broken Dreams"—a knockoff on Edward Hopper's *Nighthawks* coffee shop painting. If you have time, it's fun to order a locally brewed Schell's in here, dig in to the free bowl of pretzels, and try to figure out who all is in the painting. Let's see: Elvis is the waiter, looks like James Dean is at the counter . . .

Domeiers
1020 South Minnesota • Phone: (507) 354-4231

This delightful little shop is like stepping into an enchanted corner of the Black Forest—and whenever I'm in New Ulm, I never leave without stopping here.

Started as a neighborhood store in 1934, it offers a rich assortment of German treasures—from tins of pfeffernuesse and boxes of lebkuchen to Bavarian blown-glass Christmas ornaments, little cuckoo clocks, glitter-sparkling Advent calendars, and old-country music recordings. A line up of nutcrackers, incense burners, and beer steins will make your head spin. A nice selection of greeting cards (in German) and refrigerator magnets that state "We love Oma" and "We love Opa" are near the cash register. There should be one that states "We love Domeiers." It's a must visit.

The Backerei and Coffee Shop
27 South Minnesota
Phone: (507) 354-6011

One morning when I was pointing out the square of the Backerei's sour cream coffee cake that I wanted, the woman behind me in line leaned over and confided she drives all the way here from Mankato to buy this delicacy. "I like to heat it up just a little in the microwave and serve it warm," she told me. "It reminds me of the kind of coffee cake my grandmother used to make," she said, "only we ate her cake warm from the oven."

After my first heavenly taste of the cake, I had to agree that this is one of those things worth searching out. You may not be inclined to drive all the way to New Ulm for a taste of the best sour cream coffee cake you've ever eaten, but I think it's certainly worth checking out when you're within, say, 50 miles. Buy a square and a cup of coffee and sit down at one of the tables on the coffee shop side of this bakery, or take your sweet treasures to the nearby park and indulge.

Morgan Creek Vineyards

23707 478th Avenue; take Highway 68 to Blue Earth County 47 to 101 South; first farm on the left.
Phone: (507) 947-3547

"The romance of wine is everywhere," says George Marti, owner, along with his wife, Paula, of Morgan Creek Vineyards. One of the newest wineries in the state, it's located in a picturesque setting a few gentle, rolling miles from New Ulm. "My feeling is there's going to be a string of wineries on the Minnesota River," says George, with a smile as he adds, "sort of the Napa of the North."

The Martis planted their first grapes in 1993, and six years later they bottled their first wine, celebrating with the first harvest festival. The afternoon I happened in, the festival was winding down (I missed the grape stomp), but I did manage to check out the brand new wine shop, as well as taste the wines.

My choice? Well, I have to admit: I bought a bottle of their Morgan Creek Myst because I was enchanted with the description: "for sipping while watching the moon rise over the Morgan Creek." It sounded so, well, romantic.

August Schell Brewing Co.

1860 Schell Road; south on Broadway (Highway 14/15), then turn west on 18th S. Phone: (507) 354-5528

New Ulm's oldest industry, the Schell Brewing Company, was founded in 1860 by August Schell and has been family operated ever since. A specialty brewer long before the popularity of microbrewing began, Schell beers have won numerous awards, including a silver medal for the beer that also happens to be a favorite of mine: the August Schell Octoberfest brew. Schell also brews root beer: Their 1919 draft is a rich and creamy blend.

Even if you're not a beer lover, though, the brewery is a destination worth a visit. Beautiful brick buildings and lovely grounds and gardens are kept tidy and lush. There are pathways through the manicured landscape, and the kids will love the little gnomes—just their size—that are set up at a table high on a hillside.

Tours of the actual brewery are only available during New Ulm's major festivals, but the gardens and grounds and shop are open all summer long.

GRANITE FALLS

The Grinder
176 East Highway 212 • Phone: (320) 564-4244

This little coffeehouse/ice cream shop/café on busy Highway 212 is very cool. For one thing, when you order your latte here, you should know that the old dark wood bar that you're standing at was originally from the Skunk Hollow Bar—a Prohibition joint just outside of Granite Falls. Yes, says owner Jeri Snortum, "I've had local customers tell me, 'I stood up to this thing many times.'" It was a great find, she added, when she and her husband, Steve, were first opening up the Grinder in 1994 and looking for furniture and supplies for the place.

Other furnishings are almost as fun in here, though. In the second room, several 1950s chrome tables and chairs are laid with vintage tablecloths. The best one in the house is covered in an orange retro plaid pattern—and is located in front of sliding-glass doors that look out into the side of a bluff. A half-dozen bird feeders are set up in the wild pocket of land here. Watching the birds while lunching on one of the Grinder's made-to-order sandwiches is mesmerizing. Even better, if you really get hooked on identifying the birds, you need only step through another doorway nearby to the Wild Bird Store. It's part of the coffeehouse complex, says Jeri. Beyond that is their greenhouse. "We actually call this the 'mini mall,'" says Jeri.

The Grinder is easy to miss if you are coming from the west (heading east). It's tucked back into the side of a hill. Keep a look out.

Red River Valley

Considered some of the most fertile soil in Minnesota, the Red River Valley is a rich expanse of land that stretches along Minnesota's western border, following the Red River of the North. Fields of bright yellow sunflowers are not uncommon sights, following the sun across the big blue sky. The land is wide open here, and the wind runs free.

BARNESVILLE

Barnesville Potato Days
Held Friday and Saturday before Labor Day weekend

"What makes your lefse bubble up?" asked an onlooker as I watched contestants preparing lefse in the sun-filled kitchen of the Catholic church during Barnesville's annual Potato Days. I leaned closer to hear the answer: "The shortening," said Mabel Braton. "I use lard, butter, and cream," added this longtime lefse maker, who has often been a winner in the Barnesville competition.

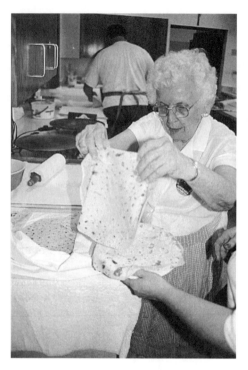

Preparing for the lefse cook-off at Barnesville's Potato Days festival

Lefse lovers are legion at this event, and the cafeteria out front is packed with people waiting to buy the made-from-scratch delicacy (all the leftover lefse is packaged and sold after judging). In the kitchen, folks are encouraged to wander around, inhaling the warm wonderful aroma of frying potato while watching the lefse makers (of all ages) flip the rounds of dough with a sweet soft swish of their lefse stick.

But the lefse contest is only one small part of this town's festival honoring its potato-producing heritage. There's mashed-potato wrestling (honest, it's gooey), there's a recipe contest (think: potato fudge pie, potato turtle bar), and, of course, there's all those incredible potato variations to eat downtown.

For example, don't miss the potato sausage wrapped in lefse that the minister is serving up. The savory hot sausage is fabulous, and the lefse it's rolled up in is warm and velvety. Then there's the potato dumpling in its pool of melted butter—cholesterol be damned, this is good. There are stands where you can buy German potato salad, twice-baked potatoes, and fish and chips (French fries). Light hitters might want to go for something such as a lemonade and a potato chip cookie. (But why?)

You can even buy a little burlap sack of award-winning recipes selected from past Potato Days Cookoffs—which includes such novelties as mashed potato fudge, potato pickles, and potato spice cake.

In the early evening, wander down the main avenue (it's officially called Front Street) pick up your free bag of hot French fries. Then join the crowds, dipping fingers into the bags of the hot salty treats, visiting with friends, and strolling by store windows where mannequins are clothed in potato sacks and window displays are collections of antique potato mashers and old French fry cutters.

Even the local gas station gets into the potato act: At the cash register there's a bucket of potatoes. "Guess how many eyes," reads a sign, "and you win." (I'm not sure what you win. Maybe a sack of spuds?) This is one of the most fun and well-done food festivals in the state.

ROTHSAY

Truck Stop Café
544 North Center Street • (218) 867-2197

If you turn off the freeway by the large prairie chicken, you are in Rothsay. If you follow the road to the truck stop where dozens of big rigs are lined up, you'll be at the Rothsay Truck Stop Café. This is a typical diner with one exception: the graham cracker pie. Rare is the restaurant that makes this old-fashioned comfort food. And it's even rarer when it's this good.

MOORHEAD

Quality Bakery & Pastry Shop
720 Main Avenue • Phone: (218) 233-6942

This is another hometown bakeshop that has been around for years and years in the Fargo-Moorhead area. (There's a location in Fargo as well.) The Quality was producing specialty breads long before the trend was even hinted at. Try the nine grain, the Black Forest rye, or the wild rice. Stumble in here during a pie special month and you could find yourself surrounded with choices: peach, cherry, blueberry, toffee bar crunch, banana fudge, coconut cream, or chocolate peanut butter. It really doesn't matter which you choose here; they're all impressive.

8. Bluff Country

Tree-shaded lanes dip down into green valleys and wind around rushing trout streams in the southeastern part of the state known as "Historic Bluff Country." Small towns with endearing names like Harmony, Pleasant Grove, and Spring Valley dot the wooded region—along with tidy farms, tiny cafés serving homemade pies, and markets selling brown eggs and crusty loaves of bread.

Roughly bounded by Interstate 90 to the north, the Mississippi River to the east, and the Iowa border to the south, the region has long seduced travelers with its natural beauty, not to mention those picturesque villages, complete with old-fashioned church steeples piercing the early-morning mist.

To be truthful, this scenic pocket of Minnesota is quite aware of its tourism appeal. Its popular Root River State Trail is one of the biggest draws in the state—and deservedly so. (Be aware: Summer weekends are extremely crowded with bikers, hikers, and in-line skaters!) But it's also the reason why you can anticipate good food awaiting you at any number of wonderful places after exploring the river trail with songbirds above and wildlife nearby.

Here you can dine in the Old Village Hall one night, lunch in a converted barn the next, pause for coffee and coconut cream pie in any number of diminutive villages, and then sleep the night away in a four-poster bed at an historic inn. In the morning, sip gourmet coffee and nibble French pastry or order up a mess of eggs and bacon and hash browns at a local hangout where folks are friendly, coffee comes in thick mugs, and the entrée arrives steaming and properly greasy.

Lanesboro—the center of the Root River State Trail—has a downtown on the National Register of Historical Places as well as several options when it comes to food. I can never resist the homemade seasoned brats squirted with handmade mustard at Das Wurst Haus; if you're lucky, you may be treated to an impromptu accordion solo by Arv, the guy who also takes your food order. At Scenic Valley Winery, sample such local fruit wines as wild plum and raspberry. Make reservations for a multicourse meal at the notable Mrs. B's or for a classic French-inspired dinner at the Victorian House.

For picnic fixings, stop at the Community Market & Deli in Preston (try their Hawaiian sandwich) and then pick up a mocha or two from The Brick House on Main (a coffeehouse in a great old storefront). Make a stop for fresh berries (or apples if it's autumn) at the Preston Apple and Berry Farm. There are plenty of beautiful waysides and turnouts for an alfresco meal. You may want to meander over to Beaver Creek Valley State Park—and lunch amidst summery wildflowers. (Know that the picnic areas in this park are so appealing that they are often used as sites for weddings and receptions). Also, trout dwell in deep pools beneath Beaver Creek Valley State Park's limestone bluffs, so if you're inclined, bring along a fishing pole.

East of Harmony, it's not un-usual to see a horse and buggy on the road ahead; many old-order Amish families farm and live in this region. You can take guided tours of the farmsteads—but it's also fun (if you have the time) to wander the country roads on your own, discovering faded signs near farms advertising blackberry pre-serves and blueberry jam or but-tery cashew-crunch candy (nu-merous brochures give detailed scenic drive instructions).

In fact, wandering back roads is how I landed in tiny Spring Grove the first time and discovered a soda pop factory that has been

Rows of fat pumpkins in Bluff Country

producing pop since 1895. Another time I straggled into Chatfield at twilight on a summer Thursday evening. When I followed the sound of music, I found a crowd listening to the Chatfield Brass Band in the park, spooning up ice cream as the stars began to shine.

After that experience, I realized, it's no surprise a first visit to this classic countryscape inspires a second and a third. The traveler who has savored a taste of small-town summer skies and fresh rhubarb wine will surely be moved to return again, to sample firsthand autumn's apple harvest or to attend Har-mony's Holiday Fest—or simply to welcome spring by peddling down a bu-colic stretch of the bike trail with visions of strawberry pie dancing ahead.

CHATFIELD

Country Crossroads Candies
Eli and Ada Yoder • Route 3, Box 108

I have a shop clerk in Lanesboro to thank for this incredible find. It was she who wrote down the perfect directions to the Amish Country Crossroads Candies: "North on 250 (9 miles). L. on 30, go straight until Hwy. turns. Go straight on gravel and turn R. 1 mi. Go L., 1 mi., go R, 1 mil. Go L. It's there at the intersection." It sounds confusing, she added before I left. Well, yeah, just a little. But amazingly, I found the place with its faded little sign on the corner of the gravel roads.

When I drove into the farmstead, with its characteristic windmill in the yard and its horses out by the barn, I also saw a half dozen? dozen? young faces pressed against the screen door peeking at us. I got out, with my son and his little buddy, and while I went to the adjoining candy kitchen doorway, they made friends with the youngsters. (By the time I finished, they were all petting a kitten while sitting in front of one of the old Amish black buggies.)

Inside the Amish candy kitchen, a mother and her daughter were finishing up a day's worth of candy making. Dozens of the pecan/caramel turtles I'd seen for sale (and tasted and fallen in love with) in Lanesboro were lined up on wax paper–covered counters. A few jars of jam and jelly sat on shelves nearby, and the buttery chocolate crunch and incredible cashew brittle I was looking for was bagged up and ready for sale, too. But the point of my visit all the way to this kitchen was also for some chitchat. How many children do you have? I asked. The mother informed me she had 12 kids: 6 girls and 6 boys—and 33 grandkids so far!! The reason for all the company today, she told me shyly, was that she had several married daughters visiting. We chatted a little longer, and then I opened the door with my purchases. My boys were wandering around the Amish black buggy by now, peering inside. Could they sit up in the buggy? Of course, said the woman with a smile. So they did.

Certainly, you don't need to drive all the way out to the farm to buy this candy. You'll find it for sale at numerous shops in the area. But if you have the time, the experience (as well as the candy) is unforgettable.

PRESTON

Preston Apple and Berry Farm
645 Highway 16 and Highway 52 • Phone: (507) 765-4486

On an autumn Saturday, do not pass through this region without a visit to the Preston Apple and Berry Farm. Located in certainly one of the most picturesque areas in southeastern Minnesota, the apple shop sits atop a bluff overlooking the lovely, delicately curving Root River.

In the fall, when the valley is at its showy colorful best, the little eatery and bake shop next to a greenhouse is filled with people, tucking into a piece of homemade apple pie (à la mode of course), sipping fresh apple cider, or munching an apple doughnut. People come from miles around for the apple and berry turnovers, and the apple muffins don't even get out of the muffin tins to cool before being snapped up. If there's no room to sit in here (there are barely four tables), simply take your purchases across the highway to the rest area and indulge in a view.

In the fall, the farm offers a good selection of apples (over two dozen varieties, including Keepsake, Fireside, Cortland, and Honeycrisp) as well as local honey, sorghum, Watkins products, and baked goods (fresh and frozen). In the summer, you'll find fresh strawberries and raspberries.

"This was just a cornfield seventeen years ago," says Carol Gosi of the acreage she and her husband, Joe, bought on the bluff in 1985. Now it's filled with 800 apple trees, four acres of strawberries, one-half acre of raspberries, and a large garden patch.

Born in Hungary, apple orchard owner Joe Gosi fled his homeland in 1956, after the revolution, to begin a new life in the United States. During the first few years he worked a variety of jobs, intermittently at an orchard near the Twin Cities. He says he knew, even in Hungary, that he enjoyed growing fruits. After being manager of an orchard for 21 years, he left in 1985 to

Some unusual wines on display at the Scenic Valley Winery, Lanesboro

begin his own orchard and vegetable business here along Highway 52 in Preston. When he's not in the orchard, you'll find him in the shop kitchen: He's usually the one dishing up the apple pie or lifting hot tins of apple muffins out of the oven.

LANESBORO

Scenic Valley Winery

101 Coffee Street W. • Phone: (507) 467-2958

Located on Coffee Street and housed in what was once the town's creamery, Scenic Valley Winery has been producing private-label country wines since 1984. Stop in on a Saturday and work your way through visitors to the sampling bar or wander around the sunny room. Whenever the door opens, the sunshine seems programmed to spotlight the bottles of gold and pink and purple wines.

These are country wines, says vintner Karrie Ristau, who works with her mother, Lucretia Brehm. Made from local fruits (ads are placed in the regional newspapers to buy hand-picked berries and vegetables), the wines have a fresh, clean taste when young. And that's when they should be enjoyed. Unlike a grape wine, whose life is measured in years, a fruit wine is measured in months, says Karrie.

At Scenic Valley, you can select from rhubarb (by far, the best seller), strawberry, raspberry, apple, wild grape, or wild plum. They also make two unique cooking wines: green pepper and onion. These were the result of the year they bought a glut of onions, says Karrie. For the heck of it, they decided to try making the onions into wine. When it proved popular with the culinary set, they experimented with green peppers as well. You can use the wines when sautéing just about anything, adds Karrie. A half cup added to homemade chili or beef stew adds another dimension of flavor, too.

Along with its tasting bar and bottles of wine, the spacious shop also sells wine accessories as well as antiques scattered throughout. Look for those old green glass plates, hand-crocheted doilies, and vintage tablecloths—perfect and fun extras for an impromptu picnic setting later . . . with a bottle of wine, of course.

From Scenic Valley Winery: Five-Hour Beef Stew

This recipe comes from Karrie Ristau at the winery. Accompanied by good bread, the stew is perfect for an autumn evening in front of the fire.

> 2 pounds of stew beef, cut up
> 6 carrots, cut up
> 4 potatoes, cut up
> 1/4 to 1/2 cup Scenic Valley Winery onion or green
>   pepper wine
> 2 1/2 cups stewed tomatoes (Author's note: I like
>   to use tomatoes and green chilies.)
> 4 stalks celery, cut up
> 1 tablespoon sugar
> 4 tablespoons tapioca (Author's note:
>   I sometimes substitute 1/3 cup barley, added
>   in after 3 hours.)

In large baking pan, mix all ingredients, except the cooking wine. Bake 5 hours at 250 degrees. Stir every hour. Add cooking wine 1 hour before serving.

Das Wurst Haus
117 Parkway Avenue N. • Phone: (507) 467-2902

"Give me the back of your hand, sweetie," Arv told me the first time I was at Das Wurst Haus and asked about the "Gentle Giant" mustard he makes and sells. When I did as he instructed, he squirted a polka dot of mustard on it. "Taste that," he said. "That's got some real authority," he added as he watched me tentatively touch my tongue to it. When I nodded my approval, he was clearly pleased.

Homemade mustards such as the one I tasted (five others include a unique caraway, a smooth honey, and a smoked variation) are only a part of the food-stuffs made from scratch at Das Wurst Haus. "Beans, potato salad, bratwurst, root beer, bread," Arv says. "We make everything ourselves except the cheese."

The cheese he's talking about is the melting Swiss stuff that tops the sauerkraut that tops the corned beef that tops the caraway bread. This is their signature Reuben sandwich (a Rachel is a specially smoked turkey version). Ordering it with a side of potato salad and beans is your decision, but be sure and accompany it with an icy homemade root beer served in a frosted-over cold mug—the kind on which you can write your name in the condensation. This is good root beer: spicily fragrant, cool, and addictive—and brewed a half-barrel at a time.

Das Wurst Haus has been serving up root beer, Reubens, homemade bratwurst, and ice cream (the front of the shop features an always-busy ice cream counter) for over fifteen years. Now that Arv's son has joined the navy, however, Arv and his wife have sold the business. "But we're still going to be managing the place," says Arv with a smile.

Coaxing a customer to try one of the special mustards at Das Wurst Haus in Lanesboro.

Owner or no, there's not a doubt that Arv will continue spouting off his famous one-liners at the restaurant: " I haven't been the same since I lost my mind," you may hear him apologize to a customer whose order arrived without the potato salad. Or when someone asks if he plays the accordion (displayed behind the cash register and under the cuckoo clock), Arv may quip: "Oh, I try to play the concertina, but right now I'm not in a violent mood."

Later, when the crowd has thinned down at the register and orders are getting caught up, Arv often picks up his beloved concertina and does play a few short tunes. It's obvious he doesn't have to try very hard, either; his talent and love for the music is apparent.

Tip: All of the mustards are available at each table, so if you have lunch here, you can sample each one and then purchase your favorite on the way out. Besides mustards to stash in the back seat, you can also buy a root beer starter kit, a loaf of bread, and even a tape of Arv and his family "band" at Das Wurst Haus.

FROM THE BERWOOD HILL INN: BELGIAN WAFFLES

Berwood Hill Inn is a beautiful Victorian country house on the outskirts of Lanesboro. If you ever stay here, you may get lucky and wake up to these waffles for breakfast. This waffle recipe from the inn's executive chef, Vin Skjelstad, is great because the batter is prepared the night before.

Note: The difference between Belgian waffles and traditional waffles is the depth and the rise of the grids in the iron (not the recipe). This multipurpose yeast recipe is made the night before and can be used as a base for a variety of dishes.

> 2 cups all-purpose flour (or 1 cup cake flour and 1 cup all-purpose flour)
> 1 tablespoon sugar
> 1/2 teaspoon salt
> 1 teaspoon baking powder
> 1 teaspoon yeast
> 2 cups milk
> 1/2 cup butter, melted
> 1 teaspoon vanilla
> 2 eggs
> 1/2 teaspoon baking soda

In a large bowl, combine first five ingredients and mix well. Pour in milk, melted butter, and vanilla. Stir until combined. Cover and let sit at room temperature overnight.

In the morning, while waffle iron is preheating, separate eggs and add yolks to the overnight mixture. In a separate bowl, heat whites until they are at soft peak stage and then gently fold into batter.

Spread one ladle of batter into iron to bake until the waffle is done, usually 3 to 5 minutes. Add toppings; serve immediately. Makes approximately 6 to 8 waffles, depending on size of the waffle iron.

Chef's note: Belgian waffles allow for spectacular presentation—perhaps filled with fresh whole berries, a dollop of Chambord-scented whipped cream on top, and a decadent drizzle of chocolate over all.

Mrs. B's Historic Lanesboro Inn
101 Parkway • Phone: (800) 657-4710 or (507) 467-2154

Walk through the old-fashioned door of this 1872 limestone inn and enter a snug, welcoming little parlor. Go up the open staircase and you'll find the cozy antique-filled rooms for rent. Go down the stairs and you'll enter Mrs. B's ever popular restaurant.

Breakfast is served to inn guests in the dining area here, and light lunches are available to the public. But for Mrs. B's legendary five-course prix fixe dinner, you'll need reservations.

The fun part—or the unfun part, depending on your expectations—is that when you dine at Mrs. B's for the evening meal, you'll be put at a table with strangers. Don't come here for a romantic, gazing-in-the-eyes-of-the-one-you-love dinner. This affair is for fun, friendship, and wonderful food.

I have eaten here several times with groups of friends. But the last time I was here, my reservation was for one. I was put at a table with two women on a shopping holiday from their husbands and an older couple who had just gotten married in the spring. At first, it was a little awkward, but by dessert, we were exchanging e-mail addresses and business cards. After dinner, the two women invited both myself and the other couple to see what their room looked like and to show us what they'd bought on the Amish tour they'd taken that day.

Oh, and dinner. That night it started out with fine parmesan and herb–enhanced polenta, with a lovely dab of rich black olive and roasted red pepper tapenade alongside. A spicy Cuban black bean soup with a swirl of cilantro sour cream on top followed. The salad of fresh garden greens was perfumed and dressed—not too heavy, not too faint—with a light raspberry vinaigrette. The main course, served family style, was a platter of turkey breast drizzled with an unfortunately bland-tasting tandoori-style sauce. Its was not nearly on par with other entrées I've had here (e.g., roast pork loin with a lush blackberry and bourbon sauce, a tasty lamb ragout with black olives and tomatoes), but it was still good enough, and the portions were generous. Dessert? A chocolate layer cake with chocolate ganache icing.

After dessert, the chef came out from the kitchen, thanked everyone for coming, and served each table small glasses of a homemade version of Bailey's Irish Cream. Called "Mrs. B's Bump," it's a tradition that started with the first chef who worked at Mrs. B's. It's a nice warming touch to end the evening.

WHALAN

The Whalen Inn
618 Main Street •Phone: (507) 467-2623

The best part about staying at the Whalen Inn is that in the morning you awaken to the scent of pies baking: rich raspberry smells and homespun cinnamon and apple aromas—wafting up the stairs and into your room. This means if you're a pie-in-the-morning person, you also get first dibs on a warm slice of the pastry. (No waiting in line!) Or you can always opt for owner Lynette Whalen's continental breakfast, which includes an oven-fresh muffin and perhaps a stemmed goblet full of cold grapes and melon.

Starting at 5 A.M. in the summer season, owner Lynette and one of her daughters (she has four, plus two sons, who all help in one capacity or another) are usually in the kitchen at the tiny Whalen Inn—four miles from Lanes-

A phalanx of fresh pies at the Whalen Inn in Whalan

boro on the Root River bike trail. Here, they prepare about sixty pies a day: among them, maple walnut, raspberry, pumpkin custard, cherry crunch, rhubarb custard, and sour cream raisin. Although all of the pie recipes (over a dozen) came with the sale of the small restaurant (Lynette and her husband, Randy, took over in spring 2000), Lynette has added a few of her own pie favorites to the repertoire: a delicate peach crumb top, lemon meringue, and raspberry rhubarb.

Customers are the hundreds of pedal-pushing bikers who pass by this little shop boasting "world famous pies" on the popular Root River bike trail. And sometimes, says Lynette, they get confused in this area of the country, known for its Amish heritage. A woman once asked her, "Are these Amish-made pies?" To which Lynette responded good-naturedly, "No, they're Irish-made pies."

Lynette grew up in the restaurant business and wanted to open a pie shop 14 years ago, but the timing and location just weren't right, she says. When she finally bought this place, she remembers her sister remarking: "I can't believe it. You always wanted to do pies." Says Lynette: "I feel pretty lucky I got to do my dream."

SPRING GROVE

Spring Grove Bottling Works, Inc.
215 Second Avenue N.W. • Phone: (507) 498-3424

At one time, every other small town had its own bottling plant, and America had hundreds of local soda pops, with fanciful names like Misty Morning, Spruce Tonic, and Spring Grove. Today, small-town bottlers are a dying breed, and Misty Morning and Spruce Tonic are long gone. But happily you can still buy a bottle of locally brewed Spring Grove Pop in (surprise) Spring Grove, Minnesota.

Introduced in 1895, the formula for Spring Grove pop still includes pure cane sugar (most pop today is sweetened with fructose; it's cheaper) and has remained essentially the same since the company was founded here in Spring Grove by G.G. Reistey a century ago. In 1964, it was bought by Arnold and Helen Morken, and today it is operated by their son and grandson Roger and Eric.

During the summertime, the pop is bottled three times a week, and on an average day, a three-person crew bottles approximately four to five hundred cases of pop. (They sell between twenty thousand and twenty-five thousand cases a year.) Their best seller is strawberry, but other flavors include black cherry, cream soda, lemon sour, root beer, lemonade, orange, and grape.

On bottling day, the bottles move along a conveyor line to the bottling machine, which dispenses sugar syrup and flavor extract. Next, bottles are filled with carbonated water, capped, and then labeled with the green-and-white Spring Grove label featuring a deer standing near a spring in a grove of trees. Finally, before they're put into cases, the bottles are gently turned upside down to mix the ingredients.

Spring Grove pop was originally bottled in the 10-ounce old-style slender-neck returnables, which you still may find here and there, but the company now uses 10-ounce nonreturnable glass bottles with screw caps—not nearly as charming to look at, but still as refreshing to drink.

Today, the pop is available in Minnesota (at Lunds and Byerly's grocery stores in the Twin Cities), northeast Iowa, and western Wisconsin. But really, the best place to experience your first taste of Spring Grove pop is in Spring Grove. Adjacent to the Ballard House Antique store, there's a little café. Here's where you can order the all-time best ham salad sandwich I've ever eaten (next to my mom's) along with a bottle of Spring Grove's most popular strawberry-flavor pop. Later, you can swing by the Spring Grove Bottling Works a couple blocks away and pick up a case of the stuff to take home with you.

HARMONY

Amish Farms in the Area

East of Harmony, don't be surprised if on a Saturday afternoon you come upon an intersection where a black buggy is parked near a clothesline hung with Amish quilts waving in the wind—and a hand-lettered sign proclaiming "Quilts and Bake Sale." Nearby, a table may be laden with jars of pear butter, elderberry jelly, pickled beets, and whole pies: peach pineapple or black raspberry ($3.75 a pie). Drive a few miles further down the road and you may

Amish quilts on display near Harmony

125

see a sign advertising honey. When you pull into the farmstead, you may find a small shed where jars of honey are lined up and a small box designated for payment is set. This is the old-fashioned honor system.

And this is Amish country. Old-order Amish families farm and live without modern conveniences in the area around Harmony. Long-skirted women and barefoot children hoe gardens; windmills mark the farmsteads, horses pull plows in the fields, and horse-drawn buggies take the black-clad Amish to town. Locally based tours of the area are popular—and often easier than navigating back gravel roads by yourself. Knowledgeable guides offer insights into the Amish lifestyle, and you also have bountiful opportunities to stop at farms to buy home-baked goods, garden produce, baskets, and even beautiful handmade furniture. But tours are not available on Sunday, and no photographs of the Amish people are permitted at any time.

ROCHESTER

John Hardy's Bar-B-Q

1940 Broadway S./929 Frontage Road W.
Phone: (507) 281-1727/(507) 288-3936

There's something about eating a barbecue pork sandwich while gazing out the window at the Starlite Motel across the street (Broadway) that appeals to my sense of culinary contentment. It seems so, well, fitting. It also seems appropriate that John Hardy, a Birmingham, Alabama, boy, was the force behind this Northern barbecue joint that's been a Rochester favorite since 1972.

Hardy died in 1986 at the age of 66 in nearby Elgin. But his barbecue legacy lives on. The two Rochester restaurants that carry his name and likeness in their logo continue to smoke ribs the same way Hardy did, over a fire of cherry and apple wood. His sauces are still prepared according to Hardy's original recipes: "Mild, Medium, Hot (proceed with caution), Spicy Hot (please sign a release form), and Big Boy Hot (need we say more?)" If you want your sauce on the side, just ask.

You can order beef, turkey, chicken, and ham here. But once you get a glimpse of those slabs of glistening dark barbecued pork ribs piled on a platter, you'll know the reason folks have kept this place in business. For the record, the hot version of the lustrous sauce is one of the best. Order the fried okra, and you'll leave a happy boy or girl.

ROCHESTER FOOD FESTIVAL

Rochester, Minnesota. Home of the Mayo Clinic, IBM, and . . . food groupies? It's true. For over a dozen years, the Kahler Grand Hotel has hosted approximately three hundred people at each of its semiannual Food Fests. Hot mulled wine awaits you as you check in on a Friday night for the November (there's one in April, too) weekend of cooking classes, tastings, and seminars. This is an event in which food lovers and aspiring cooks eat, drink, and sleep gastronomy. It's a gourmet getaway in a class by itself.

Showing off some of the goodies that make people return to the Gingerbread House Bakery in Rochester

Original Roscoe's
603 Fourth Street S.E. (two blocks east of the Government Center)
Phone: (507) 285-0501

Roscoe's North
Cedarwood Plaza • 4180 18th Avenue N.W.

Roscoe's Root Beer and Ribs is another Rochester institution. Since 1981, Steven and Barbara Ross have been brewing up homemade root beer at Roscoe's and slow-roasting their award-winning pork ribs with the hint of hickory, apple, and cherry wood that smoked them. The homemade barbecue sauce is pure and thick (although a Southern-style hot sauce is available on request). You can now eat these superb sweet ribs year round (Roscoe's second location is in Rochester's Cedarwood Plaza). But on a summer noon, it's still much more fun to stop at the minuscule shack (five stools for eat-in diners) near Mayo Park, where the Original Roscoe's is located. Order a succulent (and sloppy) pork sandwich, a pile of homemade barbecue beans, maybe coleslaw, and, of course, a cold root beer. Then head over to the park for an impromptu picnic. Get plenty of napkins. Oh, and have them bag up a bottle of Roscoe's sauce before you leave too. You'll want to try it at home.

The Gingerbread House Bakery
1104 North Broadway • Phone: (507) 288-2621

Like many things in life, beauty lies within at this nondescript box of a bakery in Rochester (it's been there forever, said the young woman giving me directions. "You'll love it," she added, and she was right).

The exterior of dreary stucco, with a sun-faded gingerbread boy and sign stating "Gingerbread House," certainly doesn't prepare one for the warmth of nostalgia and scents of a spicy past inside. Open the door, and a little bell rings with a small, sweet jingle. Inside, there's a small entry, just big enough for a carved and painted wooden chef, complete with rolling pin in one hand and an American flag in the other. Straight ahead, an old-fashioned kitchen cupboard displays packages of cream cheese muffins; long, slender cherry pound cakes; and even a tray of six tiny cream puffs—all bewitchingly enticing on a bright red cloth.

Beyond this entry, you'll find the spacious bakery itself, complete with a shining antique black iron stove in one corner. It's used as a display for bundles of bread wrapped in clear plastic bags, tied and labeled—onion bread, barley bread, eight-grain bread—all nestled alongside packages of dinner rolls and Hungarian coffee cakes.

The traditional glass case holds frosted long johns and jelly-filled doughnuts—while a blueberry pie and a pumpkin pie repose, humbly enticing on top of the glass. On shelves high above, you'll see old cookie tins, vintage tin chocolate Easter Egg molds, gingerbread boy–motif cookie jars, and gingerbread molds all cozily clutched together alongside new wedding cake tops.

At the Gingerbread House, gingerbread cookies aren't just baked for the holidays. Here, you'll find them all year long: big ones with M&M's for eyes, medium-sized ones with raisins studded in, or the ones I can't resist: those plain, crisp, baby-size honey boys and girls.

9. Minneapolis

A city of sparkling lakes (22 within its city limits) and shimmering skyline, Minneapolis is a teasing mix of peaceful green space, notable museums, numerous restaurants, and bakeries heady with the scent of cinnamon and cardamom. Besides festivals celebrating music, art, and barbecued ribs, Minneapolis has unique neighborhoods enticing those seeking everything from Chinese herbs to Polish sausage and sauerkraut.

Summer Thursdays on Nicollet Mall, you'll find flavors of the country as many vendors from the regular (traffic-jammed) weekend Farmer's Market set up stalls along part of this 12-block pedestrian avenue downtown. Bankers and lawyers on their lunch hours purchase fresh asparagus and rhubarb in the spring or homegrown tomatoes and bunches of feathery dill and basil midsummer. Come autumn, folks select perfect apple-dumpling squash and beautiful red and green peppers. And all season long, it's fun to see workers toting home bouquets of Queen Anne's lace and colorful zinnias.

Restaurants abound in Minneapolis, and three of downtown's top tables that consistently win rave reviews (and deservedly so) are the sleek Scandinavian-inspired Restaurant Aquavit on Seventh Street and the Nicollet Mall, Goodfellow's (located in the art deco showplace that was once the Forum Cafeteria), and top-of-the-line D'Amico Cucina in the warehouse district.

You can also pick up good vegetarian fare at Café Brenda, and I like to take out-of-town visitors at Christmastime for breakfast at the sunny Nicollet Island Inn (they decorate a huge old-fashioned tree in the entry way) overlooking the Mississippi River.

A short distance from downtown, one of my choice places for a light lunch (with a stunning view) is on the rooftop terrace at The Walker Art Center Gallery 8's cafeteria. You can get a slice of very good herb-scented quiche and a fresh salad—and always a lovely dessert: a fresh little tart perhaps or a piece of peach cobbler. Before you leave, stop in the museum store to browse, but don't leave without buying yourself a souvenir box of the Frango chocolate-cherry candy (they're made in Minneapolis). On the candy box cover is a great souvenir photo of the landmark Spoonbridge and Cherry sculpture.

From Gallery 8's rooftop deck, you can almost see the trendy Loring Bar and Café, near Loring Park and the Cathedral. This is another place that has long been considered to serve some of the best food (by some of the rudest waiters) in the city. Its artsy décor includes antique and flea market sofas, easy chairs, and lamps. On a star-filled summer night, request a table out back in the tiny alley: The "intime" bricked courtyard is a seductive little lair.

The Minneapolis skyline

Here in the heartland we also have great places to plunge a fork into some juicy meat: Manny's Steakhouse, where portions are as big as some of the egos that eat here, or Murray's famous "silver butter knife" steaks —a romantic throwback to the days when dining out usually meant you were celebrating something.

Pickled Parrot offers spicy Caribbean jerk–version ribs, and my sons think it's heaven to order a platter full of Famous Dave's tender pork or beef ribs, slathered with Dave's "secret" sauce. Oyster lovers will find it difficult to resist Oceanaire's oyster bar. As many as a dozen kinds of oysters glisten in the chipped ice. And the mollusks, shucked to order, arrive with two ramekins brimming in a sauce of shallots and red-wine vinegar. At Jax, a northeast landmark, you can select a fresh trout for your dinner from their legendary trout "stream," in back by their summery patio.

If you want to grill your own fresh swordfish or tuna at home, head over to Coastal Seafoods. For years, this little nondescript fish market has been supplying chefs and seafood lovers the freshest fish you'll find in the city. I usually make a stop here and then cross the street to United Noodles, a spacious and large Asian grocery store—another favorite with local chefs and aspiring cooks as well. Here you can find kaffir lime leaves; dozens of soy, chili, and fish sauces; bags of rice; paper lanterns; chopsticks; and woks. If they're handing out samples here, expect the unexpected: fish balls in curry sauce, for example.

Asian cuisine dominates on the stretch of Nicollet Avenue immediately south of the Nicollet Mall from Grant Street to 29th known as "Eat Street" (see more about it later in this chapter). And another popular locale for people watching (the pierced, the posh, the tattooed) is in the Uptown area of Minneapolis. Favorite food stops here: At Giorgio's on Lake, Giorgio himself is often in the kitchen or greeting guests to his sunny corner trattoria and adjacent wine bar. Seasonal menu changes include a roasted spring-vegetable lasagna or an autumn beet-and-apple salad that I adore. Lucia's Restaurant and Wine Bar is a vibrant hangout with exquisite fare dictated by the seasons. Chilled cucumber-buttermilk soup, perhaps, or pan-seared lamb tenderloin—Lucia's remarkable flair for making great ingredients shine has attracted a loyal following since she opened her restaurant in 1985.

Visitors should not miss Isles Bun & Coffee Company. This is where early birds find the freshest-from-the-oven, monster-sized, cinnamon-sugar bread bliss. A slather of frosting melts on, and you're welcome to scoop on even more from the container that sits on the counter. (Only a fool doesn't.)

French Meadow Bakery and Café is another high-energy urban eatery, located on busy Lyndale avenue. Its exceptional sourdough breads—more than twenty varieties—include a fantastic crisp seed baguette. I also make a point to call and find out when they're baking Anaheim pepper bread. They only bake this about once a month for customer sale, although they serve sandwiches on it daily.

At The Turtle Bread Company, the chocolate bread is another beloved of locals, and if I'm there on a Saturday morning, I always pick up the aromatic cardamom coffee braid: An almond-encrusted loaf, infused with the scent of cardamom, it's only sold on weekends.

An Urban Picnic

Perfect Picnic: Pick up sandwiches and a couple bottles of Italian soda at the Linden Hills' D'Amico & Sons deli. Then find a spot on the hill overlooking the Lake Harriet Bandshell and enjoy your alfresco meal with a free concert under the stars. Dessert: Ice cream cones from the concession stand are a tradition. If you get here earlier, stroll the rose gardens (the largest in the Midwest) and take a ride on the old-fashioned Como-Harriet Streetcar.

Still on the sweet note, not far from here is the Linden Hills neighborhood, where Sebastian Joe's homemade ice cream is another longstanding city favorite. Some folks can satisfy their craving with a single dip of the raspberry chocolate chip ice cream, but many people just get in line on weekends (and even hot summer week nights) to purchase a hand-packed pint or more of dozens of homemade cool confections.

NORTHEAST MINNEAPOLIS

On the other side of downtown, northeast Minneapolis has become a trendy food destination as well. Wine bars (Bobino Café & Wine Bar is in an old funeral parlor), espresso shops, and artists have moved in next to age-old establishments such as the Polish Palace, Kramarczuk's Sausage Company, and Mayslack's Polka Lounge—home of Stan's legendary garlic–roast beef sandwiches and live polka music every Sunday night. From the outside, Mayslack's looks rather down on its luck, but don't let that deter you. Inside, it's filled with wood booths and a large, old-time bar, complete with a braid of garlic next to the bottles. The longtime waitresses are friendly ("I wouldn't work anywhere else," one once told me), and the garlic-infused beef sandwiches are still worth ordering.

Then there's Surdyk's. More than a liquor store, this place is a true northeast institution—and its cheese and gourmet shop within the building is a city favorite. Here you'll find topnotch cheeses from around the world, pâtés, salsas, chutneys, oils, and chocolates: Try locally made B.T. McElrath superb and unusual creations: passion fruit mousse or lavender–black peppercorn truffles.

Up the block from Surdyk's is a great little Greek place: Gardens of Salonica. Infused with the fragrant Greek-inspired cooking of Anna Christoforides, the café is also a destination for university students—hearty portions, and the price is right, too.

The Modern Café
337 13th Avenue N.E. • Phone: (612) 378-9882

The Modern Café, located in a building that dates back to 1941, has a vintage counter, pink art-deco murals, and homespun cuisine—with a gourmet spin. Chef and owner Jim Grell works culinary miracles on his pan-roasted chicken, and I love his pizza with red onions and goat cheeses. The décor may be retro 1950s (very cool), but the food, even the homemade mashed potatoes, is definitely twenty-first century.

FROM THE MODERN CAFÉ:
GARLIC–BLUE CHEESE MASHED
POTATOES

1 1/2 pounds red potatoes, peeled and cubed
1/4 large head of garlic, peeled and finely minced

3 tablespoons whipping cream
3 tablespoons unsalted butter
3–4 tablespoons crumbled blue cheese
Salt and pepper to taste
Chopped parsley, for garnish

In a large saucepan, simmer potatoes, covered, in about 2 inches of water until tender, about 15 to 20 minutes. Drain.

Mash potatoes by hand or with an electric mixer, gradually adding garlic, whipping cream, butter, and blue cheese. Season to taste with salt and pepper. Spoon into a serving bowl and sprinkle with parsley. Makes 6 to 8 servings.

Delmonico's Italian Foods

1112 Summer Street • Phone: (612) 331-5466

A visit to Delmonico's is a step into a fragrant Italian past. The friendly and warm aroma of garlic and spices envelops you outside the market door, and once inside you notice old-fashioned cones of packaging string dangling from the ceiling.

Things don't seem to have changed much over the years here, although sadly, Louis, one of the longtime owners, died in 1999. His brother George, however, is still working the counter with nephew, Terry, and son, Bob. And he's still calling all little boys who wander in here "Tony" and all the moms "Hon." Samples of their pepper cheese and salami are still freely handed out on white waxed paper, too, and the guys here can always make you smile and feel like you're one of the family.

But the best part about this incredibly small shop is that it is literally crammed from top to bottom with every Italian item you could ever imagine wanting or needing—from the always-fresh ricotta cheese to Italian mint syrup, Italian cigars, Italian coffee pots, Italian baby bibs, and even Italian stomach relaxer (Brioschi).

Opened in 1929 by the Delmonicos' father and uncle, the shop cooks up an award-winning spaghetti sauce and preserves pickled banana peppers and crushed chili peppers in olive oil (these are incredibly wonderful; I am never without a jar). They also sell more than two dozen kinds of cheese (domestic and imported) and stock their meat case with Italian specialties: prosciutto, porketta roasts and steaks, homemade hot and sweet sausage, hard-to-find pancetta (a rolled Italian bacon), and several kinds of salami.

You can also get a sandwich here, made to order with whatever meats or cheeses you choose. Just make sure they put a swipe of that crushed chili pepper sauce on the bread; it definitely sends the sandwich to new heights.

Kramarczuk's Sausage Company, one of northeast Minneapolis's culinary links to the past

Matt's Bar

3500 Cedar Avenue • Phone: (612) 722-7072

It's not unusual to see someone in the Twin Cities proudly wearing a T-shirt proclaiming "Matt's Bar." For years, this unpretentious neighborhood joint has been taking top honors for making the best burger in town.

Not just any burger, of course. This one has a name: the "Jucy Lucy." At its most basic, a Jucy Lucy consists of two beef patties pressed together around a center of American cheese. But when it's grilled, watch out. The cheese turns molten, the patties succulent. Hot off the grill, a Lucy is wrapped in waxed paper and served sans plate. A waitress usually cautions you to wait a few minutes before biting in. Some people heed her advice. (They don't get a burned tongue.) But most folks can't wait and don't care—a small price to pay for the best burger in town.

Kramarczuk's Sausage Company

215 East Hennepin Avenue • Phone: (612) 379-3018

In northeast Minneapolis, the basic feature is age: This is the oldest part of Minneapolis. First settled by Ukrainian immigrants arriving in 1876, a more significant wave came ashore about 1948—after the Iron Curtain came down in Europe.

One of these later arrivals was Orest Kramarczuk's father, who started Kramarczuk's Sausage Company on East Hennepin Avenue in 1954. Today, the younger Kramarczuk runs the shop, and the deli case remains an education in the cold cuts of Eastern Europe. More than sixty authentic old-world varieties of sausage are still prepared using the original recipes. Half the shop is devoted to racks of baked goods such as Polish rye bread, traditional babka at Easter time, and heavenly kolachi: pastries filled with cheese, cherry, apricot, poppy seed, or apple.

Adjacent to the sausage shop is an old-fashioned high-ceiling deli (it's part of Kramarczuk's), reminiscent of East Coast eateries. Here CEOs and blue-collar workers stand elbow-to-elbow

"Nana" Marino and one of the house specialties at the restaurant bearing her family name

ordering huge sausage sandwiches dripping with flavor, sides of sauerkraut, and cold bottles of Polish beer.

Marino's
2205 Central Avenue N.E. • Phone: (612) 781-0920

By 6:00 A.M. most mornings, Mary Marino, well into her nineties and affectionately known to family and customers as "Nana," is already in Marino's kitchen overseeing the preparation of sauce for the mostaccioli or mixing up dressing or flipping from-scratch pancakes The spicy scent of Italian sausage wafts over factory workers, businessmen, and an elderly couple who look as if they've shared their breakfasts here for decades. "Where's Tony these days?" someone asks a waitress when she comes to take an order.

This is the quintessential northeast neighborhood café—run by a close-knit family, following recipes handed down from grandparents, and serving exceptional food at good prices.

Breakfast regulars order a stack of pancakes with the homemade Italian sausage—"split and grilled"—or eggs scrambled with sausage, onions, and peppers. (Forget ketchup with the eggs; those who know ask for a side of homemade spaghetti sauce.)

Weekly lunch specials are printed on the complimentary matchbooks by the cash register. On Fridays, the place is packed for Nana's lasagne and homemade rice pudding with cinnamon and raisins. Often served steaming hot, minutes out of the oven (customers have their orders in while it's baking), Nana calls it "crybaby pudding"—because, she says, "men here cry if they don't get any."

BEST ETHNIC MEAL DEAL

Northeast Minneapolis is a place where church bells chime on the hour and ethnic culinary traditions are intertwined with home and community. Even the local parishioners are in the food business. For years, at St. Constantine Ukrainian Catholic church, every Friday morning a group of loyal church members gets together and makes up pyrohy—sometimes spelled *pirogy, piroghi,* or *pierogi.* Whatever the spelling, the term refers to those delectable pasta pockets filled with potatoes, sauerkraut, or prunes that are indigenous to Eastern Europe. The pyrohy (approximately two thousand are prepared and sold here weekly) are packaged up for those who have called in; you do need to call ahead (612/378-9833) to order earlier in the week. If you're visiting the city, you really must stop in St. Constantine's (515 University Avenue N.E.) for the Friday noon meal of fresh pyrohy (no reservations necessary!). When you walk in the fellowship hall—take a sharp right and go up the stairs—the first thing you'll see is a long table of women, many in old-fashioned aprons, some with little flowered scarves on, making up the pyrohy. A meal doesn't get any more homemade than this! Lunch cost depends on the number of pyrohy you order ($5.50 for a dozen if you're the truck-driving type or $3.75 for half a dozen; coffee is free). The pasta pockets are best served with onions and butter, but sour cream is also offered. This is no church hall dining-line buffet, either. You sit down at the communal tables, someone comes to take your order, and then, soon after, someone brings you out a plate full of those little buttery darlings. "It's just like a restaurant," one of the women once told me. The difference is this meal is a *real* blessed event. Give thanks.

Ready Meats, Inc.
3550 Northeast Johnson Street • Phone: (612) 789-2484

I've been shopping at Ready Meats since I moved into northeast Minneapolis over twenty years ago. I've lined up before the holidays to get my ham, porketta, and fresh turkey, and I've crowded in here on summer Friday afternoons to purchase Polish sausage and ribeye steaks for weekend barbecues.

The place seems always packed, but the wait is never long. At least a half-dozen friendly guys are behind the counter, wrapping up meats, slicing sausage, or weighing a piece of steak. Two of the guys (and owners) I always like seeing are the Norwegian brothers, Dale and Dave Carlson. They've helped me out numerous times, estimating how much meat I needed for entertaining 20 or sharing their favorite barbecue grilling secrets. If necessary, they've even carried out my purchases to the car.

Ready Meat has all sorts of ethnic specialties, too, although sausages are their most diverse offering. Besides Swedish varieties, you can find Polish, Mexican, Cajun, and Italian. Their braciola, a rolled and seasoned Italian flank steak with meat stuffing, is renowned here. Others swear by Ready's fennel seed–encrusted porketta.

The market also offers plenty of other products, including my sons' favorite: the homemade meat or cheese ravioli (in the frozen case). A couple bags of those, along with a big jar of the market's well-spiced spaghetti sauce, make an easy dinnertime meal.

Every Friday, St. Constantine Ukrainian Catholic Church serves up a feast of pyrohy—pasta pockets stuffed with a variety of fillings.

Bryant Lake Bowl
810 West Lake Street
Phone: (612) 825-3737

There are not too many places where you can breakfast on free-range eggs with spinach and feta while listening to the oceanlike sounds of crashing bowling pins. The small vintage bowling alley is in back (next to the cabaret), but the front room facing Lake Street has become a café with excellent food that attracts locals, musicians, and famous folks who make it to the northland (Winona Ryder was once spotted here with Soul Asylum's Dave Pierner).

The neighborhood spot was saved by entrepreneur Kim Bartmann, who bought it from longtime owner Bill Drouches. In fact, says Bartmann proudly, many of the Grain Belt Beer bowling tournament trophies displayed on the big old 1937 mahogany bar belong to him.

"People thought I was insane when I bought a bowling alley," she laughs, remembering, but today she's turned the place into a popular hangout that serves incredibly tasty food. Goat cheese quesadillas, Thai chicken wraps, and homemade guacamole are all produced in a tiny, tightly organized kitchen at the end of the bar. "It used to be the shoe counter," explains Bartmann.

Ingebretsen's Scandinavian Center
1601 East Lake Street • Phone: (612) 729-9331

Holiday time is the busiest at Ingebretsen's, a lace-curtained, lutefisk-scented market/gift store. Customers line up outside the door at Christmastime, and the staff there "make and sell a ton of Swedish sausage a day," says Steve Dahl, whose dad, Warren owns the place. Other daily sales during the holidays include 1,500 pounds of Swedish meatballs, 1,000 pounds of lutefisk, and 1,000 three-sheet packages of lefse, made from fresh potatoes, Dahl says, not instant, like many other brands.

Other homemade specialties prepared in this store, where not much has changed since it opened in 1921, include blood sausage, Jul skinke (a sweet pickled ham, only available at Christmas), home-smoked bologna, and three kinds of sylte (Swedish headcheese). Happily, Ingebretsen's offers a free handy tip sheet for preparing many of these Scandinavian delicacies.

You can also find Swedish breads, lingonberries (fresh or frozen), cloud berries (a type of golden raspberry), glogg spices, Swedish cookie presses, and Norwegian baking irons here. And what good Scandinavian store wouldn't have a book or two of Ole and Lena jokes and an apron for sale stating "Lefse is Beautiful"?

LINGONBERRY COOKIES

These rich cookies spread with a light layer of lingonberry jam (available at Ingebretsen's) are elegant and irresistible. You can also substitute raspberry jam.

> 1 cup butter
> 1/2 cup sugar
> 1 teaspoon vanilla
> 2 1/4 cups flour

Lingonberry jam
Glaze
2 cups confectioner's sugar
Few drops vanilla
2 to 3 tablespoons water

Preheat oven to 325 degrees. Cream together butter and sugar. Add vanilla and flour, mixing well. Divide dough into four pieces and roll each the length of a greased cookie sheet, about 1 inch in width. Flatten slightly. Bake for 12 to 15 minutes.

Immediately brush with lingonberry jam and spread with glaze made by mixing powdered sugar and vanilla with water until of spreading consistency. Cut diagonally while still warm.

Excerpted with permission from *Var Så God, Heritage and Favorite Recipes and Handbook of Swedish Tradition,* compiled by members of the American Swedish Institute.

Lucia's Restaurant and Wine Bar
1432 West 31st Street • Phone: (612) 825-1572

Lucia's in Uptown is legendary. The cuisine is near perfect—using local farm bounty and changing weekly. The clientele is hip, and the place is happening. Highly recommended.

FROM LUCIA'S RESTAURANT AND WINE BAR: CHILLED CUCUMBER-BUTTERMILK SOUP

This is a smooth, summery soup and a favorite with regulars who come to Lucia's to sit outside under the umbrellas and cool off from the hot sun. The buttermilk brings out the cucumber and herb taste, and chilling the soup intensifies the flavors even more. Watson advises serving the soup with a loaf of good crusty bread and a light Pinot Grigio or French Chardonnay.

CHILLED CUCUMBER-BUTTERMILK SOUP

1 medium onion, chopped
1 large russet potato, peeled and chopped
1 clove garlic, peeled and chopped
3 tablespoons butter
3 cups chicken stock
3 large cucumbers, peeled and chopped

2 large green onions and tops, sliced
1/2 cup packed parsley sprigs
1/4 cup packed dill sprigs
1 cup buttermilk
Fresh lemon juice, to taste
Salt and white pepper, to taste
1/2 cup sour cream
Dill sprigs

In a large saucepan, cook onion, potato, and garlic in butter over medium-low heat for 15 minutes. Add chicken stock and heat to boiling. Reduce heat and simmer, covered, until potato is tender, about 10 minutes. Stir in cucumber, green onions, herbs, and buttermilk.

In a food processor or blender, process soup mixture until smooth; season to taste with lemon juice, salt, and white pepper. Refrigerate until chilled, 3 to 4 hours.

Serve soup in individual serving bowls. Garnish with a tablespoon of sour cream and dill sprigs. Makes 8 servings (about 1 cup each).

Al's Breakfast
413 14th Avenue S.E. • Phone: (612) 331-9991

Tantalizing breakfast aromas always fill this crowded, closet-sized diner, dimly lit by egg, bacon, and jalapeño pepper lights. And there are always lots of people—from all walks of life—waiting to eat at the tiny cluttered café, once a burger stand known as the Hunky Dory. In fact, folks have been known to stand in pouring rain, dripping heat, high humidity, and snowstorms for the chance to sit at the ancient counter here and eat breakfast. But why, you ask?

Because everybody knows Al's serves the best breakfast in town. An institution since it opened in 1950, the 14-stool diner fills the belly and feeds the soul, according to folks who have frequented this Dinkytown hole-in-the-wall for years and years.

Breakfast here isn't a leisurely event, however—not with some big guy standing impatiently *right* behind you, waiting for your seat at the counter (former Minnesota Viking football player Carl Eller is a regular, by the way.)

Even (and amazingly) so, the place manages to be adored for its personality and sense of counter camaraderie. Need a car, an apartment, or a new boyfriend? Bring it up while you're digging into a stack of superb "wally blues" (blueberry pancakes with walnuts) and you may leave with what you were looking for. Or at least a phone number.

Besides the remarkable pancakes, Al's is highly praised for its free-form poached eggs and its well-spiced corned beef hash. You really can't go wrong with any menu choice at Al's. It's got a flavor all its very own.

Rainbow Food Ribfest
Held annually in July

Smoke-roasted ribs and secret sauces abound at this annual event in downtown Minneapolis—and spicy aromas fill city blocks for the five days the celebration lasts. A true pig-out, at this annual event you can plan on sampling ribs in every variety: pork back, spare, boneless, St. Louis style, and country style. Likewise, expect plenty of finger-licking sauces to choose from—whether you like your ribs wet (smothered in the stuff) or dry. Peppery, spicy sweet, thick, smoky, hickory-style, tangy—the list goes on.

Almost a dozen barbecue joints set up shop at the smoky extravaganza: places with names such as C.L.'s Hawg Heaven (Pennsylvania), Pigfoot BBQ (Ohio), Razorback Cookers (Arkansas), and, of course, Minnesota's own, Famous Dave's—not to mention that bastion of barbecue, Roscoe's Rootbeer & Ribs of Rochester.

Shuang Cheng
1320 4th Street S.E. • Phone: (612) 378-0208

Another Dinkytown hot spot with a loyal following, Shuang Cheng has been popular with high-profile chefs eating out, Twin Cities restaurant critics, and of course, university students who know a good cheap meal when they see one.

The décor has been described as bargain basement, but who cares with seafood this fresh, prepared this perfectly—and at bargain-basement prices? An astonishing assortment of menu items includes melt-in-your-mouth salmon in a black bean sauce or sole—delicately stir-fried with asparagus and bok choy. Although the seafood is my choice, Shuang Cheng's huge menu also offers crispy duck, tasty chicken egg foo yong, and a sweetly rich beef with dried orange peel.

Any of the Szechuan specialties work for me, too, and their Dungeness crab is almost, dare I say? exuberant, in that spicy sauce accompanying it.

Still, if the dictionary-sized menu's choices overwhelm you, simply select an entrée from owner Daniel Lam's daily board of handwritten specials (printed in English and Chinese). No matter what you end up ordering here, you'll be glad you did.

Peter's Grill
114 South 8th Street • Phone: (612) 333-1981

Peter's Grill is a nice slice of small-town atmosphere and fare in the big city. And on a dreary, snow-imminent type of day, when I don't want to cook dinner or stop at the nearest deli—when I'm craving "mom food" (the kind this mom doesn't have to cook)—I head to Peter's Grill.

On Wednesday nights, you can't cook a meal for the family this cheap. It's just $3.75 (plus 37 cents tax, they'll tell you) for their legendary Wednesday chicken dinner special (it's been on the menu for over twenty-five years!). One-quarter baked spring chicken with dressing, cabbage salad, mashed potatoes, cranberry sauce, and homemade roll. At this price, there's no excuse for not ordering a piece of their very good and rightly famous apple pie. Even when President Clinton was here in 1995 (his place is marked at the counter), he finished off his lunch—a Canadian bacon and egg sandwich and bowl of vegetable soup—with a slice of pie.

The place is considered the city's oldest café; its history dates back to 1914, with founder Peter Atcas. Today, current operators are nephews Andy and Peter Atsidakos.

Austrian Oblaten Company
1101 Stinson Boulevard N.E. • Phone: (612) 331-3523 or 800-333-3523
Web site: www.oblaten.com

THE LITTLE-KNOWN OBLATEN

I'm always amazed that more people don't realize that Austrian oblaten, exquisite featherweight cookies made from a 600-year-old recipe and a West German baking machine, are produced and packaged in Minneapolis by the Kennedy family (the only producer of oblaten in the United States). In fact, their warehouse is not far from my home in the northeast part of the city. (And yes, I've been known to buy huge bags of "seconds" here.) But very little has been written locally about these historic, wafer-thin (try 1/16 inch) wedges.

I don't know why. I do know that these airy cookies with their fleeting almond taste are perfect accompaniments to a dish of homemade ice cream or a bowl of fresh fruit or even as a sweet served with sparkling champagne.

What exactly are oblaten? Basically, they are two wafer layers pressed together with ground almonds, powdered sugar, butter, and vanilla. Each 7-inch-diameter round is then stamped with a design and the words "Original Carlsbad Oblaten" on its face. The rounds are then cut into wedges.

The oblaten have been baked in the Twin Cities area since 1950, two years after company founders Frank and Josephine Ullman escaped to this country from Carlsbad (originally in Austria but now in Czechoslovakia). Carlsbad is considered the home of the oblaten. This also explains why the wafer design includes a geyser. It's representative of the famous geyser discovered in Carlsbad in 1349.

The Ullmans brought with them the oblaten recipe and the special baking irons and kept their business small—using seven hand-operated baking irons until the early 1970s.

In 1973, Frank sold the business to his neighbor, Marie Kennedy, who bought the company with her mother, Dorothy Sisco. Later, they fulfilled Frank Ullman's dream of buying an automated oblaten-baking machine.

Today, Marie's daughter, Kerry, is in the shop as well, and besides selling to local stores, they ship worldwide; their oblaten are also available for sale online. Although the original oblaten is still the best seller, they also make a lemon oblaten, cinnamon oblaten, chocolate oblaten, and dark chocolate-dipped oblaten.

"EAT STREET"

"Go global" could be the buzzwords on Nicollet Avenue from Grant Street to 29th in Minneapolis. Instead it's "Eat Street," and the boldly lettered signs lining the streets say it all: "Authentic special Vietnamese, best Thai, delicious *comidas dominicanas,* fine Greek, easy Mexican, German to go, Chinese herbs and gifts, tempanyaki, finest Middle Eastern, house of the best noodle soup, Oriental market and furniture, saloon burgers . . ."

Only minutes away from downtown Minneapolis's glass-and-steel towers and the glimmering skyways connecting them, this section of one of the oldest avenues in the city has become a vibrant culinary world of its own—with over a dozen different ethnic eateries represented along the blocks.

For those in search of the perfect noodle, the avenue offers a treasure trove. On these tables you're likely to find many a bubbling hot pot, as the flavors of Asia dominate the street scene. Plates—or more often bowls—arrive authentic and steaming, exotic bottles of condiments as well as ceramic spoons and chopsticks fit in plastic boxes on each table, and menus (where offered) rarely have anything that costs over five bucks.

One of the best is Quang Oriental Pastry & Deli. Beginning in a handkerchief-size café (tucked back into a strip mall off the avenue), Quang's eventually moved into bigger, nicer digs along the avenue, increasing its service and table space but keeping its incredibly fine menu of authentic Vietnamese offerings. Folks in a noon-hour hurry here can still pick up one of their famous

An Asian grocery on "Eat Street" features a section filled with herbs that are individually blended into teas.

white paper–wrapped and rolled banh mi thit (the Asian version of a sub sandwich). But those who have time dine in—slurping up steaming hot bowls of noodles, splashing on shots of chili sauce, piling on fresh bean sprouts, and cooling it all down with squirts of fresh lime juice. Caramelized chicken or grilled beef salad, a fragrant feast in a bowl—vermicelli noodles, sweet and tender marinated slices of grilled beef, aromatic greens, a tangy vinegar and soy dressing—are among my top picks. Quang's spring rolls are another must; they've been praised highly not only in every metro paper but even in the *New York Times.*

Phuong Café, hidden in the spacious basement of an Asian grocery, is another little noodle jewel. Paneled walls, folding chairs, and kids watching cartoons and giggling make it somewhat like dining in a family rec room. With a booklet menu of choices, first-time visitors are torn between euphoria and panic. Any of the dozens of soups are worth ordering, especially if they have some wontons floating around in the broth.

For more upscale surroundings, try Pho 79, a small but spotless noodle shop renowned for its enormous bowls of soup. The signature beef noodle soup is filled with veggies and rare, paper-thin beef—flavored with sausage and fragrant with herbs. There's even soup for dessert: Che nhan nhuc is a sweet soup with dried longan fruit, said to lower the body temperature.

Next door to Pho 79 is the Chinese-inspired Seafood Palace—where tables are covered with pink cloth tablecloths and set far apart for private conversations. The ambience here suggests a more serene blend of quiet and class. While the prices definitely reflect this more refined dining experience, nobody cares. The food here is exceptional. Best bets are the daily specials: Dungeness crab in a spicy garlic sauce (be prepared when a Thanksgiving-size platter of the glazed beauties are presented) and huge New Zealand mussels accompanied by a brimming hot pot stuffed with all sorts of seafood.

A longtime Nicollet Avenue favorite is the Rainbow Chinese Restaurant. Toddlers in booster seats wave ceramic spoons and watch the rainbow-hued fish in the tank while their parents, chopsticks in hand, dig in to the fantastic food. Start out with the Szechuan wontons: a plate full of delicate steamed dumplings filled with pork and shrimp and slipping in a spicy black bean sauce. Satay summer beef is excellent; adventuresome types should try the fishball seaweed soup.

The five Wong sisters and their mother have been cooking and running Rainbow for years, but now sister Daisy operates the newer Shuang Hur market down the block, a great resource for gourmet home chefs seeking authentic ingredients such as fresh quail eggs, dried squid shreds, or canned chrysanthemum tea.

Actually, Asian markets abound on the avenue. In the back of Hiep Than grocery you'll find red-glazed whole barbecued ducks—bills and all—hanging in the deli case and freezer containers filled with edible exotic sea creatures. At the well-organized Hai Nguyen Market, look for packages of dried sweet gooseberries on skewers, boxes of dehydrated fungus, live seafood as well as beautiful paper patio lanterns, rice cookers, woks, and cool stacked metal lunch carriers.

Step into Troung Thanh and the first thing you see are shelves lined with jars and jars of Chinese herbs filling the top half of one wall—with rows of curious labeled drawers below. Here's where you'll find everything from the sheddings of cicada (good for itchy skin) to scrapings of sheep horn, eacommia bark (stuff that looks like snakeskin), and dried honeysuckle flowers. According to your ailment, herbs are selected, weighed on a scale, then packaged up in large paper squares to be taken home, boiled, and consumed as tea.

Sandwiched between these two Asian shops is the Middle Eastern Sindbad's Café and Market, where the scent of freshly baking pita bread mingles with spices and Arabic coffee. Weekends find lunch lines waiting to buy the 99-cent sambosa, hot snacks synonymous with Middle Eastern street food. Standing beside tattooed teenagers, older women dressed head-to-toe in black look over the barrels of nuts and seeds in front of the deli. Lamb roasting is Sindbad's specialty, but others seek out Sindbad's jumbo medjool dates: the sweetest in the city according to several local chefs known to shop here. "You know if you present someone with one of these," owner Sami Rasouli has told me more than once, "it means you want a date with them."

A few blocks away, step into Myconos, and you're transported to a cozy Greek family taverna with blue-checked tablecloths, handsome waiters uncorking wine, and dark-haired waitresses expertly flaming the traditional kasseri cheese with Metaxa brandy at your table. For dinner, try the horiatiko: lamb sautéed with feta and spinach and wrapped in pastry.

Lunch on the best (and biggest) south-of-the-border burritos at Los Gallos, where "Easy Mexican Food" is the motto and imported bottles of pop in pastel tints line the counter. Like many shops along the avenue, English is at best a second language here, and the décor is—shall we say—basic. Two other hidden-away finds for folks searching out authentic and cheap tacos and enchiladas on Nicollet are El Mariachi and Taco Morelos.

Discover a Mexican fiesta of sweet flavor and colors at the corner of Nicollet and 27th. Marissa's Bakery is a self-service bakery (pick up a tray and tongs) where you can select from huge squares of cakes or buns sugared in bright turquoise and hot pink. I can't resist those trays full of the long twisted sugar-sprinkled churros either—they're perfect served with a cup of Mexican hot chocolate.

Next to its deli, the Strudel & Nudel, on 26th (pick up a loaf of pumpernickel rye) is the Black Forest Inn, the German restaurant that opened here in 1965. Black Forest's summer courtyard is renowned in the city, but the aged, warm, and familiar atmosphere inside (elaborate painted murals, sparkling stained glass) provides a perfect wintertime retreat. Some people make a meal of the Matjes herring & rye bread appetizer, but others order owner Erich

The mix of cultures on "Eat Street" can produce some interesting culinary creations.

Christ's homemade bratwurst. ("His mother made him learn two things in Germany before coming to America," says co-owner and wife, Joanne, "the meat trade and how to dance.") Along with a side of sweet-sour red cabbage, spaetzle—homemade German noodles—and a foaming mug of cold German beer, all that's left to this meal is to make the traditional toast: "Prosit!"

Twin Cities Food & Wine Experience
Held in early February

Midwinter in Minnesota. What could be more fitting than a weekend spent tasting wine from warm regions, listening to chefs give seminars on the perfect strawberry shortcake, and dreaming about a new kitchen? Since 1995, the Twin Cities Food & Wine Experience (produced by *Minnesota Monthly* magazine as a benefit for Minnesota Public Radio) has steadily grown in size and popularity. Besides seminars and demonstrations by top regional and national chefs, there are wine dinners, luncheons, and kitchen design classes. With over 250 exhibitors, the affair now takes place at the Minneapolis Convention Center. And even the Minnesota Opera gets into the culinary act: entertaining with excerpts of food and wine moments from famous operettas.

10. Saint Paul

When the morning sun slants over the clock tower and fairy-tale turrets of the 1902 Landmark Center and shines on nearby Rice Park in downtown St. Paul, it's easy to understand why the past is part of the charm in this capitol city. A sense of history and timelessness pervades the hilly winding streets—and places such as Mickey's Diner, one of only two diners in the country to be listed on the National Register of Historic Places, only enhance the feeling. Here you can dine at the newest Kincaid's, take afternoon tea in the elegant 1910 Saint Paul Hotel, or lunch on Harriet Island at the No Wake Café, the Mississippi's only floating restaurant and bed and breakfast inn.

Because historic settings create their own ambience and spirit, they often spin into romantic stage sets. Such is the case in the elegant 1889 brownstone housing W.A. Frost & Company—located on the corner of Selby and Western in St. Paul. Inside: fireplaces, candlelight, and oil paintings. Outside: an enchanting, old-fashioned bricked courtyard. Consistently voted by locals as the most romantic place to dine, W.A. Frost is also considered the heart of a five-block area in this Cathedral Hill neighborhood where a resurgence of restaurants is sparking citywide interest. Zander's, Z's, Tulips, and the Vintage Restaurant and Wine Bar (located in a stunning dark-brick 1888 building) are all worth a visit. One of my favorite restaurants in the neighborhood is Moscow on the Hill, where camaraderie shared between friends after a few warming shots of vodka and a hearty meal always makes for a fun evening. FYI: Nobody leaves without a final swig of Moscow's homemade (and delicious) cherry vodka.

During lunchtime in the area, some of the best subs can be found at Chicago Submarine. Here, jars of colorful homemade giardiniera line the counter and shelves. Besides a scoopful of the spicy hot stuff (cauliflower, carrots, celery, jalapeño peppers, etc.) on your Italian beef sandwich, you can also purchase a homemade pint or quart for your home kitchen; folks often make a special trip here just for that reason.

On St. Paul's Grand Avenue, you can take your pick from more than sixty-four food-related businesses tucked between one-of-a-kind shops. This 26-block-long street (from historic Summit Hill to the Mississippi River) has become one of the most popular in the city for food lovers.

In fact, some of the restaurants have even taken up residence in the renovated houses along the avenue. The Barbary Fig, for instance serves up chef Hadj-Moussa's North African cuisine upstairs in an early-twentieth-century house. In

The Landmark Center in downtown St. Paul

warm weather, locals love sitting at a table on his outdoor front terrace, savoring fragrant black olives and chewy French bread. The Lexington on Grand—a gathering spot for local politicians and St. Paul old money since 1935—offers up basic and good fare, but truthfully, it's the dark and elegant old bar I'm fond of—especially on a snowy night, sitting within the glow of antique mirrors and the patina of rich wood and sipping a "Lexstacy" (steamed milk with a splash of Frangelico).

Also on the avenue: Café Latté, beloved for its legendary turtle cake, a masterpiece in caramel and chocolate, or Cooks of Crocus Hill, where you can count on finding nice brand-name kitchenware, tart pans in any size—and even heirloom tomatoes and fresh Michigan cherries, come summer.

At holiday time, I always love to wander by Wuollet's Bakery and press my nose against the window with the kids—admiring the displays of elaborately decorated gingerbread castles. And I'm positively addicted to the dark chocolate–covered lemon creams at Maud Borup's candy shop.

Tavern on Grand has a typical "Up North" décor (mounted trophy fish, an antler chandelier, and paintings of birch trees and blue lakes). It has long been one of my choices for taking out-of-state visitors. I think it serves some of the best-tasting (and best-priced) walleye in the city—buttery and grilled with seasoning or deep-fried in the Tavern's secret batter.

As for homemade ice cream on a hot July night, look for the faded red screen door on Grand Avenue—or a line of people straggling down the block outside of it. The Grand Ole Creamery has the real homemade stuff. Buy a "single split"—two homemade flavors (i.e., Chocolate Brownie and Black Hills

Gold—a combination of caramel ice cream, pralines, and Hydrox cookies with chocolate) scooped and stuffed into a buttery waffle cone, with a large malted milk ball tucked into the bottom to keep drips to a minimum.

Of course throughout Ramsey County there are personal favorite food places of mine scattered hither and yon. In a turn-of-the-century brick building, Trotter's Café and Bakery has great old-fashioned display cases piled high with pans of brownies as well as breads made with local honey—and my particular passion, "chocolate chaos cupcakes."

Farther down Cleveland Avenue, Cecil's has been in business for over fifty years as a deli and thirty-plus years as a restaurant. Sample the hot pastrami with hot pepper cheese on pumpernickel bread. Don't skip a side of cole slaw (it could be the best in town).

The Dakota Bar and Grill, located in an old brick train building, has been serving consistently fine regional cuisine since 1985. A bowl of their rich Minnesota brie and apple soup is one of my autumn rites.

At Ristorante Luci, folks return again and again just for a plate of the handmade ravioli. Tiny Café 128, tucked in the basement of an apartment building, is another gem of place, and its creative and elegant cuisine is well worth searching out. (You *will* need to call for directions!)

Taste of Thailand, on Snelling, looks like a dive. But everyone in town knows you don't come here for the atmosphere. This is quite possibly the best Thai

At Christmas time, the enticing front window of Wuollet's Bakery

food you're likely to find in the Twin Cities. A huge menu includes over twenty assorted appetizers, plus iced Thai coffee and entrées such as traditional pad thai that can be ordered mild to hot. But know that hot means HOT here.

For American down-home flavor, folks have been cooling off at the St. Clair Broiler (with its vintage neon flames above flashing) on award-winning malts (try the hot fudge) since 1956. Not far away, Snuffy's Malt shop nearby serves their thick milk shakes and malts in a frosty aluminum-mixer container.

At the Mildred Pierce Café, a fairly recent addition to St. Paul's Randolph Avenue neighborhood dining scene, food evocative of the 1940s (when Joan Crawford starred in the movie *Mildred Pierce*) is simple but sophisticated.

Regina's candy shop is a must visit, especially before Christmas. It's one of the few candy kitchens left in the country that still makes candy canes and ribbon candy the old-fashioned way—by hand (and you can watch!).

The original Key's Restaurant on Raymond in St. Paul, started by Barbara Hunn in 1973, is a breakfast institution in these parts. Renowned for their huge fresh-from-the-oven caramel or cinnamon rolls, it's a wise soul who orders one as soon as seated here.

Finally, locals know that nothing nudges nostalgia like Porky's drive-in on University on a summer Saturday night. Shined up vintage Corvettes and freshly waxed, restored vehicles are all part of the scene. You might even catch a glimpse of that 1968 Ford Mustang you wished you'd never sold. Cruise on in under Porky's huge old sign and console yourself with a double supreme burger and onion rings.

Regina's Candies

2073 St. Clair Avenue • Phone: (651) 698-8603

A candy shop right out of a fairy tale (even its name sounds like a princess from a storybook), Regina's sells more than four hundred varieties of candy, much of it made on the premises. Buttercreams and jelly beans, peanut brittle and pastel wafers tease from behind marble-edged display cases and spill out of bins, boxes, and jars.

But while its chocolates entice and jellies inspire, it's Regina's sparkling rainbow-colored candy and handmade candy canes that make this shop truly one of a kind.

Here, the stripes are twisted in the cane, not painted on. And if you've never tasted a real candy cane, you're in for a treat. But be prepared: Once you've tasted one of these, you can never go back to the mass-produced variety.

Right after Thanksgiving, the candy cane production kicks in (Regina's also makes their own ribbon candy), and if you time it right, you can even watch the whole sweet (and labor-intensive) business of making these stocking stuffers:

Step one: Owner Mark Elliott throws a heavy mass of molten candy on an antique silver hook mounted on the wall, tossing it up and over the hook repeatedly until it changes from a translucent amber to a satiny white. Then, pieces of red, taffylike candy are pressed onto the sides of this white watermelon. Finally, Mark begins pulling and twisting out the actual candy canes, which he measures and cuts ("we don't weigh them," he says, "so some people may be getting a better deal than others"). His sister, Sue Martinez, finishes each of the still-warm peppermint sticks by gently shaping them around her finger, creating the canes' characteristic crook.

Originally called the Central Candy Company, Regina's was founded in 1926 by Mark's grandfather, Greek immigrant Frank Elliott, who eventually renamed the shop for his wife, Regina. Nowadays, besides the peppermint candy canes, Regina's candies are still cooked according to Frank's recipes in the same copper kettles he used and poured on the original marble-topped tables.

Festival of Nations

From a Serbian sausage sandwich to Korean kimchi to a bowl of borscht and a piece of baklava, some 45 food cafés at the annual Festival of Nations reflect the diversity of nationalities (over a hundred ethnic groups) found in Minnesota. Presented by the International Institute of Minnesota since 1932, the celebration, which is held in RiverCentre during the last weekend in April, includes exhibits and entertainment. It's one of the nation's largest and longest running multi-ethnic events. Plan to sample a mango shake, sip some Egyptian hibiscus tea, snack on Cambodian egg rolls, or lunch on Indian chicken curry. And oh yeah—forget hot dish.

Cossetta's Italian Market
211 West Seventh • Phone: (651) 222-3476

A St. Paul neighborhood institution (Cossetta's opened in 1911), this Italian grocery/deli/pizzeria/cafeteria-style restaurant today is a big, sprawling, and happy sort of place. A wide and old-fashioned staircase leads up to a second floor where dozens of black-and-white family photos line the walls— and tables are filled with extended families and groups of friends. Everybody is unashamedly (and happily!) digging into pizza or chowing down on thick meatball sandwiches or twirling spaghetti in huge clumps on a fork. People indeed are always everywhere at Cossetta's. There's a line for pizza. (I think the hand-tossed puffy crust and homemade sauce have been celebrated by every eating publication in the Twin Cities.) There's another line for entrées such as manicotti or sausage and peppers. Just shopping for dinner ingredients? Crowd your way through another doorway (next to the personally auto-

Twentysomethings, teenagers, and pizza—a classic encounter at Cossetta's Italian Market

graphed photo of Frank Sinatra) and you're in Cossetta's small but well-stocked Italian grocery store. Smoked hams, salamis, and cheeses hang from the ceiling. Fresh homemade peasant bread is stacked in baskets in another corner, and big wheels of parmigiano-reggiano fill the cheese case. Throughout the entire building, the spicy smells feed the soul.

The whole scene always makes me think of a big, bustling Italian family home. I always come here with an appetite. And I always leave feeling like part of a happy well-fed family.

Taste of Scandinavia
2232 Carter Avenue • Phone: (651) 645-9181

If you have time for just one or two bakery visits while you're in the Twin Cities, make sure that Soile Anderson's Taste of Scandinavia shop is on your list.

Located in the heart of St. Anthony Park, just off the bricked and tree-shaded Milton Courtyard (her other shop in a North Oaks strip mall is take-out only), you step down a half-dozen stairs—and enter into an enchanting little piece of Europe.

"When space became available here, I didn't think twice about it," says Anderson of her decision to open her second Twin Cities bakery. The character of the 1909 Bavarian-style complex—and the surrounding sidewalks where pots of blossoms sit next to old-fashioned park benches—reminded her of Finland, where she was born and raised. "I love the neighborhood," she says, "it feels like home."

The bakery sparkles with white lights in the rafters and pierced tin lanterns hanging by the stone fireplace. I love to visit before Easter when Soile decorates her shop as artfully as she arranges the fruit on a tart. ("Soile always decorates for the different holidays," a clerk once told me when I commented about the seasonal decor.)

By the entrance, a slowly twirling glass case immediately seduces with strawberry tortes, lingonberry tarts, and an R-rated chocolate cake called "Soile Sinful." In the display cases, beauteous old-world bakery goods like kringler and shiny cardamom pulla buns (a traditional Finnish treat) are for sale. Behind, loaves of glorious fresh breads fill the shelves: a popular spinach-Parmesan . . . or my son's favorite, the soft and buttery Norwegian milk bread.

For lunch, step over to the deli area and pick up a slice of layered artichoke pie or a fresh open-faced sandwich. There are plenty of small, round iron tables and chairs inside to sit at, and afterwards, if time permits, the shops surrounding Como and Carter Avenues are worth a peek. Stop in a cozy independent bookshop called Micawber's, the cool and unusual Bibelot gift shop, or Country Peddler, a packed-to-the-rafters quilt store. Or simply wander over by the grand and lovely 1916 Carnegie library that graces the corner of this neighborly, friendly spot—remembering, of course, when a trip to the library always meant a stop at the bakery afterwards.

TASTE OF MINNESOTA

As the granddaddy of Minnesota food festivals, Taste of Minnesota features feasting and fun in the shadow of the State Capitol building. Besides music and other entertainment, food booths from over thirty-five area restaurants offer all their specialties. Where else can you sample a Cajun steak sandwich, spicy fried rice, or a beer-battered brat on a stick; wash it all down with an iced mocha, old-fashioned lemonade, or an Italian soda; and finish it (and yourself) off with some cookie-dough ice cream and New York cheesecake?

Between bites, you can also enjoy culinary demonstrations (watching someone else eat a Wacky Mountain Sundae, for instance). Later, plan to spread out a blanket and collapse—happily full—under the night sky for the always-spectacular fireworks (the event is held for four days around the Fourth of July).

Buon Giorno Italian Market

335 University Avenue E. • Phone: (651) 224-1816

This shop is an Italian lover's dream, with its wonderful selection of local products and a wine section that boasts more than four hundred wine varieties from every province in Italy. Wines such as Scavino and Sandrone, rarely available outside New York and Chicago, fill the shelves alongside every kind of chianti and many other lesser-known wines from other regions. Even better, friendly owner Frank Marchionda is happy to recommend any bottle for any occasion, including marriage proposals.

He and his son, Marc, annually journey to Italy to select the wines for the shop—many from high-quality small producers.

But although the wine is one reason to go out of your way to visit this well-stocked shop (Buon Giorno is located off the beaten path on an odd corner of University), its cheeses are another. Representing a regional tour of Italy, you can find cheeses from Lazio, Emilia-Romagna, Veneto, Sardinia, and Tuscany. Their own mozzarella is made daily, and parmigiano reggiano sells for decidedly less than at some of the upscale cheese shops around. The meat case is filled with real Italian-style mortadella and prosciutto as well as sausages—hot, mild, and Sicilian style.

On the shelves sit imported honeys, jellies, biscotti, more than forty different kinds of olive oil, and exceptional balsamic vinegars (one version costs $150 per bottle). At the front of the shop, you can order huge sandwiches made on flavorful focaccia, and in the cooler you'll find cartons of the mild, brothlike traditional "wedding soup" prepared from Grandma Clara's time-honored recipe. (This is good to know—especially if that marriage proposal gets accepted.)

Dakota Bar and Grill

1021 Bandana Boulevard • Phone: (651) 642-1442

It's hard to resist a summer evening on the Dakota Bar & Grill's pretty patio. Flowers, a fountain, and twinkling lights away from the roar of city traffic make it one of the most appealing dining spots in St. Paul. But talk about off the beaten track (literally). The Dakota is located in a restored brick train shed in Bandana Square within an area called Energy Park—lots of office complexes, not much else. But even so, it's well worth searching out.

For one thing, since it opened in 1985, owner Lowell Pickett has been committed to offering menu items using fresh, seasonal, and local ingredients—long before it became the trend—and his executive chef, Ken Goff (with the Dakota since it opened), has produced Midwestern fare both innovative and pleasing for the past 15 years. Grilled portabella mushrooms with sweet corn, asparagus, peppers, and pumpkin seeds. A pot-roasted moulard duck with honey-blueberry sauce dipped over. Goff's rich and wonderful Minnesota brie and apple soup has never been off the menu. Other offerings: Walleye with homemade herb-scented tartar sauce; maple-glazed pork chops; ravioli stuffed with fontina; fresh chévre and garlic; and a good Caesar salad.

Wine selections are all American as well, including vintages from nearby Alexis Bailly winery in Hastings. Many desserts also have a Minnesota touch: some with blueberries, others using maple syrup. But my favorite here is still the traditional chocolate sundae: homemade vanilla ice cream, drizzled with hot fudge sauce that hardens as it hits the icy scoops.

To be truthful, most folks linger after dinner at the Dakota for another reason. Owner Pickett brings in some of the best local and national jazz acts you're likely to hear in the Twin Cities.

From the Dakota Bar and Grill: Minnesota Brie and Apple Soup

This is one of the signature dishes of Ken Goff, executive chef at the Dakota.

    4 tablespoons unsalted butter
    1 cup chopped yellow onion
    1/4 cup sliced leeks (white part only)
    4 large tart apples, peeled and quartered
    2 cups clear chicken broth
    1 sprig fresh rosemary, about 1 1/2 inches long
        (save a little for garnish)
    1/4 teaspoon dried thyme
    1 small bay leaf
    1 1/2 teaspoon kosher salt
    3 cups heavy cream (for a lighter soup, light
        cream or whole milk may be used; then use
        4 potatoes instead of 3)
    3 small potatoes, peeled and sliced 1/8-inch thick
    8 ounces brie cheese, cut into pieces
    Kosher salt and ground white pepper to taste

In a soup pot with a heavy bottom, melt the butter over high heat until it bubbles. Add the onion, leek, and apple. Stir to coat them. Reduce heat to medium and cook until onions are softened, about 8 minutes. Add the chicken stock, rosemary, thyme, bay leaf, and salt. Bring to a boil, reduce heat to medium low and simmer until the vegetables are tender, about 15 minutes. Remove bay leaf and rosemary. Meanwhile, in a separate heavy-bottomed pot, combine the cream and potatoes. Cook slowly, stirring frequently, until the potatoes are tender—takes about 12 minutes. Combine this with the contents of the first pot. In a blender, puree in batches, adding pieces of cheese while blending just long enough to incorporate. Add salt and white pepper to taste. Garnish each bowl with slices of green apple and a sprig of rosemary. Makes 6 servings.

Reprinted with permission from the *St. Paul Farmers Market Produce Cookbook* by the St. Paul Growers Association (St. Paul: St. Paul Growers Association, 1999).

Mickey's Diner
36 W. Seventh Street (at St. Peter Street) • Phone: (651) 698-0259

The first time I ate breakfast at Mickey's, I dragged my husband and three sons along to experience this authentic diner I had read so much about. Unfortunately, I didn't know how tiny the place is (a dozen or so stools at the counter, a few booths in back). It certainly looked as if the family would have to split up to eat. But just as I was about to sit two boys over here and one over there, the waitress pouring coffee saw us. "Move over Joe, slide down Nick. Let this family sit together," she ordered. The men complied without a murmur. This is the kind of straightforward place Mickey's is. Swift service, no chitchat, and an occasional waitress who sports a "devil waitress" tattoo. Don't expect a contrived Disney diner experience here.

Mickey's Diner in downtown St. Paul has been packing them in since 1939.

But do expect decent food. You may even rub elbows with unexpected celebs. The little red-and-yellow diner has been serving everyone from Arnold Schwartzenegger and Bill Murray to local politicians to down-and-outers since it opened in 1939. In fact, since it opened, Mickey's has been 24/7—long before the term was even invented.

Located in downtown St. Paul at the corner of St. Peter and Seventh Street, there's 30-minute parking at the side. Inside, a quarter in the jukebox will get you music with your meal, but be forewarned: The songs listed are not even close to the top 40. Still, listening to "Love Potion No. 9" while digging into an order of the "twos" (two eggs, two pancakes, and two pieces of bacon or sausage), seems strangely fitting. Buttermilk pancakes, baked beans, and Mulligan stew are all made on the premises from prewar (World War II, that is) recipes.

STATE FAIR FARE

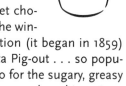

At the Minnesota State Fair, folks forget cholesterol counts and toss fat grams out the window. In fact, this end-of-summer tradition (it began in 1859) could be redubbed the Great Minnesota Pig-out . . . so popular is the food with all Minnesotans. I go for the sugary, greasy minidoughnuts and a foot-long hot dog, smothered in onions and slathered with mustard and catsup. Others are addicted to the fried cheese curds. The ice cream counter in the dairy building (it's officially called the Empire Commons, but everyone still calls it the dairy building), has the best deals on cones, sundaes, and four flavors of malts. Sweet Martha's, the Mrs. Field's of the fair, sells approximately 18 tons of cookies during the 10-day event! Of course, that still leaves onion rings and brats, roasted corn on the cob (drenched in 3,000 pounds of butter), over 30 different foods on a stick, and plenty of other fare at the fair. The event runs for 12 days from late August through Labor Day and is held at the state fairgrounds between the Twin Cities.

BLUBARB JAM

I love wandering the creative activities building at the State Fair, admiring all the home-canned jams, jellies, fruits, and vegetables—as well as the perfect plates of home-baked cakes and muffins, cookies, and bars. Later, I always look for the newspaper's coverage of the winners and clip any recipes shared. I don't remember when I cut out this recipe for State Fair blue-ribbon winner Arleyne Zima's Blubarb Jam, but I do know I've been making the jam every summer for several years.

3 cups finely chopped rhubarb
3 cups crushed fresh blueberries
7 cups sugar
1/2 tablespoon butter or margarine
2 (3-ounce) pouches liquid fruit pectin

Combine rhubarb and blueberries in a large saucepan. Add sugar. Mix and add margarine. Bring to a full, rolling boil over high heat. Boil hard for exactly 1 minute, stirring constantly. Remove from heat.

Stir in pectin. Skim foam. Fill jars to 1/8-inch from top. Process in a water bath canner for 10 minutes. Or keep the jam refrigerated for up to two weeks. Makes 9 1/2 pints.

Café Latté
Address: 850 Grand Avenue • Phone: (651) 224-5687

It's safe to say that Café Latté is an institution on Grand Avenue in St. Paul. Since it opened, this cafeteria-style place has been crowded, noisy, but always fun. Located in a building that originally housed an old Studebaker dealership, Latté nowadays also has a sleek pizza/wine bar (they also serve afternoon tea here).

While the cafeteria side still draws the lunch and dinner crowd for its homemade soups and sandwiches, everyone in town knows that the REAL reason you come to the cafeteria is desserts. Cheesecakes—strawberry-rhubarb, chocolate Kahlua—and fruit tarts such as peach crostada and pear-almond. Cakes include banana with a silky browned-butter frosting, and the café's signature Turtle Cake—a layered extravaganza of devil's food cake, caramel, and pecans, all draped over with a thick coating of chocolate—easily, the most popular item on the menu.

In fact, Linda Quinn (who owns the restaurant with her husband, Peter), says total Saturday cake sales here (totaling around 200) usually include a whopping 25 Turtle Cakes.

FROM THE CAFÉ LATTÉ: SHORTBREAD COOKIES

I'm a big fan of these buttery-rich cookies—and this recipe is a favorite of mine. Quinn says these are a good accompaniment to afternoon tea, and she's right. She also suggests making up several cylinders of dough, covering them in plastic wrap, and then stashing them in the freezer. Later, unthaw a few minutes, then slice and bake as desired.

1/2 cup sugar
3 cups flour
1/4 cup rice flour
1 1/2 cup cold butter, chopped

In medium mixing bowl, combine the sugar, flour, and rice flour. Add the butter gradually (in chunks) and mix until dough gathers around the beaters or paddle. Take dough out of bowl. Form into an 18-inch long rope (1 1/2- to 2-inch diameter). Smooth out by rolling dough between your hands and the counter. Wrap in plastic wrap. Chill 1 hour. (Or double-wrap and keep in freezer.) Preheat oven to 350 degrees. Slice into 30 to 40 cookies about 1/4-inch thick. Arrange on an ungreased baking sheet (or parchment-lined baking sheet) and bake 12 to 15 minutes or until sides are golden. Makes 30 to 40 cookies.

Café Latté's signature Turtle Cake

West Side Salsa

Smoky roasted corn, homemade tamales, and fresh salsa scent the sidewalks during the first weekend in May when St. Paul's West Side has its biggest celebration: the popular Cinco de Mayo Fiesta. Vendors sell sombreros, paper flowers, and "mucho mucho más." Dancers in bright traditional garb perform on stages up and down Concord street, and music fills the air with a lively (and loud) beat.

For the record, St. Paul's predominantly Hispanic West Side refers to the west banks of the Mississippi River. It's not to be confused with West St. Paul or the West End. In fact, the West Side is actually less than a mile south from downtown St. Paul.

Name and geographical puzzlements aside, one need only cross the Mississippi River on the new Wabasha Street bridge to enter this area filled with a fiesta of flavors and color—whether it's the season for Cinco de Mayo or not.

You can't miss Boca Chica: The exterior mural on the side of this "Mexican Restaurante" reads "Bienvenidos," welcoming visitors to the neighborhood. For more than thirty years, Boca Chica has been dishing up homemade chorizo, terrific chiles rellenos, rich mole, and a renowned Sunday brunch.

At El Burrito Mercado, mariachi music mingles with the scent of cumin, and colorful piñatas twirl from the ceiling. A grand grocery store/deli/restaurant where you can find everything from cactus salad to molcajetes (stone mortars for grinding chili peppers), their hot sauce selection is nothing short of breathtaking. A couple aisles over, beneath the bright ceramic birds, you'll find a well-stocked deli case. Tortillas filled with chorizo con papas (chorizo with potatoes) and rajas con queso (poblano chilies with cheeses) are stacked next to containers of big bowls of (hot!) pico de gallo. A bakery case displays dozens of Mexican pastries, and the cooler holds Mexican cheeses, sausages, and homemade sauces. Open bins in the market side are heaped with fresh fruits, such as guava, mango, and papaya. And if you're here on a Thursday delivery day, you might even score some of those exquisite tiny round Key limes—hard to find in Minnesota. On one of my first visits to El Burrito, I learned from co-owners Maria and Tomas Silva that in Mexico, a squeeze of fresh lime juice is used on almost everything. They recommended it on a ripe mango, followed by a shake of chili pepper; I've been hooked ever since.

Lunch is always packed on the cafeteria side of this deli/market. No wonder. It's a good deal, and the spicy, cheesy enchiladas suizas are excellent—as are the creamy refried beans. Those who know grab a tray, point out what they're hungry for, and then find a table near the sunny windows and dig in.

For breakfast, El Amanacer ("sunrise" in Spanish), across the street from El Burrito, is a local gathering spot among business folks in the area. (Order the eggs with homemade salsa.) And I also like Me Gusta (look for the sign with a sombrero over the name) on Robert Street. Here's where you'll find delicious moyetes, the Mexican version of bruschetta with cheese and pico de gallo.

At Morgan's Mexican Lebanese Foods, the sign on the door says "Abierto," but inside this colorful market, food for both Mexican and Lebanese abounds. Owners Marion and Roger Morgan can easily give you directions for preparing fresh cactus (which they sell) as well as Marion's native Arabic pita snack, falafel. The *New York Times* once reported that Morgan's is where "two cultures meet in St. Paul." Canned mango slices, guava shells, several types of corn flour, and Mexican chocolate and vanilla line the shelves along with garbanzo and fava beans, sesame seeds, and olive oils.

Don't let the rather rough exterior (and iron door!) scare you off at the tiny Don Panchos Bakery. Inside, it's cozy, fragrant, and warm. There are all sorts of wonderful things to admire and choose from—including little loaves of cheese bread (pan con queso). But I usually end up pointing to my favorite: the "Tres Leches (three milks) cake" in the cooler. The friendly help always nods knowingly at me and responds with a smile. Love in any language is understood.

Pearson's Candy Company
2140 West Seventh Street • Phone: (651) 698-0356 or (800) 328-6507

It's called a candy *bar,* but in fact, Pearson's original Nut Goodie is a round patty, about two inches in diameter. Underneath its real milk chocolate cover, you'll find a cluster of unsalted peanuts coated within a sweet maple-flavored cream—and if you grew up in Iowa, Minnesota, Wisconsin, or the Dakotas, you'll no doubt remember the Nut Goodie as part of your childhood.

Today, the quintessential Midwestern candy bar is still being made in St. Paul, although even many Minnesotans don't realize how close we came to losing our beloved favorite. According to Larry Hassler, Pearson's co-owner with Judith Johnston, when George Pearson (a nephew of one of the three brothers who founded Pearson's in 1909) retired and sold the company to ITT/Continental Baking in 1969, the company ended up altering the Nut Goodie ingredients and scrapping its traditional red-and-green wrapper.

Eventually, Pearson's was sold again to a different partnership before being bought in the mid-1980s by Hassler and Johnston, two former Pearson's employees. They returned to Pearson's original recipe for the Nut Goodie, brought back the familiar wrapper, and worked hard to put the business back on track.

If you make a stop at Pearson's candy factory these days, you can smell the sharp, frosty aroma of peppermint from the parking lot. Step inside the building and aromas begin to mingle more—mint with chocolate, chocolate with nuts, nuts with caramel—seductively hinting at what's cooking behind closed doors down the hall: namely, Pearson's Mint Patties, Nut Rolls (most of us still call them Salted Nut Rolls), and, of course, the Nut Goodie.

The factory is large by Minnesota standards, though Hassler says it is actually quite small compared to the mammoth candy-bar businesses such as Hershey, Mars, and Nestlé. ("They produce 90 percent of the candy in the country," says Hassler. "The rest of us get to compete for the other 10 percent.")

You can no longer buy boxes and bars of Pearson's products in the small main office at the facility, and unfortunately you're not allowed even a peek into the actual candy factory beyond. But if you're a food writer on a mission, you do get a tour to let everyone else know what's really going on back here: One room has king-sized kettles and drums filled with batches of the candy-bar centers. In another room, flavors get mixed in. And over at the production-line room, clusters of peanuts and chocolate glide by Nut Goodie inspectors who use a spatula to shape each one before they're sent on to be packaged in that distinctive wrapper Midwesterners know and love.

Golden Quince Bakery
3557 Lexington Avenue N. • Phone: (651) 483-3327

Arrive around noon at the Golden Quince and you can watch the fresh breads being pulled from the ovens—warm, fragrant cinnamon bread; herbed focaccia; buttery brioche; and honey-colored Armenian breakfast bread, a specialty of the Persian-born proprietor.

Although it's located in a strip mall, I love this shop. Its pale yellow walls, huge vases of flowers, and bright corner windows create a sunny, scented universe. This is the best place to indulge in an apricot-glazed chocolate-stuffed croissant or a plate-sized strawberry scone big enough for two (or even three) people. The Golden Quince serves up delicious soups and sandwiches, too, but to be truthful, it's the breads and pastries I regularly go for.

St. Paul Farmer's Market
(651) 227-8101

Most summer Saturday mornings, I pull out my flexible-handled straw market basket and head straight downtown for the bustling St. Paul Farmer's Market.

With its 148-year history, the market has seen various locations, but it has always been *somewhere* in downtown St. Paul. These days, you'll find it near one of the areas first selected in 1853 by St. Paul to house the original Farmer's Market—on Fifth and Wall Streets. Bricks pave the walkways and underneath the corrugated-fiberglass roof, about one hundred seventy open-air stalls offer the usual fresh, locally grown tomatoes, strawberries, and sweet corn.

However, with St. Paul's ever-growing Hmong population, it's also now easy to find generous trays of traditional tender French beans and succulent baby peas next to bunches of bok choy and lemongrass.

Longtime vendors include the Eichtens (Joe and Mary), who offer creamy cheese and fresh cuts of bison. Over at the Melon Patch, you'll find bunches of aromatic herbs: spicy basil, feathery dill, and sweet marjoram.

Make a note to stop at Dancing Wind's Mary Doerr's stall early on. She makes incredibly good herbed, peppered, and plain goat cheeses. Tip: Crocks full of her homemade chévre for sampling disappear quickly.

I also usually pick up a loaf (or two) of excellent sourdough rosemary/onion bread from the New French Bakery, purchase a jar of local honey at apiarist

A bountiful harvest of tomatoes at the St. Paul Farmer's Market

Bernie Brand's booth, and make another stop at a stand selling hand-harvested wild rice from northern Minnesota.

In truth, until 1997, foods like wild rice, honey, and maple syrup that were produced elsewhere in the state were not allowed to be sold at the St. Paul Farmer's Market. Unlike Minneapolis's farmer's market, vendors of the St. Paul Farmer's Market had to farm within a 50-mile radius of the Twin Cities to qualify as local growers. Today, boundaries have been expanded.

Coffee lovers tip: Before or after the market, pause for a latte and a crisp biscotti at the lively Black Dog coffeehouse nearby.

ST. PATRICK'S DAY

Besides an "Irish Celebration" at Landmark Center and a noonday parade through the streets of downtown St. Paul, you can plan on lots of green beer being consumed during St. Paul's famous St. Patrick's Day party. Whatever you do, be sure to stop in at Patrick McGovern's Restaurant and Pub. Even its locale—a building built in 1886 with a black-trimmed turret and three-story-high bay windows—seems a fitting place to tip a Guinness or two.

---

11. Beyond the Twin Cities

As the suburbs have spread around Minneapolis and St. Paul, so have the fast-food joints and the chain restaurants. Even so (or perhaps even in spite of this), the metro area still offers a rich supply of tried-and-true cafes, old ice cream shops, and family-owned restaurants filled with an ambience and spirit that only time can achieve. Happily, there also seems to be a small resurgence in one-of-a-kind independent restaurants opening out in suburbia—and finding success. This is good news, too.

EDINA

Tejas
3910 West 50th Street • Phone: (952) 926-0800

This Southwestern standby (originally located in downtown Minneapolis) remains a great address to know when you're in the mood for a good, innovative meal accompanied by a fine margarita. In warm weather, tables out on the sidewalk are coveted spots, while inside, diners have plenty of room in a friendly, upscale setting.

Oh, yeah, it's trendy (this is 50th and France in Edina, after all), so you'll want to dress up a little (black leather jacket and designer jeans work) if you're planning to dine here. What keeps Tejas on top in the Twin Cities are the talents of its chef, Mark Haugen. For the past 10 years, he has managed to keep delivering dishes that are delicious and different. Haugen, who grew up in a family where one grandmother cooked everything from scratch and the other never cooked at all ("but she took us out to eat," says Haugen), has a "rich memory palate." That's what helps spark creativity in his kitchen, he says. He's also a chef who pays attention to nuances of taste, likening the matching of food flavors to a mariachi band. "You have the brassier tones like citrus, or fresh chilies, and then the base notes like garlic, onions, banana. . . ."

The food can be a bit on the fussy side, but you're sure to find some good fare on Haugen's menu. Try the piñon-crusted gulf snapper with avocado aioli or the roasted pumpkin risotto (accented with leeks, intense with black truffles, rich with an Alpine chèvre). Among his starters, taste the smoked salmon quesadilla—a new twist on the old traditional, something Haugen does with flair—this one features papaya relish and cilantro sour cream. The popular Southwestern Caesar salad (prepared with shaved asiago cheese, hot pepper–flavored croutons, and a fragrant cumin-tamarind dressing) is another good choice. An extra bonus: Wine suggestions are offered on the menu next to the entrées.

If there's room for dessert, sample the chocolate-chocolate chip fritters—a cool combination that matches white chocolate ice cream, red raspberry coulis, and smoldering "fiery fudge sauce." For a really unusual finale, sample the banana–white chocolate ice cream cake with roasted banana salsa. It's weird but wonderful.

Two from Tejas

When pairing a dessert or ice cream with a sauce, Tejas chef Mark Haugen tries to balance the sweetness of the syrup against the richness of the dessert. For example, his not-too-sweet blackberry tequila sauce is fairly thin and adds a touch of acidity (and color) to a heavy lime cheesecake. "Tequila has that baseline flavor, while the scented blackberries hit the bright note," he says.

Blackberry Tequila Sauce

>   1 1/2 cups fresh blackberries (or 1 14-ounce bag
>   frozen blackberries, thawed and drained)
>   1/2 cup tequila
>   1/2 cup sugar

In a medium saucepan, combine blackberries, tequila, and sugar; heat to boiling. Reduce heat and simmer for 3 minutes. Cool, then puree in a blender. To remove seeds, strain this mixture through a fine sieve into another container. Stored, covered in the refrigerator, this strained juice keeps for five days. Makes 1 cup. Serve with lime cheesecake or over lemon, lime, or mango sorbet, says Haugen. It's also good with a slice of lemon pound cake.

Fiery Fudge Sauce

This is a fudge sauce you'll want to keep on hand all summer long. Skip the pepper if you like or add even more—for a real fire-and-ice combo.

>   1/3 cup light corn syrup
>   1/4 cup water
>   3/4 cup sugar
>   1/4 cup unsweetened cocoa powder
>   1 tablespoon unsweetened chocolate, chopped
>   2 tablespoons butter
>   1/3 cup whipping cream
>   1/2 teaspoon cayenne pepper (or to taste)

In a small saucepan, heat the corn syrup to boiling and boil for 1 minute. Stir in water. Be careful, as mixture may splatter.

In another bowl, sift together the sugar and cocoa powder. Stir this into the corn syrup mixture. Heat to boiling, stirring constantly until the sugar is dissolved. Add unsweetened chopped chocolate and the butter. Whisk until melted. Stir in cream and heat to boiling. Immediately remove from heat and stir in cayenne pepper. Stored, covered, in the refrigerator, it keeps a week. Reheat gently. Makes 1 cup.

Convention Grill
3912 Sunnyside S. • Phone: (952) 920-6881

A true little hamburger joint long before those golden arches existed, the grill still has the dark wood booths, counter, light fixtures and old-fashioned stools from the original restaurant—opened in 1934. Behind the counter, you can watch as hamburgers get sizzled and flipped, and malts (e.g., wild blueberry, coffee, strawberry, chocolate, caramel, honey) are swirled up. Be forewarned: these frozen concoctions come in tins that fill two and a half malt glasses to the brim!

Along with their burgers (the cheeseburger is a beaut: smoky cheddar, Muenster, American, or Swiss served on a warm homemade bun), there are hand-cut French fries, and a homey chicken noodle soup. Best of all, the hot fudge sundae arrives with a pitcher of the buttery-thick chocolate sauce.

EXCELSIOR

Lick's Unlimited
31 Water Street • Phone: (952) 474-4791 (seasonal)

Synonymous with ice cream and Lake Minnetonka, Lick's Unlimited in Excelsior is one of the most quaint and kitsch-cluttered ice cream shops I've had the pleasure to frequent. Step inside this minuscule seasonal shop (where not much has changed in over seventeen years) and the first enticement you're subjected to? No, it's not the 30 flavors of ice cream. It's the 11 (ELEVEN) varieties of ice cream CONES to select from. Neatly labeled and displayed atop the ice cream case, the cones include the following choices: double-dipped cherry, homemade waffle cup, double-dipped chocolate peanut, double-dipped chocolate sprinkles, double-dipped piña colada, double-dipped chocolate krunch . . . you get the picture.

Everybody has their favorite, but I usually go for the double-dipped chocolate cone filled with whatever ice cream happens to be the flavor of the month. If I'm lucky, it'll be Moose Tracks (a mixture of vanilla ice cream, peanut butter cups, and fudge). You can eat at a little table inside (old Excelsior photos line the walls, and a flying wooden pig and teddy bear cycling across a tightrope hang overhead) or sit on the bench outside next to the front door. One time while I was sitting on the bench, a little girl sat daintily down beside me and informed me proudly (in between licks of her ice cream) that she comes here every day and has a chocolate chip cookie dough ice cream cone.

Antiquity Rose
429 Second Street (between Excelsior Boulevard and Water Street)
Phone: (952) 474-2661

Yes, Antiquity Rose is a place for ladies who lunch. (But men are still welcome.) A combination antiques shop/dining room, you can eat here *and* purchase the dining room table that you're sitting at. (A friend of mine did just that. Honest. The chairs, too.)

The pale pink old house (circa 1879) has tables on its porch (white railings and vintage screen door) and serves a weekly afternoon tea. Lunch items tend to be light and homemade, but portions are hearty. Besides fresh tossed salads, you'll find warm muffins and savory soups: Golden Glory corn chowder or Italian vegetable soup with sausage. Desserts are also memorable: their rhubarb torte is a classic. These are homey offerings, made from good solid recipes by people who like to be in the kitchen.

St. Alban's Boathouse
21960 Minnetonka Boulevard • Phone: (952) 474-6260
Web site: www.stalbansboathouse.com

After the sun sets over Lake Minnetonka but while the sky is still pink, they light the candle torches on the second-floor deck at St. Alban's Boathouse restaurant. Diners dressed in shorts and flip-flops, sundresses and suit coats toast the twilight with glasses of Spanish sparkling wine and then dig into platters full of spicy shrimp or crisp walleye sandwiches.

I like this rather hodgepodge old restaurant on the lake. It's one of the few restaurants on the water that feels, well, neighborly. It's not filled with a bunch of tan twentysomethings, and you don't need to worry if your car isn't a brand new BMW or shiny red convertible. (In Lake Minnetonka, they pay attention to this sort of thing.)

St. Alban's has had a stormy ownership history, but the last time I was here, the servers were friendly and the food was delightful. You can sit outside on the ground-level patio, but those who know ask to be seated upstairs on the second-floor deck. The sunsets from here are spectacular.

Adele's Frozen Custard
800 Excelsior Boulevard • Phone: (952) 470-0035

Skip dessert at St. Albans and head over to Adele's Frozen Custard (it's just a short distance down the road). Have their chocolate raspberry truffle custard—they make it every other Sunday, with fresh raspberries and chunks of chocolate. Bring the kids during the day and you can even watch them making these pure, smooth confections: butterfinger, tangerine, and bear claw, a rich and creamy caramel custard with chocolate truffle and pecan pieces. They have an outdoor deck here, too—and on warm summer days and hot summer nights, it's packed with people.

CHANHASSEN

University of Minnesota Applehouse
1 mile west of the Arboretum on Highway 5: Turn north on Rolling Acres Road where it intersects with Highway 5 • Phone: (952) 443-1409

The university's Applehouse (located a mile west of the University of Minnesota Landscape Arboretum) sells apples, but its real business is releasing varieties. With more than seventy-five available, this is a shop where apple connoisseurs sometimes ask for the "1606" or the "1505"—apple varieties that never received names but are enough in demand for the university to continue growing them.

MINNESOTA APPLES

Several years ago, I asked David Bedford, a scientist at the University of Minnesota's Horticultural Research Center (and who has tasted hundreds of apples), for a list of the best Minnesota-grown varieties. He selected the following, listed in order of appearance during harvest season:

State Fair: One of the earliest-maturing apples, it's sometimes confused with the Beacon, which was nicknamed "the State Fair apple" and was for years sold at its namesake event.

Chestnut Crab: Homely looking, it's smaller than most apples but not as small as the typical crab apple. It has good texture, one of the best flavors around, and an almost perfect sweet/tart balance.

Wealthy: Widely considered one of the best baking apples, this historic variety was developed in Minnesota.

Red Baron: A mild, sweet, mid-sized apple used mostly for eating, it ripens before many other varieties.

Sweet Sixteen: Finely textured, with a nice rose-red color, it has an almost cherrylike flavor early in the harvest and then develops an anise/licorice taste.

Lakeland: Good for eating, it also holds its shape when sliced and cooked.

Honeycrisp: Expected to be the newest world-class apple, it has a crisp taste and excellent keeping qualities.

Haralson: The most widely grown—and the most familiar—apple in the state, it's one of the oldest varieties still recommended. Its tartness long ago made it a favorite for eating and baking.

Prairie Spy: Its nice balance of tart and sweet has made it popular for cooking and baking.

Honeygold: A cross between the Golden Delicious and the Haralson, this yellow apple has a sweet, honey-like flavor; it's good for baking and eating.

Regent: Similar in appearance to the Red Delicious, it has twice the flavor and is crisp and juicy. It's good for eating and cooking.

Fireside: The second most popular variety in the state, it's sweet and very hard. The redder version of the Fireside is the Connell Red; both varieties hold their shape when cooked.

Keepsake: Neither large nor especially beautiful, it's very aromatic and has a wonderful, unusual flavor. It's hard as a rock when picked, and it keeps very well.

LONG LAKE

Dumas Apple House

3025 Wayzata Boulevard • Phone: (952) 473-9538

Just a mile west of Long Lake on Highway 12 is one of my favorite apple stands, a tidy open market called the Apple House. Bushel baskets of rosy apples labeled with names like Sweet Sixteen and Lakeland and bins of the bagged fruits scent the way inside, where more apples abound. But besides the fruit, a visit here is worth it just to see the Dumas's delightful collection of antique apple-motif china lining the walls. The dishes aren't for sale—but with your apple purchase you'll get a copy of the *Dumas Family Recipes,* which will help you prepare "Grandma Gleason's pie Crust" and the "Definitive Apple Pie."

Recipes like these are just a few of the ones Kathryn Dumas has collected through the years at this family apple orchard. (The Dumas family has owned the orchard since 1925, when Kathryn's in-laws, Ed and Beatrice Dumas, first bought the property.) Today, the third generation is active in the business, soon to be followed by a fourth generation—"as soon as he's old enough to see over the counter top," says Kathryn. They grow over two dozen different varieties of apples—including the one they turned me on to the first time I stopped by the market: the Chestnut crab apple. Called the "gourmet's apple," it's a homely looking little apple, but its looks belie an almost perfect sweet, spicy flavor. The Dumas's also introduced me to the small and tangy Snowflake, another eating apple worth seeking out during the few weeks it's available. This is the place to find Dolgo crab apples, too: the best "jelly crab" according to Kathryn—although, she says, when Dolgos are baked in a pie, they taste like cherries. Traditional apple pie makers should try the Wealthy—a historic variety first developed in Minnesota. "It makes a fantastic pie," advises Kathryn, even though her first preference for use in homemade pie is still the long popular Haralson.

FROM DUMAS APPLE HOUSE: APPLE COBBLER

I love the way the Dumas family thinks about apples. This recipe for apple cobbler suggests trying it "warm, ladled with cream for a truly self-indulgent breakfast." Kathryn says this is their most requested recipe, and describing it, she notes, "It's more like a butter cake over cinnamon sugar–spiced apples."

> 5–6 apples (peeled, cored, and sliced)
> 1 tablespoon cinnamon sugar**
> 1 cup sugar
> 8 tablespoons butter (room temperature)
> 2 eggs (beaten)
> 1 cup all-purpose flour
> Pinch of salt

Place the apples in a buttered 8-inch square pan. Sprinkle with cinnamon sugar. Beat the sugar and butter together with a spoon. Stir in eggs and flour. Drop mixture over apples (it will spread as it bakes).

Bake at 325 degrees for 40–45 minutes.

**Make cinnamon sugar by stirring 1 teaspoon of cinnamon in 1 cup sugar.

MINNETRISTA

Minnetonka Orchards
6530 County 26 • Phone: (763) 479-3191 (seasonal info)
Business phone: (763) 479-6530

Driving into this postcard-pretty apple orchard, you feel as though you're about to enter a secluded retreat. The two white posts have hanging baskets of lush petunias cascading over painted antique milk cans. A lovely old tree ablaze with autumn color sits in a puddle of bright orange leaves, and just beyond is where you park your car on the side of a gently rolling hill bordered by more trees.

I especially love to visit here during the orchard's annual Ciderfest (the second weekend in September). This is when owner Lowell Schaper sets up his 1874 antique bright-red cider press, and kids and adults are invited to toss in the apples or take a turn cranking the press. After the aromatic juice has finished splashing into a filtered bucket, it's poured into another container and then ladled out for everyone to taste. The cold sweet cider is fabulous, and sipping it amidst the apple trees, with that evocative smell of fruit and autumn air, is something akin to harvest bliss.

Checking the cider press at Minnetonka Orchards in Minnetrista

Like many orchards, this spot also offers free hayrides on fall weekends—with one unusual spin. The wagons are pulled by one of Schaper's classic tractors. Schaper owns six of these vintage vehicles—with their dates of birth ranging from 1939 to 1955—and including a nice looking old Minneapolis Moline. If you decide not to hitch a ride to the apple trees to pick your own apples, however, you can always simply stop in the building where the Schaper's have already bagged up the fresh beauties for you. They grow 15 different varieties of apples—including a new variety called Zestar (developed by the University of Minnesota).

Whether you decide to pick your own apples or buy them already bagged, if it's Ciderfest, plan on lunch here. Follow your nose to the tent where the "cider brats" are being served up. Marinated in apple cider before they are grilled, these juicy numbers are stuffed into a soft warm bun, then loaded with chunks of warm apples and slices of onions that have been sauteed together in more apple cider.

Although the orchard also puts together a decent apple caramel sundae, I can't resist the freshly fried hot apple donuts gently shaken in a bag with cinnamon sugar. If you're simply too full, buy a half-dozen of the hot sugared treats to take home: They'll scent the car all the way there.

WAYZATA

Blue Point Restaurant and Oyster Bar
739 East Lake Street • Phone: (612) 475-3636

"Eat Seafood! Live Longer!" the neon sign that doubles as a clock over the door at the Blue Point encourages. If you can get past the toney-looking women in designer wear whining about why there is no coat check person, you'll find this place has wonderful seafood prepared with style and flair.

Skip the oyster bar; it's too smoky. But reserve a table in the dining room where the air is clean and the atmosphere clubby. Tony Bennett croons on the sound system, dark wood paneling surrounds, and red plush banquettes are inviting. With old-fashioned touches such as boxed souvenir matches and a chic menu printed with the night's date on it, you'd swear the place has been here forever. (In truth, it's been open a few years over a dozen.)

Start out with a fresh half-dozen Malpeque oysters, dabbed with a bit of Blue Point's freshly grated horseradish, and you're on your way to heaven. The clam chowder is justifiably good, too, but for a burst of spicy satisfaction, sample the Louisiana shrimp grumb, a perfumy mix of andouille sausage, okra, shrimp,

The neon clock over the front door of the Blue Point Restaurant and Oyster Bar, Wayzata

and crayfish. Executive chef Patrick Donelan's entrées reflect his philosophy of clean, simple taste: He doesn't like throwing twenty things on the plate, he says. Sample his San Francisco–style Dungeness crab and you'll know what he means. He pairs blackened Florida swordfish nicely with an accompanying simple salad nicoise.

After dinner, take a stroll along Wayzata Bay. Walk amid the landscaped blossoms and admire the restored yellow-and-red Minnehaha Steamboat carrying passengers back and forth across the bay. Then watch the sun set and the stars pop out over the shimmering, glimmering water.

Gianni's Steakhouse and Supper Club
627 East Lake Street • Phone: (952) 404-1100

Make no mistake. Gianni's is a spot for big appetites and big spenders. Still, my husband and I have had fun here, dining at the bar one summer Saturday night when we didn't have reservations. Order the juicy Delmonico ribeye—it takes the word *succulent* to new heights—and accompany it with a bottle of Rolling Rock beer or a biting good Bloody Mary. Peppery grilled pork chops are beauties, and side orders of mashed potatoes are plenty big to share. Don't miss the garlicky string beans, which are sparked with Szechuan fire. Tip: If you're here on a Friday night; you'll understand why all those playing cards are on the ceiling.

Black's Ford
862 East Lake Street • Phone: (952) 473-2940

The newer Black's Ford location in the Wayzata Shoppes strip mall lacks some of the crowded neighborhood bedlam found at its original storefront shop up the street, but the place is still serving its tasty homemade fare, and it's still a popular part of the Wayzata lakeshore scene.

At lunchtime, join the crush of customers, all ages and all pocketbook sizes. Order an old-fashioned egg salad sandwich and a Buddy's orange float. Or sample a black bean burrito. Homemade soups range from a light Manhattan clam chowder to a rich sweet potato–pumpkin soup. Have a glass of wine or a microbrew. Early-morning types get their cappuccinos and muffins here.

WHITE BEAR LAKE

Pine Tree Apple Orchard
450 Apple Orchard Road • Phone: (651) 429-7202

Everybody loves Pine Tree Apple Orchard. This is the kind of place where you can smell the apple pies baking from the parking lot. But besides apples and wonderful apple baked goods available here, this place sells every possible apple gadget and gizmo produced. Along with at least four types of apple corers, there are apple parers, apple slicers, apple-shaped cookie cutters, apple potholders, apple pie–top cutters, and apple cookbooks.

Outdoor Cooking Store

2225 Fourth Street • Phone: (800) 4-COOKOUT or (651) 653-6166

Talk about gizmos and gadgets—and grills. This shop is a barbecue afi-
cionado's smoky-infused daydream. With 2,400 square feet of showroom floor
space, here you'll find just about everything related to cooking in the great out-
doors. Whether you're looking for sauces and seasonings, camping grills, accessories, barbecue cookbooks, or fancy backyard built-ins, the Outdoor Cooking Store has them all. Recipes and grilling tips abound. This is the place to
find shish kebab baskets, circle kebab skewers, roasting racks, charcoal chim-
neys, potato bakers, drip pans and ash guards, square woks for the grill, and
even aprons that state "Real Men Fry Turkeys."

My husband loves all the barbecue "toys," but I adore perusing the jars and
bottles of sauces, marinades, and seasonings. There are dry rubs such as Cajun
Dust, Porky's Delight, and John Henry's Apple Rub (John Henry also has a
cherry, a pecan, a jalapeño, a hickory, a mesquite, and an herbal rub). There
are wet sauces such as Bone Suckin' Sauce, Spankin' Sauce, Hogwash (a sweet
pungent mixture tasting of orange juice, brown sugar, with a "wild slap" of
horseradish), Southern Ray's Roasted Garlic and Ginger Sauce (highly recommended), and Prairie Smoke, a thick and hearty sauce made as a class project by high school students in Walnut Grove, Minnesota. Marinades worth a
try include Chef William Jamaican Jerk Injectible Marinade and Chef William
Polynesian Pineapple Injectible Marinade.

You can also buy dinner bells and strings of lights for the patio: weeny
roast lights (hot dogs in buns!), chili pepper lights, mess o' trout lights, and
pack o' piggies lights!

Phil and Sue Ann Muller started this business in 1990 after a trip to Texas and
Phil's first look at a Lyfe Tyme smoker. As Sue Ann says, "I saw that look in his
eyes and knew we would own one. I never guessed we'd be selling them, too."

The retail store also conducts cooking classes in the fall and winter months,
has a 72-page catalog, services grills and similar equipment, stocks over twenty
thousand parts year round, and competes in a limited number of barbecue
competitions.

WACONIA

Nancy's Landing

318 Lake Street E. • Phone: (952) 442-4954

Brunch at this unpretentious beachfront restaurant in Waconia (adjacent to
Clearwater Marina) is highly recommended. Chefs Paul and Laura Laubignat pull out all stops, serving up a buffet-style spread with a different
theme/cuisine every week (for example, Hawaii, India, the Orient).

Lunch or dinner in the airy, white and blue dining room with picture windows overlooking Lake Waconia is just as worthwhile. The best dishes sampled

here seem to happen when this husband and wife chef team weave in the bounty of their garden along with aromatic herbs—fresh string beans, oven-roasted rosemary chicken, or lemon verbena mousse spooned over strawberries.

The entrées are fairly basic but always with a classic French touch (Paul is a native of France). Sample the grilled beef tenderloin served with a green peppercorn sauce. Tender medallions of pork might be sautéed with mushrooms, and artichoke hearts in a lush port wine.

Desserts are showcases at Nancy's Landing. During the summertime, the exceptional sweet finales are often enhanced with herbs from the Laubignat's garden. Laura likes to subtly flavor (and scent) poached pears and chocolate syrup with a sprinkle of untreated lavender blossoms (sublime). Other indulgences found on their dessert tray might be a European hazelnut torte or a bowl of ice cream topped with cherries sautéed with chopped sage and walnuts (unusual but wonderful).

FROM NANCY'S LANDING: GOAT CHEESE ROSEMARY PINWHEELS

Don't overchop the herbs, says chef Paul Laubignat, "or all the aromatic oils and flavor end up on your cutting board, not in your food." Tender and rich, these hors d'oeuvres taste best when served with an oaky Chardonnay or a light red wine.

> 1 sheet frozen puff pastry, thawed
> 3.5 ounces chèvre, at room temperature
> 1–2 tablespoons chopped fresh rosemary
> 1 teaspoon freshly ground pepper
> 4–5 slices prosciutto
> 1/2 cup freshly grated parmigiano-reggiano cheese
> 1 egg
> 2 teaspoons water

Place puff pastry on a lightly floured surface. In a small bowl combine chèvre, rosemary, and black pepper. Spread mixture on puff pastry. Lay prosciutto on top. Sprinkle with parmigiano-reggiano cheese. Roll puff pastry tightly; cover loosely with plastic wrap and chill for 20 minutes (or overnight).

Cut roll into 1/4-inch pieces and place onto an ungreased baking sheet. In a small bowl, beat egg and water with a fork until combined. Lightly brush on each pinwheel. Bake in a 400-degree oven for 8 to 10 minutes. Serve immediately.

Makes about 30.

Tackling a gargantuan chocolate-glazed doughnut at Hans' Bakery in Anoka

ANOKA

Hans' Bakery
1423 Fifth Avenue S. • Phone: (763) 421-4200

Hans' Bakery is a personality-plus bakery. It's always busy. And if you get here in the afternoon, when the middle school next door lets out, be prepared to wait. Students line up to buy the oversized chocolate glazed doughnuts (they require two hands for eating).

But it's not the doughnuts that are the siren song here. It's Hans' legendary "beehive." I have not tasted anything like this anywhere else in the state. At its most basic, it appears to be two flaky pastry rounds with a Bavarian cream filling in the middle—then dusted on top with powdered sugar. Because it's kept refrigerated, when you sink into the first bite, you get several sensations: the confectioners' sugar is sweet, cold, and powdery; the filling, smooth, creamy, and cool; and finally the pastry, featherlike and ultratender. Who can resist?

Besides the beehives (which come in individual or crowd size: The large ones serve 12), at Hans' there is a whole counter full of their "All Butter Coffeecakes," which include variations from plain to pecan to cherry. A chalkboard proclaims "authentic German Brotchen," and these are some of the best traditional hard rolls I've tasted, too, especially the Dutch crust. Breads include a

179

seven-grain, cobblestone, Black Forest, German whole grain, and a Bavarian farmer's bread with a perfect crispy crust. A sign proudly states that everything you see is baked fresh daily.

In the shop itself, you can sit at any one of many tables (the place is large). Or admire the tortes and decorated cakes that spin around in glass cases in the middle of the store. The girls in their red aprons behind the counter are friendly and knowledgeable, and the whole place seems to evoke a happy sort of mayhem.

12. Towns along the Way

As I traveled throughout the state, it always seemed there were a few towns I'd go through on the way to somewhere else that didn't quite fit in with the area I wanted to write about. I loved Pie Day in Braham, but where would that fit? It's on the way north, but would it go with the "Up North to the Lake" chapter, which was farther west? Or should it be a part of the "Iron Range" chapter? What about Schumacher's in New Prague? And how could I leave out Costas's Candies in Owatonna? Would that work in the "Bluff Country"chapter? What to do? Give them their own chapter.

NEW PRAGUE

Dozinky Festival
Held the third Saturday in September

Every September, the scent of sauerkraut and grilling sausages wafts over the sidewalks and down the streets of New Prague during Dozinky, a Czech harvest celebration.

Mingling with such definitive aromas, the old-fashioned accordion music drifting about seems a perfect accompaniment. Families in old-world outfits create a brilliant street scene with their splashes of bright red skirts and fancy embroidered vests. Those not in traditional dress are wearing pins with the words "Czech Power" or T-shirts stating "So many kolace . . . so little time."

To be truthful, I didn't find any of those fruit-filled yeast-dough delights called kolace or kolacky (except in the town's Bohemian bakery) during Dozinky. But I did find the most remarkable strudel—and a whole lot more.

The strudel I stumbled upon was displayed on tables in front of the sign saying "St. Scholastica." Actually, it was the two enchanting little girls with headbands of flowers in their hair who first caught my attention here. They were standing alongside their moms, serving up the strudel to customers and pointing out the tea rings for sale. As it turned out, there were five generations of the family at this particular stand, and they had been making the strudel to sell at Dozinky for several years. This is quite possibly the best strudel you'll ever eat. And for $1.50 a slice, it's a bargain to boot. One bite and bits of nuts, raisins, and coconut crumbled from my mouth. Catch them in your hand—you'll want to savor it all. "A gentleman comes here every year and buys $50 worth of strudel and sends it to his daughter in another state," one of the women working here told me. Trust me. You'll want to get to this table right away.

A road through the wide-open spaces of western Minnesota

Besides the food stands set up during Dozinky, there are also crafts and beautiful Czech colored glass sparkling in the sun for sale. Wander down the main street and you'll also pass old guys on accordions and antique button boxes playing music in little shaded alleyways. Old folks sit on folding chairs lined along the brick wall, conversing or simply listening. Grandkids skip in and out, sit on a lap, run off.

Near lunchtime, I found myself at a stand where a friendly man and woman in authentic garb were serving up fat sausages, draped with tongfuls of sauerkraut, in homemade buns. As I pulled out my $3.00, I asked, "What makes a sausage a Czech sausage?" "Well," said the costumed gentleman, "Czech sausage actually has a lot of barley in it. It was really called poor man's sausage." Not exactly a ringing endorsement, I thought, but one taste of this delicious sausage sandwich changed my tune.

The sausage they use at the festival is made at the meat market in Lonsdale. "It's the closest we can get to the real thing," the fellow told me. Then he explained how Lonsdale, along with Montgomery nearby, is part of this little pocket of rolling farmland in the middle of the state with strong Czech roots. Montgomery's bakery is known for its kolacky, the ethnic fruit-filled delicacy. In fact, the town hosts an annual Kolacky Festival, I was informed. "You should try to go to that next year," he recommended.

Later in the afternoon, after I'd passed up the sauerkraut balls, I decided to sample the intriguing little flatbreads called zelnicky. Actually, they're more like crackers, said the woman behind the stand who answered my questioning stare at the small cellophane package of the savory snacks. "They're made with equal amounts of flour and sauerkraut," she explained. "I mix it all together, then he [she nudged her husband] pats it out into a big flat jelly roll pan." Are they a special holiday food? "Well," the woman told me with a half-embarrassed smile, "my mother used to make them—to serve with beer."

After a taste of these pungent treats, with their chewy consistency and salty slick flavor, I can see why they would be great with a cold brew.

I bought a couple extra packages and then began heading to my car. It was getting late, and the stands were starting to close down. Even so, the music continued. A couple guys were still up on a small stage with their accordions. Farther down the street, an impromptu gathering on the sidewalk included two gray-haired men playing their antique concertinas surrounded by a half-dozen younger men unabashedly singing in the old language. I watched them for a while, and it was impossible not to smile.

Schumacher's New Prague Hotel

212 West Main Street • Phone: (800) 283-2049 or (952) 758-2133

Situated in a restored 1898 hotel, Schumacher's New Prague Hotel and Restaurant has been a dining destination for over twenty years. The place is pricey, and a dish or two doesn't always hit, but if you're in a celebratory mood anyway (many anniversary types are here), the place works very fine.

Owner and chef John Schumacher's style in the kitchen includes fare both wild and hearty—in the generous spirit of Central Europe. This is not food for sissies. Red elk loins, char-grilled with onions and red pepper, are satisfying and unusual—with a bit of John's horseradish alongside like an exclamation point. Pheasant braised in a Burgundy wine sauce is nicely done. Wiener-schnitzel and roast duck are other options. Traditional entrées such as shrimp and pork medallions are on the menu, too.

Serving up some Czech sausages at the Dozinky festival in New Prague

Many of Schumacher's desserts are European in form as well. An elegant apricot-raspberry linzertorte or the signature torte made with thin sheets of meringue and pecans—heavy on the whipped cream—are both worthy of a sample.

After such a meal, it's no wonder that most people rent a room here for the night. Or maybe it has something to do with the romantic atmosphere. The inn bespeaks European charm and comfort: lace curtains, Austrian linens, and eiderdown comforters.

FROM SCHUMACHER'S NEW PRAGUE HOTEL: GERMAN POTATO SALAD

John Schumacher, owner and chef, says he get requests for this recipe all the time. It's a staple on the hotel menu and a favorite dish all over Central Europe.

Chef's Tip: This recipe will last in your refrigerator for about one week. It's a bit difficult to prepare well. Once you've mastered it, though, you'll make it again and again.

9 medium-sized potatoes
1/4 pound raw bacon, diced 1/4 inch
3 heaping tablespoons flour
2 cups hot water
3/4 cup white vinegar
1/4 cup sugar
1 teaspoon salt
1/4 teaspoon white pepper
1/2 teaspoon celery seeds
1/2 cup raw onion, thinly sliced
2 tablespoons sweet red pepper, diced 1/4 inch
3 sprigs parsley, chopped fine
1 cup water
2 teaspoons capers

Boil potatoes with skins on until just tender to the fork. Remove from heat and drain immediately. Let potatoes sit uncovered to cool.

In a heavy sauce pot, render bacon until dark brown. Add flour and cook for 2 minutes, stirring to keep from burning. Add water and vinegar, mixing well. Combine sugar, salt, white pepper, and celery seeds. Add to base. Stir to keep from sticking to pot. Simmer for 5 minutes on low heat.

As soon as potatoes are cool enough to handle, peel and cut into 1/2-inch cubes. Place in a large bowl. Quarter and finely slice onions. Add to potatoes. Clean and dice red peppers. Add to potatoes. Add chopped parsley and capers. Add bacon base and stir gently to combine.

Taste and adjust seasoning with salt and pepper. Serve hot.

Serves 6–8.

Reprinted with permission from *John Schumacher's New Prague Hotel Cookbook* by John Schumacher (International Cuisine Publishers, 1991).

BRAHAM

Braham Pie Day
First Friday in August

If there is poetry in pies, then Braham's Pie Day is a masterpiece. Lucky the traveler who happens into this tiny town on such a day—for he has stumbled into pie paradise.

At the city park, a dazzling array of pies, pies, and more pies—sugar-sparkling crusts shining in the sunlight—stretches before the eyes. Rhubarb. Cherry. Blueberry. Peach. Lined up on tables set beneath a huge blue and white–striped tent, each pie has initials pricked into the top crust to identify the juicy contents. Servers in bright aprons cut wedges of pie and then scoop out balls of vanilla ice cream to plop on the plate alongside the slice you select. Will it be raspberry (R) or perhaps cranberry apple (CA)? For a few more bucks, you can take home a whole pie, maybe cherry rhubarb (CR)—which also gets you the souvenir tin the pie was baked in.

Proclaimed the Homemade Pie Capital of the state (it's stamped on the pie tin), Braham has long been referred to as that town "where they have those good pies." For years (before Interstate 35 changed the scope of vacationers' drive time to "the lake"), Braham's Park Café—with its assortment of pies—was a popular stopping point on a shortcut Up North. When the town, which is located about sixty miles due north of the Twin Cities, needed to come up with a civic celebration in 1990, longtime resident Phyllis Londgren said there was no question: Pie was the answer. (She was quickly appointed coordinator.)

Since then she's been involved in every Pie Day, doing her share—including shifts at Braham High School, where over five hundred pies, in a tightly organized pastry production, get rolled out, fitted into pans, filled, and fluted by hand several days before Pie Day. On Pie Day proper, the crusts are filled

This is what all the shouting is about at Pie Day in Braham.

and baked and then loaded up into vans and delivered to the park, where hand-lettered signs stating "Parking for Pie Delivery vehicles ONLY" are taken seriously.

Besides the customary pie-eating contest (junior and senior divisions), Pie Day events also include a "pie race." Running with pie and coffee, eating pie, mixing pie dough, and rolling out a pie crust are all components of the zany race. The highlight of Pie Day, however, is still the pie-baking competition. Past winning entries have included everything from a bumbleberry pie (a mixture of blackberries, blueberries, strawberries, and apples) to the controversial Senator Durenberger's Creamy Peach Pie—made without peaches. (For his winning entry, Durenberger won $30—and "in Braham, that's big money," said Londgren at the time.) The senator's sweet little scandal also got his name in the newspapers in Texas, California, and Oregon.

Of course, the best part about Braham's pie-baking contest is that after the pie entries have been tasted and ribboned, they're auctioned off at the end of the day. Yes, in a grand and sweet finale, each precious poem in pastry goes to the lucky highest bidder.

For several years, a pie recipe contest was conducted before Pie Day proper. Entries were made and taste tested at the Park Café and then typed and compiled in a special Pie Day cookbook. Fogcutter pie, musical pie, banana fudge pie, double-chocolate Almond Joy pie, and watermelon dream pie were just a few of the recipes to make it into the spiral bound recipe collections. Today, the pie recipe contest is no longer conducted, but winning pie entries in the pie-baking competition are published in the local newspaper.

FROM BRAHAM PIE DAY: BUMBLEBERRY PIE

Marles Riessland of Riverdale, Nebraska, has won her share of pie contests, including Braham's. This bumbleberry pie is rich and juicy with fruits of the season. It won first place in Braham in 1999. And it looks as beautiful as it tastes. Pastry for a double-crust 9-inch-deep dish pie (recipe follows)

Filling
2 cups peeled apple slices, 1/4-inch thick
1 cup fresh blackberries
1 cup fresh blueberries
1 cup fresh strawberries
1 tablespoon lemon juice
3/4 cup sugar plus 2 tablespoons for sprinkling
3 tablespoons tapioca
1 slightly beaten egg white for top crust
Butter to dot top of crust

Preheat oven to 450 degrees. Mix together all ingredients except egg white and butter. Let stand 15 minutes to soften tapioca. Turn into pie shell. Dot with butter. Adjust, flute, and vent top crust. Brush top with slightly beaten egg white and sprinkle with sugar. Bake at 450 degrees for 10 minutes. Reduce oven temperature to 350 degrees and bake for 25–30 minutes longer or until golden brown. Cool on wire rack. Makes one 9-inch-deep dish pie.

Pastry
3 cups flour
1 teaspoon salt
1 teaspoon sugar
1 cup plus 1 tablespoon butter-flavored shortening, chilled
1/3 cup ice-cold water
1 tablespoon vinegar
1 large egg, well beaten

Stir together flour, salt, and sugar into mixing bowl. Cut in shortening with a pastry blender until mixture resembles cornmeal. Combine water, vinegar, and egg. Add liquid 1 tablespoon at a time, sprinkling over flour mixture and tossing with a fork to form soft dough. Shape into three discs. Wrap with plastic wrap. Refrigerate 3–24 hours. Extra pastry may be frozen for later use.

OWATONNA

Costas's Candies and Restaurant
112 North Cedar • Phone: (507) 451-9050

There are at least two reasons to get off Interstate 35 and visit this small but fine candy shop and café in downtown Owatonna. One reason, of course, is the selection of hand-rolled creams, homemade caramels, and chocolate-covered English butter toffees. The other is to buy a half-dozen of the feather-fine and powdered sugar–laden Greek kourambiedies (butter cookies).

This is probably one of the few candy shops you'll find in the state where you can arrive at 7:30 for breakfast as well. Costas's candy counter is in the front part of his small family café, serving breakfast, lunch, and dinner.

When it first opened in 1919, however, the place was part candy shop and part ice cream parlor—typical of many towns' sweet shops in those days. To make ends meet, the café was added, says candymaker Costas—although his heart is still in the candy kitchen. The caramels here are rich and buttery, poured on a stone table, set overnight, and then individually hand-wrapped in clear cellophane. The creams, which come in more than a dozen different flavors (for example, cherry, maple pecan, vanilla, peppermint, orange, or raspberry) are also mixed and then allowed to set overnight before being hand-rolled and dipped in chocolate. Finally, each one is delicately wrapped in a square of tissue paper. They are definitely little labors of love.

It was Costas's uncle who owned the candy shop and brought Costas to the United States from Greece in 1955. Upon entering the candy shop after he arrived, Costas says with a smile, "The first minute I came in, I liked it."

Now about those kourambiedies, the butter cookies. Baked by Costas's wife, Mary (she also makes baklava for sale), you'll find them on a tray in a display case below the cash register. They're easy to overlook, and if you don't know about them, you may just pass them by. Tip: Don't. Buy a couple. Maybe four. Oh, heck why not half a dozen. These crescent-shaped butter treats, buried in powdered sugar, are the best.

Don't head back to the freeway without stopping at Owatonna's charming parklike town square, either. Within walking distance of Costas's, the small green space, with its park benches, huge old trees, historic 1893 water fountain, and pair of unusual 1909 drinking fountains is reminiscent of the squares you might see down south, say, Savannah way. It's the perfect place for a picnic or even sitting on a bench, eating one of Costas's chocolate creams, perhaps thinking about life à la Forrest Gump.

WINTHROP

Lyle's Café
102 East Fourth Street • Phone: (507) 647-9949

This little hometown café located in tiny Winthrop is one of those places it's easy to cruise by on your way to somewhere else . . . say, New Ulm for example. But for years it's had a reputation for pies. In fact, "the Pie Lady of Winthrop" is something of a local legend in the state—and her pies were known far and wide.

Sadly, after forty-some years of pie baking at Lyle's, the pie lady has passed on. But Lyle's still puts together a pretty decent slice of pastry. A warm-from-the-oven, quivering orange meringue one Saturday noontime was luscious; a cool, fresh banana cream another day was dreamy.

The café is actually bigger than you think, with a room in the back where paper placemats on the tables proclaim "Welcome to Lyle's" and are bordered by the town's businesses. But it's more fun to sit in the front in a booth or at the counter where wooden stooltops on iron posts rattle noisily around— and the smells coming from the kitchen remind you of dinner at grandma's. Town boys park their bikes out front and stop in for cokes, while local moms rush in to pick up a specially ordered lemon meringue pie for a family reunion. A dry erase board states the specials of the day: a Mexican hot dish, tossed salad, and dinner roll, $4.75. Another board lists the day's soups: Chili, sauerkraut, bean and ham, hamburger wild rice, or cream of vegetable. And you can also get Lyle's famous "commercials," homemade gravy poured over a hot beef or hot pork sandwich.

Folks are friendly here, and if you're asking the waitress for directions, don't be surprised if later, on your way out the door, some guy in jeans and a baseball cap advertising corn or seeds advises you to be extra careful at that four-way stop just up the road where you have to make a left turn.

MORA

The Sportsman's Café
67 North Highway 65 • Phone: (320) 679-2322

You'll see the billboard along Highway 65 first: "FAMOUS FOOD STOP SINCE 1954" it states. The Sportsman's Café.

One of those typical on-your-way-up-north eateries, it's next to a bait shop and near the busy intersection of highways 65 and 23. Sure, The Sportsman's Café appears a bit aged and worn (and the neon sign is missing a couple lights). But as my friend Rosemary said when she walked in, "This is a slice."

And not only a slice of Americana, this place is a slice of pie. As in order one. Sour cream raisin, cherry cheesecake, chocolate-chip walnut, lemon sour cream, rhubarb custard. Which is best? Well, they were out of the sour cream raisin and the rhubarb custard when we were there. So that tells you something. Still, the lemon sour cream was good, and the chocolate-chip walnut even better: rich, nutty, with just enough chocolate (although this chocolate lover would have preferred even more.)

If you're looking for dinner and don't know what to order, simply take a gaze at plates around you (with 17 stools at the counter, it's fairly easy to do). Yep. It looks like I'll have the hot beef sandwich—with the mashed potatoes and gravy.

MCGREGOR

Minnesota Wild Winery and Shop
North of McGregor on Highway 65 • Phone: (800) 328-6731

"You want something to go with that grouse dinner tonight?" asked Jay Erckenbrack, when two hunters in orange vests walked into this winery one rainy September day. "Yeah," said one of the men, "the grouse."

True story. I know because I was sampling wine when I heard it. Obviously, this place is not your typical winery. For one thing, it's located in northern Minnesota. For another, the wines are made with Minnesota fruits that have been gathered by residents of Leech Lake and White Earth Reservations. Stop in this sparkling, clean shop and you can sample the all-fruit wines such as chokecherry and wild plum. You can also sample several of the fruit-flavored honeywines (for example, blueberry, pin cherry, or black currant). Personally, I always take a bottle of the plain Charred Honey Wine home with me.

Jay Erkenbrack is the owner and cofounder of this winery—part of the Minnesota Specialty Crops in McGregor—which manufactures and markets Minnesota Wild products. He and Lori Gordon, now the company's general manager, founded the company in 1990. Erkenbrack started making wine in 1995.

A short walkway separates the winery from the jam shop—and this is where you'll usually find Lori. In this spacious room, the shelves are stacked with wild rice, honeys, salsas—and jams, jellies, and syrups, prepared from hand-picked fruit like the wines. Be forewarned: Once you have tasted the deeper, richer flavor of a wild plum jelly or dipped a spoon into a tart old-fashioned chokecherry jelly—it'll be difficult to return to the standard Smucker's. Minnesota Wild also now makes honeywine syrups, jellies, and even fruit cooking wines. Like the jams and jellies, the varieties include grape, blueberry, pin cherry, highbush cranberries, crabapple, wild hawthorn, and rose hip.

Fireside
Highway 210 and Highway 65 • Phone: (218) 768-3818

If you are traveling through McGregor on a Friday night, put the Fireside on your eating itinerary. That's fish-fry night. Broiled, this cod is flaky and fine. Deep fried, it has a crisp, golden crust and luscious inside. You get your choice of how you want it prepared. Can't decide? They'll bring you some of each.

Even better, at the Fireside, the salad bar that goes with the fish fry is a notch above standard supper club fare. Check it out. How often do you find REAL bacon bits offered? Yes, bacon that has been fried and chopped up. It's here. The Southwestern Beef soup wasn't prim and proper either. This stuff had some good spice and bite.

The ambience is country friendly, starting with the sign at the door: "Howie and Alice welcome you to the Fireside." Inside, the clientele is all shapes, sizes, and ages. Another "slice," as my friend likes to say, of real, small-town Americana. Good food, too.

Schoolhouse Café
Country Lane • Phone: (218) 768-2403

The first time my friend drove me up to this place, I admit I almost grimaced. The Schoolhouse Café. On Country Lane. Too cute.

But what a find. Joan and Judy are the cooks here. And what cooks they are. Huge homemade cinnamon rolls with almond frosting, muffins, cookies, peach pie, and apple pie. The girls waiting on you are sweet, chatty, and friendly—the type who'll ask you if you want a "middle" or an "end" cinnamon roll.

Details are just as important: Breakfast is served on bright Fiesta ware, soups such as chicken dumpling and split pea are hearty and homemade, and sandwiches such as the veggie grill are loaded with the good-for-you stuff and prepared with tender loving care. Lighter lunches arrive on those old-fashioned glass luncheon plates that all our moms used to have—you know, the kind with the place for a punch cup. Only at the Schoolhouse, that's where the homemade blueberry muffin goes.

The room here—it really is an old-fashioned one-room schoolhouse—is stuffed to the max with old elementary school kitsch, but it's not corny or precious. Retro, maybe. All those Dick and Jane pictures. And remember those pull-down maps? They're the window shades. Antique scooters, wood desks, and globes hang from the ceiling. Tables are squeezed together; it's crowded and noisy, with the espresso machine hissing in the background. But this place definitely goes on the honor roll.

NORTHFIELD

The Tavern
212 Division Street • Phone: (507) 663-0342

Follow the walkway that leads down to the river behind the Archer House restaurant, make a turn onto the old brick sidewalk at the bottom, and steps later, you'll be at the door to The Tavern.

The name is misleading—at least gastronomically. The Tavern does serve liquor, but it's certainly not a bar. It *is* reminiscent of an old-fashioned pub, though, with its low ceilings and dark wood booths, all tucked underground like it is. Or at least the first room you walk into gives that cozy (almost claustrophobic) sort of feeling. In fact, in this room, you'll feel like you should duck your head when you enter (and if you're over six foot two, you probably should). But the spacious dining room beyond has windows that look out to a small terrace, and from here you can see the Cannon River, which winds through this picturesque town.

The menu at The Tavern is all over the globe. (This is a college town, after all.) Tacos, lamb pitas, spaghetti, burgers—and everything here is homemade. The Pesto Pasta (made with fresh basil) is nice; the homemade soups include a popular turkey wild rice and my favorite—a creamy rich Minnesota chowder, thick with ham and vegetables. Do sample The Tavern's signature potatoes: cooked baby reds, cut in chunks, seasoned, and sautéed in olive oil. Dessert? Oh, it's the homemade carrot cake. Hands down.

Quality Bakery and Coffee Shop
410 Division Street • Phone: (507) 645-8392

A sweet old bakery, this little shop (now expanded to include a coffee shop) has been around since 1903. For some reason, I always seem to be here in the fall—when they have their bakery window filled with Halloween decorations and delights. Inside, you'll find orange frosted cookies and decorated cupcakes for the season—plus the standard bakery fare. Do try their mini caramel apple pie. Perfect for two, it makes a small afternoon delight. Pick up cappuccinos over at the Goodbye, Blue Monday coffeehouse and then stroll down to a table by the river and make a toast: To apples and autumn and pretty college towns.

CANNON FALLS

Lorentz Meats and Deli
305 West Cannon • Phone: (800) 535-6382 or (507) 263-3617

Lorentz Meats sells a great sub sandwich if you 're looking for picnic fare, but it's really famous for its commercially marinated pork loin roast. A machine massages, or "tumbles," the seasoned marinades deep into the muscle of the roast, allowing the flavors to completely penetrate the meat within a few hours. Just taking it out of the plastic bag and putting the garlicky, spicy piece of meat in your roasting pan (it's also superb on the grill) is intoxicating. And after it's cooked, it's so tender and moist, it seems to melt on your tongue.

The Edgewood Restaurant and Motel
Route 1, Box 213
Phone: (507) 263-5700

I'll be honest. I don't always stop at this supper club for dinner. But I love the place for a Friday-night beer in the bar and their incredible onion rings. However, if you're here for dinner, don't skip dessert. Marie Hernke's pies are legendary, especially her lemon meringue.

Note that The Edgewood is not really in Cannon Falls; it's actually 7 miles south of town on the west side of Highway 52. Tucked back into the woods, the restaurant has been a family tradition for over forty years. Keep a look out for it though; it's not the easiest to spot from the highway.

Cookies for every occasion, including Halloween, are on display at the Quality Bakery and Coffee Shop.

MAHNOMEN

Minnesota Wild Rice

Ancient traditions surround this food that grows in the water. Actually the kernel of an aquatic wild grass, wild rice has been an integral part of Ojibwa life in Minnesota for hundreds of years. Near Mahnomen as well as several other places throughout the state, September is the moon of wild ricing.

But ricing isn't done beneath the moon. It's done early in the morning, when Native American ricers take their canoes out to the lakes. And watching those two-person canoes slip into the water and weave through the rice bed truly seems a glimpse of a moment lost in time. Once in the wild rice grass, one person poles and guides the canoe while the other uses a pair of cedar sticks (about two feet long), bending the grass over the canoe and knocking the kernels loose into the bottom of the boat. When the canoe is filled, the ricers head back to shore, where the rice is scooped into gunnysacks. Later, it will be parched and threshed and, finally, bagged and sold.

This hand-harvested rice looks and tastes completely different from the cultivated wild rice often found in supermarkets. For one thing, because cultivated wild rice is bred to survive harvest by machines, it has a harder hull, which requires a much longer cooking time.

Hand-harvested rice cooks faster and tastes better. It's organic. It's more expensive. But make sure you get the real stuff. It's worth it.

WILD RICE SOUP

Among Minnesotans' wild rice favorites is soup. At Byerly's—dubbed the "designer supermarket" of the Twin Cities and considered one of the best in the business—they not only sell the hand-harvested wild rice but also offer a best-selling version of the soup in their deli. The following recipe, provided by Byerly's home economists, is similar to but not the same as the secret recipe used for the soup in their stores.

> 6 tablespoons margarine or butter
> 1 tablespoon minced onion
> 1/2 cup all-purpose flour
> 3 cups chicken broth
> 2 cups cooked wild rice
> 1/2 cup finely grated carrots
> 3 tablespoons chopped silvered almonds
> 1/3 cup diced ham
> 1/2 teaspoon salt
> 1 cup half and half
> 2 tablespoons sherry (optional)
> Snipped parsley or chives

In saucepan, melt margarine or butter; sauté onion until tender. Blend in flour, gradually adding broth. Cook, stirring constantly until mixture comes to a boil; boil 1 minute. Stir in rice, carrots, almonds, ham, and salt; simmer about 5 minutes. Blend in half-and-half and sherry; heat to serving temperature. Garnish with snipped parsley or chives. Makes 6 cups.

Recipe reprinted with permission from *The Best of Byerly's*, from the test kitchen of Byerly's home economists (Edina: Byerly's, Inc., 1985).

FREEPORT

Charlie's Café

115 Main Street • Phone: (320) 836-2105

It's hard, indeed, to miss Charlie's Café in Freeport, especially since the big sign pointing the way to the place is painted on the side of a house.

Here the motto is "Have a meal with your pie"—and the pies are mighty fine. Charlie Heidgerten doesn't own the place anymore. Ever since about 1990, brother Bud has been running it. It's a friendly spot and always busy. The food is all the tastier in this nostalgic small-town setting. Try the baked chicken. And don't forget the prerequisite cup of coffee and slice of banana cream pie for dessert.

Index By City

Index

Index by Type
of Establishment

Index